THE MOVIES IN MY HEAD

THE MOVIES IN MY HEAD

SHORT STORIES,
ESSAYS,
RUMINATIONS,
FLASH FICTION
AND A NOVELLA OR TWO

WESLEY R. HARDEN III

This is a work of fiction. Names, characters, places, and incidents either are the product of the author's imagination or are used fictitiously. Any resemblance to actual persons, living or dead, events, or locales is entirely coincidental.

ISBN: 978-00-9888806-8-9

Contents

Flying ... 3

Cry Babies ... 4

You People ... 5

Evolution ... 14

Ask Me ... 15

A Perfect Microcosm ... 16

Insula ... 30

Species ... 51

Trout in the Milk ... 53

The Captive ... 59

The Swansong of Perphrobisher Barbash, III ... 74

Task Force Boston ... 78

The Dead of Night ... 93

The Season ... 94

Shelter from the Storm ... 95

Flight of the Valkyries ... 102

The Songs of My Father ... 103

When We Were Young ... 108

Longing ... 114

The Hammer of God ... 115

A Rock in the Sun ... 121

The Patient with Bad Taste ... 130

For the Glory of France 131
The Speed of Light 146
Green Bank 150
Weekly Report 154
Betsy 160
The Big Dog 163
The Irresistible Hum of Deep Space 165
OK, You Win 169
The Algorithm 175
Ask the Astronomer 177
The Cora Burst 182
Cora 190
Light You Can Hear 194
Protocol of Urgency 201
The Rental 206
Wrong Number 207
Alone 208
Fat 209
Rene 215
God and Ford Motor Company 222
Smegma 224
Fun 226
Somebody's Red-headed Stepchild 227
Passage 231
Advert 235
The Strait 236

Smiles......242
Rocky' Eyes......244
Football over Cabernet......249
Thirteen Days......253
The First White Woman......386
Siren......396
The Beast of Train 317......397
The Chihuahua......407
Paris or the Lost Generation, part duex......409
When to Quit......422

Flying

I took the window seat. She sat down beside me. She was young with more than enough makeup on to make her point. When she crossed her legs, I could see her expensive heels. Her short skirt also sent a message. We exchanged obligatory smiles but that was the extent of it.

After takeoff I dozed off and on. We were well above the clouds when the bang occurred and there was a sudden change in the engine noise. A second later the oxygen masks dropped like yellow-headed snakes from a hundred tree limbs. I looked out the window as the engine, not a dozen feet from where I sat was engulfed in flame.

This it is. She grabbed my arm and turned to me. Her face was streaked with tears and running make-up. Our eyes locked oblivious to the blood-curdling screams that drowned out all other noise.

Pinned to our seats, plunging at an impossible angle, I turned to her and held her hand.

"Don't worry," I said calmly. "You won't feel a thing."

Cry Babies

Babies in Pyongyang. Seoul, Shanghai, Freemantle, Mumbai, Mosul, Caracas, Baltimore all look different. Except for the occasional application of the knife, they all pass through similar birth canals into a cold, uncompromising world. And, when they cry, they all cry with the same voice.

You People

Carl left the campsite to take a wicked pee. The bladder could only hold so much beer waste. He was a little tipsy and it was dark but, was confident he could find his way back. He went a respectable distance, unzipped, extracted his little member and let it rip. He played his stream back and forth over a poison ivy plant. A high-quality beer piss could last awhile, so he looked around. He saw a flicker of light under a tree in the distance. At first, he thought he was mistaken. Then he saw it again. He and his pals were the only ones in these woods, he thought. Nobody around for miles. Best fishing stream in the whole forest and best kept secret.

For reasons he could not explain, he decided to seek the light. Couldn't be that far, fifty yards, he guessed.

He came upon them sitting on a log in a small clearing. Their little fire was a neatly controlled burn. They were big. Sitting, he thought they were each at least seven feet tall. They had big heart-shaped heads with a row of fine hair down the center indentation. They had large, round, unblinking eyes with dark pupils and two holes for nostrils and ears. And a mouth that only appeared when they spoke. Their skin was smooth, gray and thin.

They did not seem surprised to see Carl.

The two strange looking gentlemen sitting on the log seemed perfectly reasonable and Carl was not frightened. Even by the fact they wore no clothes and looked like something out of a science fiction comic book.

"Hello," said the one on the right as if he had been waiting for him all evening.

Carl was speechless.

"Hello, my friend. Have a seat," the other one said pointing a spindly little arm and finger at a log opposite them.

Carl felt a trickle of urine against his inner thigh.

"Please. No need to be frightened. We will not hurt you," Left said. The one on the right exchanged a glance with the one on the left but showed no outward emotion.

Carl noted they spoke with a weird accent that was at first incomprehensible. Like they were from England or Harvard or something.

"Who the fuck are you?"

Right said, "There's that word again."

"Yes. Rugged and endearing at the same time," Left said.

"Yes. So versatile."

They exchanged glances and chuckled. That's what Carl assumed it was. It was more like clearing one's throat. But all outward appearances suggested it was a laugh mutually shared.

"We're criminals," Right said.

"Exiles, really. We were criminals at one time. Now we're exiles."

"Yes, precisely."

Practically every time one spoke it would look at the other as if for validation.

Carl was convinced he had fallen and hit his head. That he would wake up with a bloody lump on his scalp and dried leaves stuck to his face.

"Where are you from?"

They both pointed up.

"Outer space?"

"A galaxy far, far away." Exchanging glances, they chuckled again.

"Holy shit."

"Another."

"Are you for real? You Martians or something?"

"No. Mars is too hot in the summer."

"Not nearly as much fun either."

"We were offered a choice and we selected the third rock from the sun what you people refer to as earth."

Right continued, "We got into some minor difficulties."

"More a misunderstanding, I would suggest."

"—and punishment is exile. We chose here. It's really quite an amusing place. We are curious to see how it plays out."

"Plays out?"

"Oh, yes. The Drake Equation is spot on."

"Huh?"

"You people are doomed. We've seen it all before."

They looked at each other and Left said, "Shame we can't snap our fingers and make him sober."

"It would be a waste of a perfectly good snap of the fingers," Right countered.

They fell into their own conversation as if Carl wasn't there.

"Did you ever try snapping your fingers?" Left asked.

"Why no. In all the time we've been here I never had occasion or need to snap my fingers."

"Perhaps you should try it."

"Why yes, let me see if I can remember how it goes." Right tried snapping his long, thin, gnarly fingers to no avail. After several failed attempts he quit trying.

"Disappointing."

"Yes, very much so. Billion years of successful evolution and we can't even snap our fingers like these people."

"Well, I would hardly call that a biological advantage."

"Yes, but—"

"Hey," Carl snapped. "I'm over here!"

"Oh, right."

"How long you dudes been here?"

"Dudes. Oh, I just love this place."

Right said, "Several thousand earth years. It's been a hoot."

"Went by in a flash. Your equivalent of a quiet afternoon."

"Craziest thing we've ever seen. I'n it?"

"Quite."

"We chose British English because at the time it seemed the most refined."

"Erudite."

"Yes. That too."

Carl spoke. "Well, what do you guys eat? And how come nobody ever found you before?"

"Photosynthesis. We get a little sluggish on cloudy days."

"Ah, yes." Right said. "One of the few things you chaps got right. And we have the ability to fade into background by instantly altering our chemistry. Sort of like chameleons. Or that gecko."

"Oh, I so love that little guy."

"The only one who saw us and got it right was the guy who invented Kanamits."

"Funny story. To Serve Man. I can see why they are so frightened of us."

"Yes. The rest all thought they were hallucinating or written off as loony."

"Yes," they exchanged another chuckle. "All this UFO nonsense. The others have avoided this place like the plague. Besides there is a universal agreement not to interfere with your destiny and or harvest you."

"Or anyone else for that matter."

"Quite."

"I don't fucking believe this," Carl muttered.

"There it is again. Lovely," Right said, "and the timing and accentuation are perfect."

"You people aren't getting off this place alive. You're trying—"

"We get a big kick out of Elon Musk, by the way."

"—but it's too little too late."

"All your stories on the telly involve either fornication, mind-altering substances or weaponry."

"Or sometimes all three."

"Quite. You people pay no attention to institutional memory and you have no soul. Just a bunch of miscreants. When little kids can be killed in a crossfire over some petty display of machismo or territoriality you have lost any right to exist let alone persist."

"What he's trying to say is you people have no purpose. You're all going to die. It may be too late to change."

"Oh," Right said softly. "I already think it is. Look at this specimen."

"We thought gunfights and religion were part of a retained primitive evolutionary imperative."

"We were wrong. You are all doomed."

"You have some fat, dopey-looking pipsqueak with a funny haircut in a place called North Korea who kills people for farting too loud and wants nuclear weapons and rockets to hurl them. It's incomprehensible. All while his citizens starve. And you let it happen."

"Oh, yes. You missed your chance long ago. The problem became irreversible when you decided to compete for a mate."

"Everything else went south from there as you like to say."

"Is there something wrong with the south?"

"No, it's just a direction," Carl said.

"Yes." Right nodded to Left and said, "You're right, you know. Wrong evolutionary choice. At that point, it could have gone either way. Now…" He shrugged his narrow shoulders. If one could call them that.

"You people are fucked. There I said." Right turned to Left, "Did I say it correctly? Proper context and all?"

"Yes. You did." He was visibly proud of his companion clapping his miniscule hands feebly accentuating his delight. "You've waited a long time to say it. Bravo."

By now Carl was focused like a laser.

"We love what you've done to the place."

"Oh, yes. You're managing to destroy the place all by yourself."

"What you call history we call battle of the tribes. It never ends."

"But do so enjoy your holidays."

"We like to play practical jokes on people."

"Especially old ladies with weak hearts and gullible children in day-care centers."

"Oh, and the occasional politician."

"Our favorite holidays are Halloween and the Haj."

"What? Where are you guys from, really?" Carl asked.

"We are forbidden to say exactly but, it is one of your Kardashev Type II Civilizations with our own Dyson swarm. Nobody ever dies unless they want to. Everyone has free will but an understanding. When our star starts to burn out, we will move to another one."

"How can you do such things?"

"We've been at this a long time."

"Five billion years."

"Imagine what earth will be like in five billion years."

"Oh, no," Left said. "Their sun will have gone red giant long before then. This whole place will be a long-forgotten cinder."

"Oh, right."

"So how did you manage to do it?" Carl was genuinely curious.

"Look at all your faults, every last one of them, and know that we managed to expunge all of these negative traits through cooperation not coercion."

"And the occasional ablative surgery," Right added.

"We did not use violence or the threat of violence. Not like Churchill who wanted to strangle Bolshevism in its cradle, but by persuasion initially. After that, any other course of action never occurred to anybody."

"So, what happened to you two?" Carl asked.

"There are always outliers."

"Everything, *everything*, occurs at some point on a bell curve. Ours is extremely narrow."

"Which end were we on?" Left asked.

They chuckled at their private joke.

"We have a council called the Fornix. Very democratic. Ordinary citizens are selected to serve on the Fornix and have uninterrupted sex for the equivalent of an earth month to clear their heads then get to work. Our people are quite anxious to serve. It's easy to survive when you have no disease or pretension."

"It must be boring."

"To whom?"

Left spoke, "And what is your preoccupation with lopping people's heads off? Genghis Khan, the French, the Japanese. Now Arabs. What's with you people? You march thirty people in orange jump suits onto a beach and cut their heads off one by one in the name of an ideology belonging in the Dark Ages."

"Nobody will want to sunbathe with little Johnnie on that beach again, or a romantic, moonlit stroll alongside the surf, eh?"

"We did not particularly enjoy witnessing the Dark Ages. And that business with Caligula was quite disturbing," Left said.

He continued, "You, none of you, have any sense of equivalence. Hitler was a piker next to Stalin and Mao yet he's your prototypical evil genius. You people have no goals worthy of the word. Your Jesus Christ was a very clever magician. Walking on water and feeding all those people on a few pieces of fish. We were very impressed until David Copperfield made the Statue of Liberty vanish. Did I use piker correctly?"

"Yes, you did."

"And your obsession with politics. This Clinton woman should be in jail already. Bernie Sanders has the right idea but he's not at all clever and Donald Trump worries us."

"Why? I kinda like him," Carl said.

"The hair. Anybody who preens that much cannot be trusted to stay focused and keep his word. We've seen it all before."

"We had hope when you formed the Fucking Hippies. Peace, Love and Rock and Roll."

"No, no, no," Carl said. "They were just Hippies. Not Fucking Hippies."

"Instead, you have free enterprise. There's nothing free about it. The Tragedy of the Commons, dear fellow. Pure communism works perfectly when you remove self-aggrandizement, greed and suspicion. From each according to his ability, to each according to his need—"

"With unlimited sex and sunlight for everyone."

"—and the people least likely to make a positive contribution to the future of the planet are reproducing, consuming finite resources and spreading across the globe like bacteria on a warm petri dish. Did I use that analogy accurately?"

"Yes, you did," Left said.

"And killing each other and their offspring at prodigious rates. Again?"

"Yes. Spot on."

"And they've completely abdicated their responsibilities as parents. They would rather turn over the future to the cynical generosity of the government." He turned and looked at his Left.

Left nodded.

Right continued, "Instead these people should be sterilized prior to puberty so they can fornicate at will and the multitude of uncontrolled, undesirable offspring should be halted. The genetic argument that more births increases the likelihood of a happy mutation is specious. They need to cull the herd."

"Now, we discussed this," Left said. "There are sensitivities at play here and we said we would keep these observations to ourselves. This is what they call a touchy subject." Left turned to Carl and gently shook his head as if to disclaim the discussion.

"It will never happen here. Your DNA took a wrong turn."

"Everything can be reduced to a biological explanation. Look hard enough and you will always find one. If you can't find one, you didn't look hard enough."

"It is amazing you have survived as long as you have seeing as how you have consistently failed to make the right choices."

"The Doolittle Raid and polio vaccine were good choices."

"Correct choices. Right and wrong have become too pejorative."

"You consistently revert to primitivism as if that's really some valid fallback position to every dispute."

"Do you believe in God?" Carl asked.

"Who?"

With that, Carl stood up and walked away.

Left shouted after Carl, "And another thing. You people are so hung up on the speed of light." Then a little louder, "It contaminates your thinking and your vision. Crazy Einstein."

When he woke up, he pulled the sleeping bag up over his head and thought, what a crazy dream that was. He would have to remind himself to Google Kanamits.

Evolution

Why did the whales, seals and otters leave the rocks for the sea? Or, instead, why did the elephants, rabbits and hominids leave the water?

Ask Me

Ask me anything, she said.
I did.
Her lip quivered. Her eyes welled. She slapped me.
I asked the wrong thing.

A Perfect Microcosm

The Call

The crash of glass in the fireplace surprised everyone including the person who threw it. The petulant act filled Noel with a satisfaction he had not felt in a long time. The downside, the glass was a crystal, holiday tumbler, part of a prized set handed down to his mother from her mother. Years of poorly veiled disappointment and not-so-subtle ridicule on the part of his parents, people who ostensibly loved him, had reached a point of no return.

The clash had been festering for a long time, his parents were PhDs, recognized authorities in academic circles; his father in Philosophy, his mother in Feminist Studies. They were unhappy when he chose such a pedestrian field as biology. They could not conceal their chagrin when he attended a state university. Even when he finally earned his PhD in zoology, it was not enough. Their woke, New Age way of life held no room for the mundane. They were too self-absorbed to understand the impact of humiliation, especially when rendered so publicly.

The precipitating event on Christmas Eve was a conspicuously flattering remark about a colleague's son who could be in line for a Nobel Prize for his research on cancer. It made his dissertation on the circadian rhythms of large Eurasian nocturnal, semiaquatic rodents seem trivial and even comedic. There is no benefit to mankind, his father said after a third martini, researching when and why French beavers decide to sleep and fornicate. You are wasting your time son, he said. You might as well be a painter of houses. That launched the glassware. He stormed out of the Baxter brownstone vowing never to return until he had achieved his 'how do you like me now' moment.

...

Devin Coates entered the office, placed his briefcase on his desk saying, "I heard you were back early. Have a nice Christmas?"

Noel was in no mood for idle chit-chat or painful recollections. Devin continued to retrieve his sandwich and soup thermos out of his briefcase. It was the same every morning since they started sharing the same office a year ago. Like some academic 'odd couple.'

Noel had developed a fondness for the guy and his quaint, unsophisticated charm. He reflected on their similarities. Two PhDs stuck in a backwater college teaching dull millennials devoid of any interest in mitosis and the intricacies of biological systems. They had developed a mutual respect and friendship facing common challenges. Publish or perish. He also understood their differences. The naturally upbeat, no-worries Devin seemed perfectly happy right where he was. Noel felt trapped in a death spiral of ennui, wasted opportunities and a bitter disappointment to those he loved.

"You had another fight with your folks, didn't you?"

"Sort of."

"Sort of," Devin muttered under his breath. "Snap out of it, my friend. I have your next great project. Something that will put you on the map. I heard there was this island in the Indian Ocean so far out in the middle of nowhere nobody knows about it."

"What's it called?" Noel asked off-hand.

"It doesn't have a name. Just GPS numbers."

"And?"

"Just that it's probably the most pristine microhabitat remaining in the world."

"You don't say," Noel said, demonstrating no particular enthusiasm

"Can you imagine what might be on that place? Like the Island of Doctor Moreau or Jurassic Park without the cages."

"Well they didn't turn out so good now, did they?"

"You ought to check it out."

"I think I will," Noel said, his mind suddenly piqued by the possibilities. Maybe he could find a new species of something and name it after himself. Wouldn't Dad be proud.

"How did you hear about this place?"

"It was mentioned in an article about a missing airliner."

"Do people live on it?"

"Not as I know of. Why?"

...

Intrigued, it took Noel less than a week to research the place about which Devin spoke so casually. For such a bold expedition to such a very remote place, very little was known about it. For centuries mariners had just thought of it as a worthless dot on a map; something to avoid bumping into. It was not part of an archipelago or cast-off of a nearby continent. Just a single, jungle island in a remote corner of a vast ocean. Un-named and known to few. Probably, Noel figured, the result of an isolated, incidental Pre-Cambrian volcano arising from a crack in a tectonic plate, so far removed from shipping lanes that anybody with knowledge of the place gave it no thought or concern. Not even the closest natives; any indigenous population would have to be restless enough to paddle their outriggers hundreds of miles into a vast open ocean using flawless navigation and an awareness of something just beyond the horizon. A regular Kon Tiki. So far removed Google didn't even have it on a map. Just a strange, long-forgotten seismic eructation.

It did exist and there was no record of human habitation. The UN had no record of it. Its biome was unknown.

Noel was determined to find out all he could about the place. It wasn't much. It had no mention in Wikipedia. There was only one mention of it in maritime literature (with a puzzling footnote: if you come across this island, you are probably lost) and the solitary article in The New Yorker recapping the frustrating, protracted saga of search and rescue of the disappearing Malaysian airliner. He was not deterred. He wrote to the Royal Australian Air Force, Search and Rescue, for the precise coordinates of the island as mentioned in the magazine. He said it was for scientific inquiry. Several weeks later, they gave him very precise longitude and latitude as well as GPS coordinates of 'Island, Unnamed.'

Noel said, "It is hard to imagine that through history there remain places on earth upon which no human foot had ever trod."

...

A few weeks later, he took Devin aside in the faculty lounge. "I found the place."

"What place?"

"The lost island in the middle of the Indian Ocean, you numbskull. The perfect microcosm. You should try to get funding for a little expedition."

In short order, Devin became obsessed with the little island and a started to put together an expedition to explore it.

Devin Coates reiterated to anyone who would listen. Noel broke his silence with his father. It was a brief exchange. The Professor displayed limited interest. 'You know, Mother is still cross with you.' Perhaps an article in Science or Nature might change her attitude, Noel thought. 'Good luck son. Send us a postcard when you get there.'

Both men held PhDs in biology. Devin's thesis was on the circadian rhythms of Northern European salamanders. Noel's was the biochemical changes in brown fat in arctic terns when exposed to subtropical climates. It was a difficult project as there is very little brown fat to be found in arctic terns.

Over time, as Devin's interest grew, Noel's waned.

...

Devin nicknamed it "Insula," Latin for isolated place or island. It was as good as any for there was no registered name he could find. Noel mockingly called it Coates' Folly, Shangri-La and Point of No Return.

Undeterred by wisecracks or ignorance, Devin devoted his next three months of his spare time to quietly sorting out biological, ecological and evolutionary imperatives to predict what such a remote, uninhabited habitat might contain. Whatever lived on it could be mundane and well-described or incredibly unique with finds and species heretofore unknown. He finally put together a proposal for an expedition. Ancient animals creeping along the jungle floor whose lucky geographical isolation allowed them to escape extinction.

He had Noel consult the IUCN Red List and catalog what to look for. Devin also insisted they catalog plant species, especially recently extinct ones, but Noel seemed uninterested. He was only interested in fauna; flora was boring.

During the months of drafting and redrafting the grant proposal, Devin increasingly relied upon Noel's opinion and expertise, especially when it came to issues of survival and outdoor living. Noel was frank to admit that he and his girlfriend had never encamped at any one location for more than a week and never more than a two hour's car ride from the nearest Walmart. The proposal called for the two of them to remain on the island as unobtrusively as possible for a month. They would be taken by a merchant charter capable of offloading several airline containers of equipment and provisions from Cocos Islands to Coates' Folly about three hundred miles due south. They would set up a base camp and carry out their exploration.

Noel consulted expeditions to Antarctica and even the International Space Station culling for unanticipated crises and responses. Unlike, Antarctica or the International Space Station, in cases of a critical nature they were a three-hour seaplane flight from Cocos.

The more he became structurally involved with the details; the more Noel's enthusiasm rekindled. They agreed on thirty days. The island was not so big that between them they couldn't see all of it in a month. They decided to take enough food for thirty days, forty-five if they dieted. They made lists. Snorkel and fins. Machetes. A desalinization, survival still; a pedal operated emergency electrical generator, batteries, solar panels, satellite phone and compact shortwave radio. iPads, computers, flash drives and forty-megapixel cameras. A fairly comprehensive first aid kit. Igloo-type tent. Noel suggested bug repellent, but this was vetoed by Devin so as not to introduce a foreign chemical into the environment. Same with sun-tan lotion. Sleeping bags. Toilet paper. Lots of toilet paper.

They also agreed that if they did not see all they thought they needed to see in thirty days they would be back.

The details were concise and frugal. The guiding principle that harnessed their focus and plans was that of syphilis and Columbus. If the island was the pristine, perfectly balanced ecosystem they both expected, they would do nothing to disturb or contaminate it, including leaving nothing behind except buried feces, urine residue and footprints. The smallest perturbation might ripple through the island's biology and grow to a tsunami that would eventually wipe out everything. They would not kill or remove anything. They called it the 'Smoky the Bear Promise' to leave their campsite the same as they found it. They shook on it.

Their proposal had three goals. Look for any species that might be extinct elsewhere; catalog the fauna and flora (grudgingly); and establish the food chain to identify the largest animals and apex predator that could flourish in an otherwise completely isolated environment.

They were proud and pleased and, two months later, the proposal was summarily rejected.

. . .

To say Devin were disappointed was an understatement. The proposal was perfect in every way. It defined a purpose, a plan and, like all scientific inquiry, room to be surprised by the discoveries. So, they tweaked it and resubmitted it.

Two months passed and it was again rejected. Devin began to lose whatever interest he had left.

They changed the words and sent it in a third time. Less than a month later, rejected. This time with a cordial, but firm admonition that they were wasting their time, inferring not to submit it again.

Several months passed and the expedition was rarely mentioned. Devin, so terribly disappointed at the rejection of what he thought was a clever plan, found himself thinking less and less of the advancement of science and the need to direct his interest elsewhere. They were sitting on Noel's deck cooking hamburgers and a veggie burger (Devin's wife, Millie, was a vegan), drinking beer and wine when Devin announced, "Maybe I ought to go to PA school."

"What?" Millie asked."

"Do something completely different. Go to physician's assistant school. I have a PhD; how hard can that be?"

"You're joking," Noel's girlfriend, Carol, said as she placed the Corelle platter of burgers on the picnic table."

"No," he sighed. "Without some grant money and published original research my stay here will eventually come to an end."

Everyone remained silent except Devin as they started to eat. "No accolades. No tenure."

The meat juice erupted out of the bun as Noel chomped down on the hamburger slithering down between his fingers like oily, brown lava. His mouth full, loudly crunching on the lettuce and onion, he turned to Devin and said, "I think you're going about this all wrong."

Piqued, Devin sat up, also through a mouth full of food, said, "What?"

Noel washed the burger down with a swig of Dos Equis and made contortions with his lips and tongue to free meat particles from the crevices of his mouth.

"You're going about it all wrong, Dev," Noel said offhandedly. "Tell 'em it's a study on global warming, climate change, the effects of rising sea-levels on an isolated tropical microcosm. Betcha, they'll fund that."

"Brilliant," Devin muttered as he slowly lowered his burger to his plate. "But you don't believe in global warming."

"So?"

...

In less than a week, the new grant application was laced with such evocative phrases as "climate change," "ravages of global warming," "unpredictability of biological systems," "rising sea levels," "extinction rates" and the like.

Two weeks later, a grant for $2.7 million was approved by the university.

...

Devin wanted to pack their bags and leave the next day. Realistically, however, they knew it would take a month or more. Being complete novices at expeditions to strange, distant places, took two months. To save space, they decided to live on Prepper foods. They took several hundred gallons of fresh water in one-gallon plastic containers and a de-salinization kit for back up. Noel purchased a new facemask, snorkel and fins, and a tent with a floor large enough to accommodate two sleeping bags comfortably, aluminum cots and two stadium folding chairs with cup-holders for relaxing, post-exploratory evenings by the campfire. And a hermetically sealed container with enough weed for the entire stay.

Frugal as well as practical; anything they saved would be used as seed money for their next big adventure.

But they were determined and set a target date for the end of April, two months hence, and met it. They had a nice little send off at the airport for the long flight to Australia. Everyone was excited. Carol and pregnant Millie waved vigorously as they passed through security. The Boys, the two women called them, never looked happier. As they walked away from security, they hoped the explorers would not be arrested for transporting marijuana.

This was going to be an opportunity of a lifetime. It's only for a month. Imagine what we will find. Pterodactyls, dodos, cycloptic marmosets.

The flight from Los Angeles to Sydney was uneventful. Knowing the duration of the flight, they both slipped into alcohol-induced comas and slept until they were only about four hours out. From there they flew to Perth and spent two days on the phone with their agent on Christmas Island. He assured the scientists everything was moving along on schedule. Catch the Virgin Australia plane from Perth to Christmas Island, stay overnight and catch the daily seaplane flight to Cocos. In the meantime, take in the sights and relax.

...

Arriving in the late morning, they dropped their luggage off at the hotel, a small, unkempt and weathered two-story affair that would have gotten an Auto Club rating of two stars anywhere else in the world but in Cocos atoll was high luxury. It had air conditioning, a pool with filtered water and the room was clean. They hired a cab to take them to the marine office at the port; another dismal affair with two small, rusted inter-island freighters and a scattering of fishing boats and scuba diving launches. Noel was not surprised for he had done much diving in the Caribbean Islands and it all looked very familiar. Devin was expecting something along the lines of San Pedro marine terminal. His disappointment was apparent.

They found the office of their port agent and quickly introduced themselves. The man was overweight, shirtless and sweaty seated behind a cluttered desk. His rotund belly protruded over a dirty, beltless pair of cargo shorts. When he spoke, his thick Aussie accent was diminished only slightly by the wet cigar stump locked in the corner of his mouth.

"Ah, yes. The finch-chaser from America."

"Yeah, Devin Coates and this is my partner, Noel Baxter."

"Nice t' meet you, gen'lemen. We been workin' on your inventory of items and I have a bi' of bad news for yer."

Devin immediately stiffened.

"What bad news?"

"Some of yer items 'ave not yet arrived."

Noel noticed Devin's hand start to tremble.

"Yeah? Like what?"

"Yer food."

"The food?"

"And yer gear."

Noel thought Devin might faint. As a precaution he made Devin sit.

"What *is* here?"

"Almost none of it."

Devin looked ill as if he was about to vomit.

Noel spoke. "Gee, well we called the agent when we got to Christmas Island and he confirmed everything was moving right along. We thought we'd be shoving off tomorrow. Next day the latest."

"Well, I'm sorry, Mates. The stuff 'asn't come yet."

Devin, his head in his hands abruptly bolted to his feet. "That's it? That's the best you've got. 'Sorry, Mates'?"

Suddenly concerned Devin might have a breakdown, Noel ushered him out of the office and sat him on a bench at the edge of the wharf. The sun was blazing hot. The white concrete of the quay and reflection off the water was blinding.

"Sit here and cool off. Let me go in and find out what's going on. Okay?"

Devin only nodded.

Ten minutes of conversation with the agent yielding the following story: the airline cargo containers had been hard to come by as few airlines in these parts used them or knew how to get them and you and your mate wanted five of them. Secondly, the thirty-day supply of freeze-dried Prepper meals had not yet been delivered to Christmas Island. The shipment was expected today, tomorrow at the latest. The gear you gentlemen shipped yourself is in a locker a hundred yards down the pier. Everything should come together, be loaded onto yer little steamer to bring if from Christmas Island and arrive the day after tomorrow. Then you can climb aboard and set sail for your little lost island of mystery tomorrow night or the day after.

"Okay," Noel told the man, fair enough. "We'll check back this afternoon."

"Good."

"Sorry about my partner."

"Go for a swim. Work on your tans. Use lots of SPF."

Noel found Devin sitting trance-like on the bench in the exact position he left him. His forehead was beaded with sweat and his face was red with early sunburn and mounting frustration.

"So?"

"We are to check back this afternoon on the status of things. In the meantime, we are to relax and enjoy our stay."

Devin leaned forward and spread his arms, "Look around. What's here to enjoy? And after all the money we paid that guy to have things ready."

"How much did we pay him?"

"I don't recall exactly. But it was a lot."

Noel leaned over the edge of the wharf to look at the bottom of the bay. He could see small schools of black minnows darting in spontaneous unison one way then the other. The water was crystal clear. The bottom was at least ten feet.

"Give me your cell phone."

"Use yours."

"I left it in the room."

Devin leaned over and pulled it from his front pocket. He handed it to Noel who tucked it safely away. With one fell swoop Noel grabbed Devin and launched him into the bay.

Surfacing, Devin yelled, "You son of a bitch!"

Laughing, Noel leaned over and said, "You looked hot."

...

After two more anxious and irritable days, they finally got a call from the agent that the *Miasma* had set sail from Christmas Island and would be there in the morning. After refueling, they should be ready to depart by late afternoon the next day.

...

Noel and Devin were standing on the wharf when the little freighter pulled up and was lashed to the pier. It was an old ship which had seen better days. Its hull streaked with rust. There were two holds and a crane to support the loading and unloading. There was also a curious-looking, shallow draft, flat-bottom launch resting transversely in front of the forward hatch.

Devin was brimming with excitement. Even though it looked to him like the nautical "Little Engine That Could" he knew his future would be carried forward on the little, rust-stained ship.

"*Miasma*. Strange name for anything." Devin turned to Noel, "Wonder if the Captain knows what it means."

"Think we should tell him?"

"No. And as long as it gets us to Insula, I don't care what it's called." After a moment, "I'll call it the *Beagle*."

After the gangway was lowered, the captain strolled over to Noel and Devin. He held a sheaf of papers in his hand. He was wearing a white, sweat-stained loosely fitting linen shirt, grimy khaki shorts and flip-flops. His white hair was topped by a woman's large straw hat that bent to the wind. He had a deep, almost impenetrable Aussie accent.

"You Coates?"

"I am."

"Then you must be Baxta'."

"Correct."

"My name is MacKenzie. I'm to take you to your island of mystery."

He lit a cigarette and continued, "Here is the cargo manifest. Everything you requested is there. I've billed the University under the number you gave me. I've taken the liberty of putting the things in the five airline cargo bins like you asked but you might have gotten away with just three."

"We held out some room for specimens," Devin replied.

"Aw, right," MacKenzie took a long drag on his cigarette and stared at Devin for a moment.

Clearly, Noel thought, MacKenzie thinks we're nuts.

"Go on board," the ship's master continued, "and meet up with Jesus Bitanga. He'll take you into the holds so you can inspect your kit. All yer gear is accounted for. Later we'll meet up for dinner and you can tell me all about your little romp in the woods." He handed the boys the papers and headed for town at a slight trot.

Bitanga, the diminutive Filipino first mate, led them into the forward hold and, armed with flashlights, went through each bin inspecting and accounting for each item on the lists. It took two hours in the sweltering, airless confines of the hold.

Satisfied, they checked out of the motel and moved into the cramped, spartan cabin.

Toward evening, the Captain returned and had them come to his mess for dinner. He pulled out a new bottle of Maker's Mark and they began to drink. The food was excellent. They explained in detail what their plan was.

"Did it occur to you how you were going to get those bins onto the island?"

They exchanged glances instantly on the verge of panic. Obviously, they had not. It was a critical detail they had overlooked.

MacKenzie chuckled as he poured more drink explaining he anticipated the problem of getting their bins and gear safely onto the beach. Since the island was uninhabited there was no pier to offload their cargo. The ship had no means of beaching itself on an unknown island for fear of damaging the hull. It would be impossible to wheel the things through the sand once they did get them onto the island.

Devin held his head in his hands. To have come this far and be ruined by an unanticipated logistical impossibility was more than he could take. Noel thought his friend might actually start weeping.

Noel thought MacKenzie was enjoying their eleventh-hour crisis. Damned, fool college kids.

MacKenzie poured three more glasses of Maker's and started laughing.

"Ahhh, don't worry yourselves, mates. I got it all figured out. You'll see."

Devin lifted his head and looked at the Captain who winked.

The drinking continued and, though Devin did not care that much for bourbon, he was thoroughly drunk by the time the little party had concluded. The Captain told Noel to take him up to the deck and get him some fresh air before turning in. MacKenzie seemed absolutely sober.

Arriving by the railing all they saw was the Indian Ocean and the setting sun. They had been unaware that they had left the port during dinner. The ocean was calm. There was not a cloud in the sky. The only sound was the splash of water beneath the bow and the humming of the engines deep inside the little freighter. Noel leaned over the railing and saw two bottle-nosed dolphins lunging effortlessly in and out of the bow waves. Perhaps their first contact with man. He took this as a good omen.

Insula

On the third day at sea, Devin and Noel were awake before dawn almost giddy with anticipation. The Captain was on the bridge and explained to them that he had worked out the best landing place based on what limited knowledge he could obtain about the island but admitted he was really not sure what he would find. He planned to circle the island before choosing a spot amenable to their task.

They were standing beside him on the bridge when he first spotted the place on radar. The first rays of light were reaching into the night as they approached. The darkness rapidly receded.

"There it is," MacKenzie said softly pointing to a spot on the horizon that only a mariner could see. "There's yer li'l island paradise."

Anxious and eager, they finally saw it. A dark speck on a flat blue horizon.

Devin became a man possessed. He fidgeted and shifted from one foot to the other until finally he stepped out onto the bridge wing and stared at it sniffing the air to pick up its scent.

The island was not as big as Noel expected. He anticipated

something between Ellis Island and Oahu. It was clearly conical, retaining its volcanic origin. Covered with dense rain forest it was dark. The pinnacle had been worn flat over the eons. Drawing closer it was easy to make out the light rim of beach, the white fluff of breakers and the aroma of rotting vegetation.

Mackenzie took them to within a mile or so of Insula, concerned for unchartered reefs or shoals, and began a careful circumnavigation. The boys and the Captain started looking for the optimal place for a landing. Something with a flat open beach or a protected cove. None was apparent. They circled again. MacKenzie seemed concerned. When asked, he estimated the area to be about ten or twelve square miles. Height of the pinnacle about two thousand feet, virtually all of it covered by a thick rainforest.

At last, MacKenzie's discerning eye found a placed. It was on the eastern side. A moderately calm, shallow cove with a narrow but accommodating beach. Slowly, cautiously so as not to damage *Miasma*'s bottom, MacKenzie expertly delivered the ship to the mouth of the cove and dropped anchor.

Inexplicably, Devin ran down the stairway to the main deck and, without breaking stride, jumped overboard. He swam to the beach much as Columbus or Drake might have had they been unimpeded by decorum. He pulled himself to his feet on the beach and waved back at Noel with unbridled joy. The first human feet to violate the sand of this obscure, little island in the middle of the Indian Ocean.

Devin yelled, "The *Beagle* has landed."

Noel turned to MacKenzie and said, "He's gunning for the Nobel Prize for Enthusiasm."

...

As soon as Noel's feet touched the sand, he knew he had made a big mistake. It was like a subliminal message telling him he should not be here. So much was riding on this little expedition that the thought of failure weighed heavily. Six months of stalking beavers in German and Polish bogs was one thing, stuck on an obscure, uninhabited island in the middle of a vast ocean, isolated beyond imagining, was quite another.

The amphibious operation was surprisingly uncomplicated as it started to unfold. It was a clever affair utilizing the ship's forklift, crane, pierced steel planking and strong backs. The boys placed them as far onto the island as removed from the water's edge as the beach and vegetation would let them. Devin took the satellite phone and called his wife. He could barely contain his excitement. While the unloading continued, Noel searched for a campsite.

The laborious, cleverly executed, amphibious landing completed, the Mackenzie wished them well, gave them a bottle of bourbon and said he would pick them up in thirty days, weather permitting, reminding them that it would take anywhere from three days to a week to reach them in an emergency or four hours by Aussie Coast Guard seaplane. Shortly and unceremoniously, he weighed anchor and backed *Miasma* away from the cove entrance, turned the little steamer and sailed away.

As he was pitching the tent on the beach, Noel stole a glance as the little ship reached the horizon, a tiny gray wisp of smoke the last thing he saw.

...

With hacking machetes and an ax, they proceeded to carve out a niche in the jungle close to the cargo bin repository a short distance down the beach and beyond the reach of the ocean. Noel put together the solar panels and in a few minutes was collecting juice from the declining sun. It was well past midnight when their nervous energy was finally consumed and they sat by the campfire, smoked a joint and went to bed. Noel noted for the first time the absence of jungle noises. What if the place was sterile, devoid of life? Impossible.

Well past dark, they sat beside their campfire and toasted their accomplishment with bourbon.

Noel said he was surprised that it was so quiet. No jungle noises or birds calling out. The only sound was the rhythmic crashing of the surf.

"Maybe the flora and fauna have been stunned into silence by all the commotion," Devin said, hoisting his drink in another toast. "We'll wake 'em up."

Sometime in the middle of the night he thought he heard muffled banging coming from the bins. He was too exhausted to investigate.

...

The night remained eerily quiet except for Devin's soft snore.

At first light, Noel leapt from bed and explored the area behind the tent. He looked under rocks and up into the canopy of trees. He tried to identify tiny, gnat-like insects that skated across the surface of a stagnant puddle leaving little wakes. He heard Devin cough.

Starting their first full day on the island, they ate breakfast and completed the few remaining logistical chores then the science would begin. Noel thought their expedition was off to a good start.

Devin had a game plan. They would immediately hack a path into the rainforest with the aim of carving their way to the summit. Noel figured it would take the better part of two days. They would make observations and catalog what they found. After surveying the island from the perspective of the freighter, Noel was convinced it would take perhaps twice as long. He kept this observation to himself so as not to dampen Devin's fervor.

Noel looked around their little basecamp and put on some coffee. The little two-burner propane stove lit right up. He could hear Devin start to stir inside the tent. He jotted some notes in a small spiral notebook. It would become a diary more than a specific record of the ecology of Insula. And he would keep it to himself. He recalled the banging and trotted down to the bins to inspect for damage while the coffee continued to brew. He found nothing. Not even tracks in the surrounding sand. No evidence of a disturbance whatsoever.

As he sat in the folding chair, he heard a twig break. A pudu deer about the size of a mature cocker spaniel stared at him, its curiosity overcoming its sense of potential danger. It was a shared moment of discovery: the pudu had never seen a human and Noel had never seen a pudu. He quietly retrieved his iPhone from his pocket and snapped pictures. It was a male as it had two small spikes emerging from its head. Rudimentary antlers. What was odd was that the pudu was indigenous to the west coast of South America, specifically Chile and Argentina. It was on the endangered list. His next thought was that it was not a real pudu but a similar species. He jotted down the encounter in his notebook. When he looked up again it had vanished. If it was a pudu, how did it get here?

This was going to be fun.

Holding his head, Devin emerged from the tent clad in gym shorts and flip-flops.

"Good morning, Sunshine. How'd you sleep?" Noel asked.

"Bad headache."

"Maybe you have boat lag. Here, have some coffee and I'll get you some aspirin. Did you hear the racket last night?"

"No. What racket?"

"There was noise by the bins."

"Noise? What kind of noise?"

"Like someone banging on them."

Devin appeared alarmed.

"You think we should put the locks back on?"

"No," Noel answered with a slight chuckle. "The latches are difficult enough for us. Unless there is an intelligent, dexterous being on this island, nothing is going to be able to open those things."

Devin poured some coffee.

"Boy, it's getting hot already."

Devin sat in the folding stadium chair opposite Noel and said, "I'm pooped. My arms are killing me. Christ. All the work we did yesterday."

"We could hold off trying for the summit today and walk around the beach and see what we can find. Start tomorrow."

"Good idea. See anything interesting?"

"I saw a pudu."

"A pudu deer?"

"Yep. Right over there by the woods."

"Couldn't be. Pudu are only found on the west coast of South America. Argentina, Chile. Impossible. You might sooner see Babe, The Blue Ox. If you really saw one. How do you suppose it got here?"

"It was a male. Had antlers. Maybe a bird dropped a seed."

"Do you know how ridiculous you sound?"

"It was a joke."

Devin did not seem amused.

"I took a picture." Noel pulled up the picture on his iPhone and handed it to Devin.

Devin stared at it a moment and turned to see where the deer had been standing.

"Well, I'll be damned." He stared at the picture for a long time before returning the phone.

Noel said abruptly, "Look, a blue footed booby. He's watching me." He turned and pointed.

"How odd."

"It's just a booby. Stupid looking one at that."

Devin leapt to his feet and stared at the bird. The bird stared back.

"*Sula nebouxii*," Devin opined.

"Yeah, so."

"Christ, Noel. The furthest west they are found is the Galapagos!"

Noel abruptly stood up spilling his coffee. He reached for the cell phone but by then the booby had slowly walked off as if bored with the two odd-looking strangers.

They gathered their cameras and ran after it but by the time they and reached the beach it was gone.

Noel returned to his seat and started writing a copious note about the booby who had no business being here. His hand shook with the release of excitement, his eyes welled with joy.

"Oh my God, Devin. Can you imagine the implication of this? Listen."

"Jungle noise."

"Yep. Jungle noise. Let's get going."

They set off down the beach in the direction the booby had taken.

"Let's reconnoiter the beach. I'd like to see if we can walk around the island. We can catalog what we see. If we're finished before it gets too dark, I thought I'd go snorkeling for a bit and see what's in the water."

"Good. Sounds good."

Devin stared out over the water. The place was magnificent. A place of unmolested beauty. There were some distant cumulus clouds rising in the distance but no contrails.

"Have you seen any planes flying over or ships passing."

"Nope. There's a reason nobody has paid attention to this place. It's as isolated as you can get."

As Devin ate his breakfast, he kept looking over his shoulder to see if the pudu returned and likely confirm the picture as genuine not some picture from Wikipedia Noel downloaded to mess with him.

The campsite was nicely shaded in the morning, but it was already starting to get very hot. The sea breeze only served to move around the steamy air.

Before the beachcombers started out, Devin felt compelled to lay down the ground rules yet again. Noel knew he was quite serious about this expedition, so he humored him yet again.

Devin referred to it as the Heisenberg Rule. Insula was a laboratory, perhaps unique in all the world: a geological burp far enough removed from everything to be its own experiment, free from the perturbations of man. They would observe. Even that, as Heisenberg might say, would be enough to disturb the ecology and disrupt the island's future. He had great fear they would inoculate the place and introduce a species of bacteria or dust mite that could ravage the place and leave it sterile or worse. Like Columbus and the treponeme. They would go so far as to put all their trash in one of the bins and bury their feces. Observe, catalog and leave, reiterating once again that, if they played their cards right, they might get to be the lead article in Science or Nature.

He also invoked the Smokey the Bear Rule: Leave your campsite as nice as you found it.

Noel humored him with serious, focused attention even though he had heard it all before sober or intoxicated.

They gathered up cameras, stuck snacks and a canteen into a small rucksack, dropped floppy hats onto their heads, and set out in the direction that seemed most promising.

Devin would occasionally poke into the woods and underbrush like a man searching for an errant golf ball, but otherwise they found nothing unique. They passed several established freshwater streams that found their ways to the sea and some brackish ponds which held promise. There were some small fish, mosquitofish, Noel thought. Nothing more than a species of minnow.

The beach proved surprisingly narrow. In some places the vegetation came to within a few feet of the surf. Large palms reached out over the water's edge at impossible angles. All they saw were fiddler crabs, an occasional fish carcass and ordinary gulls, grebes and noddies. They were nearly ubiquitous in the world, found on almost any beach or body of water on the planet. They could have flown here from practically anywhere without a booby in sight.

Noel suddenly yelled for Devin to come quickly.

"Huh." Noel pointed to a salamander on a rotting log. He picked it up by the tail and placed it in his palm.

"Yeah. Salamander."

"No, you idiot! This is not just *any* salamander. This is a Southern Torrent salamander. It's only found in the Pacific Northwest, you dummy!" He returned it to the log.

"So, Dev. How's your headache now?"

"Still there." He rubbed his temple as if to demonstrate its persistence.

"When we get back, I'll get you some more aspirin. Do you want to go back now while I press on?"

"No! We're on a roll here."

Noel smiled but did not respond. He superficially examined the moss-covered log for a few moments and continued his inspection of the beach. Devin resumed his prodding of weeds and stepping over logs.

After travelling what Noel figured was two miles, they were stopped by a large breastwork of fallen trees and brush extended out over the water. It had been there a long time as it was covered by new growth ferns and vines. It was too big to climb over, so they detoured around it. The sun was high, and, despite a sea breeze, they were sweating profusely. Noel suggested they get out of the sun and rehydrate.

Devin agreed.

They found some shaded rocks and sat to drink their water. Noel's speculation about finding unique species was confirmed. The problem was they were unique to somewhere else, thousands of miles across open ocean on different continents. It was confounding to Noel. Not so, it seemed, to Devin. There was a simple, natural explanation, Devin said, all they needed to do was figure it out. There was no enthusiasm in his voice as he said it. The unbridled zeal he displayed only a short time ago had left him. Maybe it's the heat, Noel thought; maybe it's the headache. Maybe he was just homesick or worried about his pregnant wife.

Noel told Devin he needed to take a leak, so he moved further into the woods. He was just about finished when he felt the disturbing sense someone was watching him. Looking back over his shoulder, he saw a bleached human skeleton entangled in the roots of a fallen palm, mouth agape, staring up at him with empty eye sockets.

"Hey Dev, I think we finally found Amelia Earhart."

"What?"

"Come here. Take a look."

"Holy shit, man," Devin said as he stepped closer to examine it.

"I thought you said no human foot had ever touched this place before ours." Noel said.

Devin stared at it for a moment then said, "No, it's definitely a male. Look at the pelvis and the cheekbone. Besides, in Tommy Bahama trunks? I doubt it's her."

"Poor bastard probably washed up from the tsunami."

"Or fell off a cruise ship," Devin said as he pulled the camera to his eye and clicked off a dozen pictures from different angles close but not so close that the skeleton might reach up and grab him. Noel documented the finding in his log.

The skeleton must have finished Devin off, Noel surmised. Whatever interest Devin had in continuing was gone and he said he wanted to go back so they retraced their steps.

They sat down, jotted their observations for the record and went for a swim, both naked as jaybirds. They saw great schools of fish but nothing one might not see on any tropical beach anywhere else in the world. The ocean was as clear as either could recall seeing. Standing in the waist-high water, Devin peered back at Insula and speculated aloud if they might see evidence of the Tsunami of 2004. He figured it was close enough to the epicenter, he said, that it should have knocked down everything ten feet above sea-level and the island would still in a recovery-growth phase. But he saw no evidence of it. At least not from this vantage point. He looked to the east lest a monstrous wave was approaching that would trap him in the surf. It must have given him a fright and he left the water quickly.

Returning to camp, Noel insisted Devin drink some Gatorade, take something for his headache and lie down. He complied. Once Devin was settled, Noel prodded around the woods behind the campsite. He did not find anything extraordinary.

When Devin woke up Noel told him he wanted to go snorkeling. He had an underwater camera strapped to his wrist and a harness around his waist.

The harness had been the source of a heated argument. Devin insisted that if Noel was going into the ocean, he had to be tethered to the beach by a long, nylon boater's rope as a precaution. That way, he explained, Noel would not get swept out to sea by an unanticipated current, or stung by jelly fish and become paralyzed, attacked by sharks or get lost. Noel was convinced the umbilical was as much for Devin's peace of mind as it was for his own safety. The fact that Noel had experience snorkeling in many oceans, coral reefs and lakes was insufficient to hold sway and he ceded the argument for his friend's peace of mind.

Every so often they would each tug at the rope as a sign all was well. Noel would come up for air, clear his snorkel with a blow and disappear again. It was reassuring. Bored, sitting on the folding chair near the water's edge, he desperately wanted a cold beer but was too afraid to let go of the rope. He could suppress his thirst no longer and, tying the rope to the chair, ran back to a cooler and opened a Budweiser. He sat back down, gave the rope a tug and received a confirmatory tug in return.

Once in the astonishingly clear water, Noel saw groupers, a black-tipped reef shark, a few clown fish and a moray eel around a small coral binnacle. Nothing unexpected. What was surprising was that about fifty yards beyond the water's edge the bottom fell away into a dark abyss. He went down as far as his lungs would take him, but it only became darker. Deep, very deep, as if the ocean floor fell into nothingness; a hole in the seabed that went straight down to the magma.

After swimming for an hour, Noel dried off in the tent, changing into shorts and boots,

Noel watched as Devin's eyes darted to the sea and back to his beer. Perhaps, poor Devin was waiting for a prehistoric kraken with bad intent to leap from the ocean and gobble them up leaving no trace except an abandoned campsite, scratched bins and empty beer cans.

After a prolonged silence, Devin entered the tent to take more aspirin and another nap. Noel went back into the water to cool off. A little while before they would start dinner, Noel decided to reconnoiter the woods behind the camp.

As he glanced upward into the trees for birds or their nests, he suddenly felt something touching his boot. A foot-long, reddish-brown centipede with a body as big as a jumbo hot dog walked leisurely across the instep as if the boot were part of the terrain. Following the instant of recognition, he flicked it off his boot into the woods. He saw it impact a tree, fall to the ground and scurry off. He glanced around for more but saw no others. He had never seen anything like it, nor did he feel like chasing after it just for a photograph. The Amazonian giant centipede was known to grow up to a foot. Capable of eating lizards, frogs and even catching bats on the wing. He would be sure to tell Devin. For now, he was too creeped out to continue. He would look for one later and get its picture. He went back to the camp watching each step.

He made notes in his journal, writing so fast he worried he would not be able to decipher it later. He took a blank sheet, drew a rough map of the world and tried to come up with a theory of how these disparate animals ended up here. The possibilities were baffling, almost illogical, and required extraordinary circumstance. Two species derived from a specific clade separated over millions of years by continental drift and geological happenstance might produce similar appearing animals, though not necessarily identical. It would be difficult to imagine biological or environmental events that would make them evolve into identical species in two places separated by ten thousand miles and millions of years. Every few minutes his mind would be halted by the intrusive memory of the skeleton in the Tommy Bahama trunks. The animals and maggots probably feasted on him for days.

He checked on Devin again. He was still sleeping. He figured Devin might be hungry, so he touched his shoulder gently. Startled, Devin bolted up in his sleeping bag.

"Hey, Dev. Easy, man. Just wanted to see if you were hungry. You slept the rest of the afternoon."

Devin wiped some drool from the corner of his mouth and said softly, "I guess I was dreaming."

"What about?"

"I'm not sure."

Devin looked disoriented. For the second time, Noel thought, coming here might have been a bad idea. Maybe the profound isolation exposed some cracks in Devin's psyche. He would save the intense centipede encounter for another time.

At the end of supper, Noel contemplated asking about the headache but as Devin was almost his normal self again, he deferred. They talked theory. Convergent versus parallel evolution, synapomorphy, atavism and the like. Noel told him about his swim and the fact he saw nothing that was not present in any tropical body of water.

Devin made no attempt to hide his displeasure and became extremely animated that Noel had gone into the ocean without his knowledge. What if he were swept out to sea by an unanticipated current or end up becoming a hungry shark's lunch. That Noel had experience snorkeling in many oceans, coral reefs and lakes would likely prove insufficient to alleviate Devin's fears, so he decided not to argue the point. Nor did he mention the black abyss where Devin's kraken undoubtedly dwelled.

"It would be a little inconsiderate if you disappeared and left me here, don't you think?"

Noel gave thought to apologizing and explain he had only gone in waist deep but decided not to for fear things might escalate. This was not the happy-go-lucky assistant professor with whom he shared an office.

They finished the evening chatting about the weird biology and then went to bed.

Around two AM, they were awakened by the banging of metal and immediately bolted from their sleeping bags. Noel grabbed the spear gun and ran in the direction of the metal storage bins. Devin was close behind.

As he ran up the beach, Noel saw several dark figures, perhaps half a dozen, on top of and around the containers. Approaching the bins, he could make out amorphous animated shadows scurrying around in a moonless night lit only by the stars. Upon his approach the vandals dispersed with remarkable agility, melting into the dark, dense jungle.

Devin ran up behind with a flashlight. But whatever had assaulted the cargo bins had vanished.

Breathless, Devin croaked, "What the hell was that?"

Noel grabbed the flashlight and walked toward the bins shining the light over them. The beam fell on the locks. They had been pummeled but were intact. The bins had acquired large scratches to the paint and numerous dents. Except for the cosmetic damage they remained intact.

"Jesus, look at this," Devin said.

"Well, at least we know one thing. There are primates on this island. I think they were chimpanzees."

"How do you know that?"

"It takes an opposable thumb to grip a rock."

"Not if you're a Peruvian spider monkey or a colobus. How many of them were there?"

"Half a dozen maybe. About the size of a small chimp as best I could tell. Clever little beasts. Look at the tracks."

"Well," Devin sighed. "A least they didn't get the locks off. Even if they did, these bins are hard enough for us to open. Let alone a bunch of monkeys."

"Chimps."

"Yeah, sure. Chimps."

"They don't belong here either. How in the hell did they get here from the Congo?"

Satisfied that the damage to their stores had been only cosmetic—a few dents and scraped paint, they returned to the camp.

"What time is it?"

"Around two," Noel said. "I'm going to make a pot of coffee." As he lit the Coleman lantern, he saw the campsite had been tossed. The chairs had been knocked over and items scattered. "Relax, Dev. I doubt they will be back."

"How do you know that?"

"I'll lay in wait tonight and spear gun one of them. That way they'll know we mean business."

"We agreed we wouldn't kill anything. Remember?"

"Okay, I'll try and reason with them first. Explain to them that theft is one of the Ten Commandments. But for sure we will have to lock everything up at night. Once they figure out there is nothing to be gained by tearing up the place and no easy food to pillage, they'll leave us alone."

"You think?"

"Yeah, pretty sure."

When Noel handed Devin the hot mug of coffee, he noticed Devin's hand was trembling.

"You okay?"

"Headache's back."

After a time, excitement over, Noel suggested they go back to bed. He told Devin he wanted to start working on the path up to the summit in the morning to see if they could find something else that wasn't supposed to be here.

As they curled up in their sleeping bags, a brisk flutter of wind momentarily ruffled the tent then a calm returned.

Perhaps it was the excitement of the attack on the bins, perhaps it was the coffee. Noel watched his friend in the dim light of the lantern. Devin's eyes remained fixed at the top of the tent. He rarely blinked.

Devin broke the protracted silence, "Some continents, like Australia, have never had indigenous primates. This likely means that primates never rafted or island hopped from there."

"Go to sleep."

The unmistakable cacophony of howler monkeys in the distant jungle started. Noel smiled.

Sometime during the night, Noel was awakened by an amber glow. It shown through the mesh windows and filled the tent. Devin was absent.

Noel unzipped his sleeping bag, slipped his feet into his flip flops and stepped outside. The glow engulfed everything leaving virtually no shadow. He peered out over the ocean and the moon, made huge by the refraction of light, was half above the horizon. It was pure white except for the scattered, gray textures of its geography. He found Devin mesmerized by the light. Devin quickly arrived at a scientific explanation. Recalling the 2010 eruptions of Eyjafjallajökull in Iceland when ash covered whole continents, it was probably a forest fire in Australia or a volcano in Africa, he said. The sky was tinged with soot.

Noel was in Germany chasing and cataloging beavers at the time of the eruption. He didn't see anything like this.

They returned to the tent, but Noel did not sleep. There were too many mysteries.

Up early, Noel stared at the curtain of jungle as a sculptor might survey at a monumental piece of rock. Where to begin? It might take a full work crew with bulldozers to carve a respectable path to the summit. They had two machetes and twenty-eight days.

Undaunted, Noel picked a place to begin their assault and together started hacking away at the vegetation with machetes. They succeeded in clearing a bridle path-sized track into the forest. They passed a mangrove swamp and stopped to peer into it. Tadpoles, newts. Nothing unique. As they got deeper into the heavy growth, they heard the distinct yell of the howler monkeys. Noel, in the lead, stopped dead in his tracks. He turned to look at Devin who heard it too. The howler was a New World monkey. Like the pudu, they shouldn't be here. Repeated howls from different directions, the sound unmistakable, echoed against the hills, a chat, no doubt, about the uninvited guests. Devin smiled broadly. He pulled out his phone and recorded a minute's worth of the simian conversation. As he held the phone above his head he trembled with excitement.

They resumed their attack on the tall grass and fronds, Devin scraping his arm on the Kunai grass causing it to bleed. Undeterred, he continued slashing with renewed enthusiasm. The deeper they went in the easier it seemed to become. They found a few open areas and paused to catch their breath and drink some Gatorade. Noel took their bearings. He could not see the pinnacle for the canopy but had a clear understanding of the direction they were to go. He had made a general mental survey of the island as the *Miasma* circled it. Now, using a compass and some notes to guide him, he kept the location of the peak clearly fixed during their ascent.

Figuring they had cut a path about half a mile long, to an elevation of about a five hundred feet, one and a half widths of a man's shoulders, they decided to quit. Reaching another clearing, they rested for a moment, finished their water and turned back. The descent was easy. They would resume in the morning.

They washed the sweat off in the ocean and shared the bottle of Maker's bourbon. It was one-third empty by the time they got around to eating dinner.

Sitting around the campfire eating their reconstituted stew, Devin abruptly yelped and slapped his forearm. Delivering another forkful into his mouth, Noel looked up.

"What was that?"

"A huge black spider was crawling up my arm."

"I thought we agreed we wouldn't kill anything."

"Geez, it took me by surprise. I just reacted. How about one climb up *your* arm, tit-head?"

"Did you happen to see what kind of spider it was before you so arbitrarily smashed it? Old World, New World. Carnivorous?"

"No," he answered clearly annoyed by the question. "Arachnoid entomology is not my strong suit."

"Come on. Figure it out."

Devin was picking the carcass off his arm distressed at the dark yellow liquid the body had released on impact. "Genus spider. Uh, species *blackus*, subspecies *scared-a-me shitless*. Happy?"

Noel snickered as another morsel approached his mouth. "Wouldn't have had much to comment about at the end of his cruise if Darwin smashed the head of every little bullfinch he saw."

"I know exactly what he would say, 'Where was the fucking casino and why do I have to tip the assistant cabin boy?'"

"Did he bite you?"

"No."

"Pity."

...

Halfway into a large doobie, they took stock of what they had seen in their several days in their unique paradise. Two mammalian species that had no business being here, one a primate, all manner of birds, amphibians, a variety of fishes and a purple frog a squat, ugly critter about the size of his hand that reminded Noel of a bloated tick. It was another alien animal that could only have gotten here after a very long swim, a clever trick considering it only hung around in marshes and subterranean habitats. Noel did not mention the bottomless abyss.

It was not enough to identify and catalog. They had to explain.

Devin leaned back causing his canvas chair to audibly protest and asked if this was the result of symplesiomorphy, the ancestral similarities of two geographically diverging species to explain the boobies and pudu.

"Huh?"

They laughed robustly. Probably giving pause to the howlers.

...

Next morning, they resumed hacking and slashing at the jungle. They were close to two thirds of the way, Noel figured. A good strong push and they should be there before supper. At a small clearing they paused to look out over the top of the canopy. They could hear the howlers in the distance and see the deep blue ocean carry to the horizon. It was empty. Noel half expected to see a sailboat or a white Carnival cruise liner drifting slowly over the waves. The expanse gave him a shudder. It reinforced his sense of his sense of isolation isolated from the rest of humanity, but this was the first time he could put it in such perspective.

As they went higher, the noise of the monkeys became muffled and the chirping and songs of birds became more prominent.

Off to the west Noel noted the approach of a dark, sinister squall line stretching across the horizon. It was still many miles away. He resisted the temptation to continue and told Devin they should head back. Once Devin saw the bank of clouds, he agreed. They turned and trotted back down the hill. Arriving back at the encampment about five minutes before the approaching deluge they succeeded in securing their loose gear and strengthen the tie-downs of their tent before the sky exploded with roaring rain, lightning and an extraordinary wind.

Devin must have led a sheltered life, Noel thought. He appeared frightened. Devin had not taken as naturally to roughing it as he thought he would, thinking the sense of high adventure, novelty and the unbridled thrill of discovery would overcome the isolation and unknown. It was one thing to put on waders and glom around a local swamp looking for snakes and be home by dinner. It was quite another to be hundreds of miles from the nearest other human and ten thousand miles from home.

Noel smiled and put the best face on it by cracking wise but Devin could not be distracted especially as the tent was pushed and pulled violently by the wind, the noise of the rain drowning out all but the deepest thought wondering if Devin was suffering from a case of the heebie-jeebies or was just homesick.

...

When the storm abated to a small, steady rain, they left the tent. Palm fronds and torn vegetation littered the campsite. Since they were in the lee of the rainforest, little had been damaged or displaced. Noel had been through many of these events and was pleasantly surprised at how well the little homestead had weathered it.

Noel told Devin to call home on the satellite phone. Check on his wife. Maybe it would settle his nerves. Atmospherics prevented contact serving only to reinforce their isolation.

Despite the lack of significant injury to the camp, Devin appeared despondent. They went about cleaning up the area, removing the fronds and scattered torn branches. By late afternoon, the place had been restored and the sounds of the jungle returned.

The storm left the island thick with moist heat. Before it got dark, they decided to cool off in the surf. Devin seemed restored. They chatted over their reconstituted spaghetti and meat sauce. Noel again speculated about the appearance of several species that had no business being there.

Except for the bleached bones of some poor, unfortunate surfer, they had seen no trace of anything connected to humanity. Once the *Miasma* had sailed over the horizon, they were truly alone, as alone as an astronaut sealed in a capsule hurtling toward Jupiter. They expected to find some detritus of civilization. A beached container. They routinely fell off ships and could be found bobbing in all major bodies of water around the globe. No debris from the Tsunami or the passage of ships. Devin speculated that the island was caught in a maritime vacuum of currents. They flowed past each other making and enormous eddy that allowed virtually nothing to come ashore. Plausible, Noel conceded. Everything just floated on past.

"I still can't explain the pudu, New World primates, Burmese snub-nosed monkey or the stiff in the swim trunks."

"Myanmar snub nosed monkey," Devin corrected.

"Ah, yes."

"Where is the apex predator? Who's at the top of the food chain?"

"Maybe the island is too small to support one."

"Perhaps. But almost every ecosystem has one."

"Besides, they are usually nocturnal, and we may not see them."

When they finished eating, they cleaned up and sipped some Makers. It had been a long, strenuous and stressful day. They would be back at it in the morning. They went to bed.

Noel slipped into his sleeping bag. A soft, cool breeze came in through the mesh windows. Soon Devin was snoring. The jungle had quieted down. Most of the animal noises and calls were absent this evening. Likely some residual effect of the recent storm.

He dozed off.

Species

They awakened refreshed and after conferring about the day's plan, decided to forgo driving to the summit. Instead they put on waders and decided to explore the mangrove swamps. Their intent was to have a day of less taxing activity and gather tardigrades, mosquitoes and any aquatic specimens that might deign to be caught.

The brackish water contained an abundance of different species, all of which were endemic to this part of the globe. Devin appeared quite enthusiastic in his exploration. His fortitude restored, he did not flinch when a black snake emerged from the dark water onto his boot and slithered across it into the underbrush much as the centipede had. He estimated it at four feet in length. When the red tail appeared out of the water, he immediately recognized it as a red-headed krait. It was rare. And extremely poisonous. He had no interest in catching it to prove the species.

Devin gingerly ventured knee deep into the dark, heavily shaded pond, placing his foot gently on the bottom, feeling for any hidden log or irregularity that might trip him sending him into the brackish water. He placed each step warily with tentative purpose.

He felt something soft, like a mound of silt over a rock. As he placed his weight onto the rock it jerked and darted from under his foot in animate surprise. Devin fell into the dark, malodorous pond, his waders instantly flooded with water. Instantly terrified, the permutations of his demise were no doubt endless. Whatever it was left a wake across the inky water.

He righted himself quickly and stepped carefully toward the edge of the pond, perhaps ten feet. Noel laughed as he extended a large branch over the water. Soon, after a protracted struggle, made difficult because of the waders bloated by water, Devin climbed onto the top of the bank of the mangrove.

Instead of joining in on the hilarity of the episode, Noel noted the panicked expression on Devin's face. Struggling to relieve the waders of their load, it took several minutes for Devin to regain his composure. He smelled of stagnant, dirty water. Devin stripped and cleansed himself in the surf. They broke for lunch, making copious notes. They agreed they would tackle the remaining quest for the summit in the morning.

Devin speculated on what he had stepped on. He said it felt like, discounting the lack of tactile differentiation afforded the thick-soled waders, a large horseshoe crab. Although, he admitted, it could have been a crocodile or alligator. Whatever it was, it did not like being stepped on. They speculated about large predators again and what was banging on the bins each night. They smoked a large doobie and went to bed. Before he dozed off, Devin spoke quietly, "This place is kind of creepy."

That night Noel awakened to a full bladder. There was no yellow glow only the nightly banging on the bins which had become so much nocturnal background noise. Flashlight in hand, he walked down to the beach to inspect them. The dark objects working at the lids suddenly bolted into the jungle, too dark and quick to assess what they were. Large monkeys or pigmy cannibals. He checked the bins. They were in the same shape, even though scuffed and battered, as they were when the *Miasma's* crew placed them there.

Trout in the Milk

They were up early anxious to complete their ascension before the oppressive heat of high sun and clouds took hold. They resumed their slashing with machetes clearing a path through the vegetation to the summit. Noel judged they would be done by noon. Devin, who seemed back to his normal mental state, could not conceal his excitement. He was particularly animated as they carved out the trail. There was no mention of headaches. Noel thought Devin's enthusiasm was excessive but did not question it.

Along the way they spotted a blue-eyed lemur sitting calmly in a tree. They both knew it was a critically endangered species found only in Madagascar. Frightened by the noise, two terrified southern pudu deer scampered away as soon as they approached. They were on the IUCN Red List as threatened. Noel jotted a quick note.

The sun was fully up when they reached the apex of their prior efforts already the steam off the rain forest was stifling. This did not deter them. They hacked away following what appeared to Noel as the path of least resistance. Noel noted the efforts became easier the further toward the top they went. The underbrush thinned and the trees were smaller.

As they were about to break through to the top, Noel saw two mito mitos, a pheasant-like bird which was extinct-in-the-wild. The birds spied the humans and, sensing no threat, casually walked away like peacocks in a zoo. He snapped pictures and wrote about the finding on his note pad.

"Devin, what *is* this place? Practically every species we've seen are on an endangered list or belongs somewhere else."

"I have no explanation, Noel. Everything about this place is a mystery."

Devin eagerly pressed on, scything at the deep brush until he was out of sight. Noel widened the path.

"Noel, come here."

"In a minute."

"Now."

Noel stood up, wiped his brow and followed the narrow trail to the edge of a clearing. He stood beside Devin and just stared.

Barely above a whisper, Devin asked, "What the hell is this?"

"Damned if I know. The bigger question is who put it here."

They stepped toward it. The ground for several yards around the base was clear of all plants except for a thin layer of grass that appeared to have been recently mowed.

Devin grinned as he stood in front of it. He arched his back to see to the top.

The machine or relic or whatever it was stood tall enough such that they had to step all the way to the far edge of the grass to take it all in.

The object was a perfect cone sitting on its base. Originally, it was probably black but was now faded dull, dark blue by sun and weather. It obviously had been here a while. It towered, Noel estimated, at least four stories. It stood in front of a barren, guano- streaked rock wall that rose another story or two behind it and was likely all that remained of the volcano that formed this place. On the periphery of the escarpment grew trees and brush like a green fringe. There were no clinging vines or grass from the crevices of the rock wall facing the object. The most curious feature of the thing were paired appendages that projected horizontally near the apex. They were tear-drop shaped, and appeared as if a pair of swimmer's goggles had been slipped over a dunce's cap. Each had a yellow lens, about the size and shape of an oblong kitchen table.

Devin moved several tentative steps forward and placed his palm on it. He snapped back and yelped.

"Electric shock?"

"No, hot."

"Well, what were you expecting? It's sitting out here in the sun like West Texas asphalt."

They walked slowly around the base until they had completed their inspection.

"What the hell is this thing?"

"Boy," Noel replied. "No windows, no doors. Not even a seam. It's like one solid piece of metal. Must weigh a bijillion pounds."

Noel rapped his knuckles on the side to test its density. He was expecting the hollow sound of an empty oil drum but, there was no internal echo. It was solid.

"What the hell is this thing?" Devin asked.

"beats me, Dude."

Devin stared at the lenses.

"It's alive," Devin barely whispered.

"Jesus, Devin. It's as inert as the rock it's sitting on."

"No." Devin turned full face toward Noel. "That yellow glow the other night?" He pointed to the lenses.

Noel peered up at the appendages. "Don't be silly."

"I mean it."

"Devin, we have found no trace of a human presence anywhere on this island, save Amelia Earhart's brother. I contend nobody was ever here before us."

"So how did this thing get here?" Devin muttered.

They continued staring at it as if they were staring at a sacred archeological site that at last answered all questions.

Finally, Devin spoke as he held the camera to his eye stepping around it to capture every detail from every angle. "'Some circumstantial evidence is very strong, as when you find a trout in the milk.'"

Noel shook his head.

"It's looking at us," Devin said softly. "It knows we're here."

Devin seemed mesmerized by the relic; his stare transfixed.

Bewildered, Noel decided it was time to go. He interrupted Devin's hypnotic stare and took him by the arm. "Let's go. I need lunch."

As they turned to leave, Noel noticed an old monkey carcass the size of a baboon under a tree as if it wanted to be close to the thing when it died.

In their descent, no words were spoken.

They ate lunch in silence each mind speculating on the possibilities. Noel was quite puzzled, but Devin seemed profoundly shaken. He barely touched his meal.

Devin looked up at Noel, his face contorted by bewilderment.

"We have to call home tonight and tell the girls what we found."

"I'd advise against that."

Perplexed, Devin asked why.

"They might worry."

...

In their descent no other words were spoken.

They spent the rest of the day poking around the local rain forest. Neither found anything. They weren't looking very hard.

After dinner, they drank some of the bourbon their discussion dominated by the relic. All mention of biology ceased.

"Clearly, that thing is not from these parts," Devin said calmly.

"Not of this planet, you mean?"

"Yes. Possibly. Perhaps probably."

"This is silly. There must be a plausible explanation that does not invoke aliens or the supernatural. Or that we suffered a shared mass hysteria at an apparition brought on by our isolation."

"Clever," Devin said, "but, I don't think so."

Devin stared at the fire. He appeared to be listening to something only he could hear. Noel finally convinced Devin to go to sleep. They would resume their conversation in the morning.

As he adjusted himself in his sleeping bag, Devin said softly, "We both touched it. Did it seem like a shared apparition to you?"

...

Noel realized they had gone to bed having not done the one thing they should have: talk through their thoughts of the relic. In bed, Devin tossed and turned. Noel would surreptitiously look at Devin and saw his eyes were still open every time he looked. Noel contemplated early termination of the expedition. If Devin didn't snap out of it, he would recommend it. That thing had squashed the naturally inquisitive, happy-go-lucky Devin like a bug under a heel. Noel's friend and fellow explorer was clearly spooked.

It was after midnight when the first large drops arrived on their tent. Within minutes it was pummeled by a tropical downpour. The sound on the jungle and the tent was hypnotic. It allowed Noel to sleep.

When Noel woke up the rain had stopped, and Devin was gone. Noel quickly climbed from the sleeping bag and left the tent. Devin had prepared breakfast. He was his usual sleepy, morning self. He had reconstituted eggs and coffee ready to go. They sat on their folding stadium chairs and talked about the thing.

Devin was convinced it had been there a long time and had been placed there by a human hand. In this remote part of the Indian Ocean, it probably served as a lighthouse or navigational aid back in the days before GPS.

Noel did not tell him a sexton and a little knowledge would have obviated the need for it.

Maybe the Japanese constructed the thing at some point in their conquest.

Noel did not tell him that this place was poorly known and of no earthly martial value.

"Are you surprised there were no vines covering it or that the place had not been overgrown by the restless, relentless jungle? Who cuts the grass?"

Noel said he did not know. He did not tell Devin about the large baboon skeleton he had seen on their initial inspection. They had not seen one. It was a major find, but Noel kept it to himself. It was, after all, long dead

Then Noel verbalized what he knew they were both contemplating. After the words left his mouth, he regretted it. "Maybe you're right, this thing is not of this earth."

Finally, they gathered their gear in silence, put on long pants to prevent chiggers and headed up the trail, Devin setting the agenda. Noel was apprehensive about ascending the trail but withheld objection. At one of the clearings about half-way up the slope, Devin veered off into the tall grass, heading for the tree line. Doing so, he mentioned quite casually that, whatever it is, it knew they were there.

In unguarded moments, Noel caught Devin snatching glimpses in the direction of the summit.

The Captive

For two days everything went smoothly. They were approaching the halfway point of their expedition. They had identified several dozen species from spiders to primates that were not indigenous to this part of the globe. It was a mystery for which they still had no explanation. How did these widely varied animals get here?

The general mechanics of the ecosystem remained unresolved as well. For an island this size and biologically complex, they should have found several large predators, cats most likely. They had not. The evidence was not there. Except for the relic and the stiff in the Tommy Bahamas trunks, they found zero evidence of a transient or indwelling human presence.

Then one afternoon following a raucous romp in the surf, Noel noticed a strange look on Devin's face. He kept tugging at his ear. He tilted his head and thumped the side of it.

"What's eating you?"

"I have a ringing in my ears."

"Ocean."

"Perhaps, but I had it in my ears before we got in the water."

"Allergies."

Devin shrugged.

Later that night Devin's earache became oppressive. He became unsettled.

Noel gave him some Tylenol and suggested he try and sleep. They turned in hoping tomorrow the ringing in his ear would be gone and things would be back to normal.

In the middle of the night, Noel woke up to check on his friend. Devin tossed and turned again. Noel, hoping his friend would be fine by morning, pulled the sleeping bag under his chin and fell asleep.

...

When he awakened, Devin was gone again. His first hope was that he was making breakfast again. He rolled out of the sleeping bag and left the tent. No breakfast. No Devin.

Noel walked down to the beach then over to the bins. No sign of him. Odd, he thought.

Wherever he is, he'll be back. Noel proceeded to make coffee.

After forty-five minutes and no Devin, Noel put his on boots and trotted up the trail.

Devin was seated Indian style on the grass staring up at the relic.

"What are you doing?"

"Listening."

"To what?"

"I can feel it. Can you?"

"You can feel it listening?"

Maybe it was like the elephants chatting back and forth in wavelengths only they can hear.

"You alright?"

"Sure." Devin turned to him and smiled.

"How's your earache?"

"What? Oh, it's gone." Devin was smiling.

"Why don't we go back down? I have some fresh coffee on."

Devin resumed staring at the thing. "Sure, I'll be down in a minute."

"No, Devin. Let's go now."

In an instant, Devin's expression turned hostile. "I said, I'd be down in a minute."

Noel hesitated, "Well, okay. Easy boy. I'll start on the eggs. Don't dally. You hate cold eggs."

His gaze returned to the relic. Devin said, "No, I'll be fine with some cereal."

"Okay, cereal it is." Noel turned and left.

...

An hour later, Devin trotted down the hill and returned to camp. Noel was writing in a notebook when he arrived.

"Whatchadoin' there?" Devin asked,

Noel looked up at him. "Just writing some notes about the lizard stampede. You missed breakfast."

"Okay, I'll have something later."

Devin poured coffee. Noel noticed again the small, barely perceptible, tremble in his friend's hand.

"Are you okay?"

As if insulted, he snapped, "Of course I'm okay. Why do you ask?"

"You were staring at that thing. You said it was talking to you. That's kind of weird, man."

Devin sipped his coffee.

"What was it saying?"

Devin sat quietly for a moment, then abruptly threw out his unfinished coffee and stood up, "Let's go see if we can find whatever it was I stepped on in the pond the other day."

Noel studied his friend for a few moments then said, "Sounds like a plan."

...

The rest of the day proved uneventful. Devin did not look up at the summit and they discovered the strange animal in the pond was just a large turtle similar to anyone might find anywhere in tropical Asia. Devin grabbed it, cataloged it, apologized for stepping on it and released it.

By late afternoon, they went for a swim and worked on their notes. Devin was particularly quiet. Noel found him staring at a page in his notebook, pen in hand, and not write anything for half an hour.

Noel fixed dinner, stew out of a can, and Devin turned in early. No observance of the sunset, no marijuana or alcohol. And no conversation.

Noel thought it through. He was finally convinced that it had nothing to do with the relic. Devin was homesick. That had to be it. Periodic chats over the satellite phone to his pregnant wife half-way across the globe only added to his isolation.

Tomorrow marked the halfway point. They still had much work to do; more than he thought they could accomplish in just fifteen days. But Devin's mental state, staring blankly into middle distance and his short temper gave him pause. Perhaps they should end it sooner, Noel thought. Call up *Miasma* and tell MacKenzie to take them off as soon as feasible. Devin might protest harshly but it would be for the best. They had enough to write a paper, several perhaps, and certainly enough to satisfy the grant.

Devin went to bed. Noel stayed up to stare at the stars. The Southern Cross was particularly beautiful. He thought of the relic. It was as inert as the rock it sat on. The idea that it could communicate with Devin was the result of isolation and a vivid imagination or perhaps hallucination. Noel knew there had to be an explanation. There was always an explanation.

When Noel climbed into his sleeping bag, Devin was snoring softly. He would be good for the night.

Later, Noel looked for the amorphous lump in the bed, but it was gone. He was probably at the altar of the relic. Noel went back to sleep.

When Noel stepped out of the tent next morning Devin had breakfast ready.

Devin looked and acted particularly animated. He was ready to take his binoculars and make a serious effort to catalog the birds near the canopy. He thought he saw a Ceylon Paradise Flycatcher. Unusual but not out of the realm of possibility that it flew here to take up residence. The camera with the foot-long telephoto lens clicked away at the sight of a beautiful Great Hornbill. Noel saw it, too. It was magnificent. Devin was smiling broadly, proud of his find. Noel mused about what the Hornbill knew of the relic.

After a successful, essentially normal day, they took the stadium chairs down to the surf, watched the lightning dance across the horizon and downed the last of the bourbon. There was a cool breeze off the water. They talked for a while. Devin waxed philosophical. With all the SETI and astrobiology and planetary discoveries, was it not possible there was intelligent life elsewhere in the universe?

No, Noel answered, this is it. The odds are against it. Conditions have to be perfect. More than perfect. Were it not for a single asteroid strike we'd be lizards.

Devin countered. "Sure, there is life elsewhere. The universe is brimming with life that we cannot even imagine. Ignore the Fermi Paradox. Or the Drake equation for that matter. He didn't take into account the number of Universes or galaxies within them. The odds are just too great. If you put an infinite number of monkeys in front of an infinite number of typewriters and give them an infinite amount of time one of them will write War and Peace.

"Or that life originated on the earth when some extraterrestrial visitors found nothing interesting about the place, tossed out their garbage inoculating the planet. The 'Rotten Tomato Theory' of the origin of life on earth."

They exchanged glances and laughed, but Devin's laugh seemed forced.

"Devin, are you okay?"

Devin's mood suddenly darkened, snapping, "Of course I'm okay. Why do you ask?"

"You were staring at that thing. You said it was talking to you. That's kind of weird, man."

"No, I said I was listening."

"That damned thing looks like something out of a 1920's horror movie. A big, clumsy, martian rolling over things, twisting stiffly one way then the other just to see where it was going, knocking down trees, snapping flagpoles, crushing pedestrians and trashcans, making burping sounds and guttural noises, shooting death rays at cows out of some unseen orifice."

Devin grew sullen, his stare fixed on the lightning.

Noel thought again about ringing up MacKenzie.

"Let's call the girls. We haven't spoken to them in a couple days."

Devin gave no response.

"We're out of bourbon. Want a joint?"

Nothing.

...

The moon was waning gibbous and by two in the morning it was bright enough to awaken Noel. He stared at the gentle undulation of shadows of palm trees on the tent. The rain forest was alive with the distant, muffled sounds of animals up and active, going about their nightly business. Devin snored softly.

A short time later, he looked over at Devin, but the sleeping bag was collapsed. Devin was gone again.

Noel slid out of his sleeping bag, slipped on shorts dropping his feet into his boots. He took his flashlight and walked over to the entrance of the path and started up the hill.

He used the light to keep him on the narrow path, watching where his footsteps would take him. He was startled by the sudden appearance of a dozen six-inch long, black snakes that slithered through the circle of light on the ground. He had never known snakes to demonstrate social behavior or herd-like activity. Where were they going in such a hurry? The biologist in him would investigate in the morning.

He waited for any stragglers to cross the circle of light on the ground before proceeding.

He felt the heat of the fetid breath on his face. Even in the dark, without benefit of light, he could see the bared, yellow canines inches from his face. It roared and vanished into the bush with the loud disturbance of vegetation. The surprise knocked him onto the ground. This was the closest he had ever come to a baboon. He trembled as he pulled himself erect. The baboon's mouth was big enough to snatch off the front of his face.

Terrified but undeterred, Noel resumed his journey.

When he reached the clearing, he found Devin seated Indian style at the base of the relic staring up at it in the white moonlight, the shadows sharp on the ground, the scarp and the relic. Devin seemed humble and small as a student might before a revered Tibetan monk or ancient demigod. Devin played his flashlight beam over the thing, perhaps trying to wake it. Maybe get it to turn on *its* lights on. He looked up at the lenses no doubt hoping they would pivot down toward him in acknowledgement.

Alas, if it knew Devin was there it gave no indication.

"You know me, don't you?"

Nothing.

"We've met before."

No sound, no vibration of the earth, no amber glow.

"What do you want? Why are you here?"

He came to his feet and walked over and touched it. It was still, deadly silent and likely warm from the day's high heat.

"Speak to me."

The thing remained silent.

Devin acted like it was aware of his presence. Perhaps it was incapable of giving a sign. Devin talked to it. "How did you get here and why? What are you saying? Who do you report to? Speak to me.?

Suddenly as if exhausted beyond resistance, Devin curled into the fetal position at the foot of the thing and instantly fell fast asleep.

Noel walked over and touched Devin's shoulder. He awakened with a start.

"Devin."

He awakened like a child from a dense dream wiping the drool from his cheek. He appeared disoriented as if not knowing where he was or how he had gotten here.

"Come on, pal. Let's go back down and I'll make breakfast then you can tell me all about it."

Devin staggered weakly to his feet confused as if aroused from a coma. Noel knew Devin was bewildered; not sure by what force had placed him there.

"Come on. Let me help you."

With no words exchanged, Noel guided his friend back down the trail as if he might a doddering old man and arranged him into his sleeping bag then zipped the tent flap behind him.

Noel walked down to the beach and tried to raise MacKenzie to come get them.

There was no answer.

...

Noel heard the tent zipper.

Noel turned to look at Devin who had emerged silently from the tent.

"Do you know I saw a baboon last night?" Noel said.

"You don't say."

"Now that requires an explanation," Devin said blandly. "An Old-World simian on such a remote place. How can you explain that, pal?"

"Devin, you were with the thing last night. I found you asleep in front of it."

"You did? Not possible."

"Devin."

There was a long silence.

"Do you want me to fix breakfast?" Noel asked.

There was no response.

Noel poured him some coffee.

"Dev, ever since we discovered that thing, you've been acting weird, man. I am getting real concerned." He did not want to mention the apparent rupture of Devin's sanity. "I think you are very homesick."

Devin pondered the statement and sipped the coffee.

"Perhaps we should take a break and fly home. We have enough data to keep us busy for months. Besides we can work on what questions to answer and come back if we need to. We have enough grant money."

Devin stared down at the coffee and said softly, "I don't want to leave."

Trying to be as conciliatory as he knew how, Noel spoke again, "Devin, I think it would be best. You need to see your wife."

"You saw a baboon last night."

"Yes, I told you."

"And a herd of snakes."

"Yeah. A bunch of little ones

...

Devin ate little but claimed he was feeling well and refreshed enough to dress and walk into the rain forest in search of Noel's band of roving snakes. Maybe even catch one. Or two. Noel noted Devin took no notebook or camera.

He called after him, "Be back for lunch."

When he was out of sight, Noel walked down to the beach and called MacKenzie. "What's wrong," the captain quipped, "Out of bourbon?

He told the captain that Devin had taken ill but would not elaborate. They needed to be taken off the island as soon as it could be arranged. MacKenzie told him it would be three days. If they needed to get off sooner, he should call the Royal Australian Coast

Guard. If things worsened, Noel told him, he would do just that.

Devin pushed his fork around his pile of ham and beans. He conceded to Noel that perhaps he was a little homesick and his wife was pregnant with their first child. Concern for her only added to his loneliness. And, even though she sounded okay, he was worried. He had not spoken to her in several days so perhaps apprehension had been part of it as well. Noel hoped this was the case.

After supper they ran down to the beach and relaxed in the warm surf. Noel found a particularly large starfish and pointed it out. Devin stared at it for a moment then turned back toward camp saying, "Reef starfish, *Stichaster australis*. Not usually found in these waters. Nice find."

...

The next morning Devin looked and acted particularly animated. He was ready to take his binoculars and make a serious effort at cataloging the birds near the canopy. He thought he saw a Ceylon Paradise Flycatcher. Unusual but not out of the realm of possibility floating over the trade winds. The camera with the foot-long telephoto lens clicked away at the sight of a beautiful Great Hornbill. Noel saw it. It was magnificent. Devin was smiling broadly, proud of his find. Noel mused about what the Hornbill knew of the relic.

After a successful day, they took the stadium chairs down to the surf, watched the lightning dance across the horizon and drank the last of the bourbon. There was a cool breeze off the water. They talked for a while. Devin waxed philosophical. "With all the SETI and astrobiology and planetary discoveries, was it possible we are the only intelligent life in the universe?"

"This again?" Noel quipped. "No," Noel answered, "this is it."

"I'm pooped," Devin said. "I'm gonna turn in." He got up and without carrying back his stadium chair. Noel stayed up as long as he could to see if Devin would conduct another evening foray, but all was quiet, and he finally turned in.

Through the night Noel woke up to periodically check on his

friend. He was an amorphous lump in the sleeping bag. Noel returned to sleep.

It was well past midnight when the first large drops arrived on their tent. Within minutes it was pummeled by a tropical downpour. The sound of the rain on the tent was hypnotic. It allowed Noel to sleep.

Noel woke up, checked his watch and saw that it was three AM. The rain had stopped. He turned to look at Devin. His sleeping bag was empty. A quick glance showed the campsite was empty as well. The jungle was peculiarly quiet. No nocturnal banging on the bins. No howler monkeys. He put on a pair of gym shorts and boots. Grabbing the flashlight, he stepped out into the night. It was clear and quite dark as the moon had not risen. The stars were pinpoint specks of light from horizon to horizon.

With the cone of light from the flashlight guiding his steps, he wondered how hard it would be to persuade Devin to leave the relic and come back to bed. He kept an eye out for stampeding little snakes and irate baboons.

He ran up the wet trail. Without revealing his presence, Noel caught up with Devin but stayed a dozen yards behind. Devin's flashlight beam played back and forth on the ground. It seemed to be ascending at a leisurely pace.

Noel, keeping his distance, saw Devin sit down in front of the relic.

"You know me, don't you?" Devin asked softly

Nothing.

"We met earlier."

No sound, no vibration of the earth, no amber glow, no bolt of lightning.

"What do you want? Why are you here?"

He came to his feet, walked over and touched it no doubt still warm from the day's high heat.

"Speak to me."

The relic remained silent and inert.

Suddenly, Devin curled into the fetal position at the foot of the relic and fell instantly asleep.

Noel watched in frightened amazement. Realizing he could not leave him here, Noel helped Devin to his feet like an old man who had fallen and did not have the strength to lift himself from the ground.

"Come on pal. You're not Pendrick and that thing is not Doctor Moreau."

Guiding his friend step by step down the path like an invalid, he finally got Devin into his sleeping bag.

...

Devin slept well into the afternoon.

Later, Devin picked at his dinner in silence and again complained of a headache. There was no mention of last night's foray. He turned in early.

Noel stayed up as long as he could to see if Devin got up again, but all was quiet, and he went to bed also.

Through the night Noel stirred periodically to check on his friend. Each time he was reassured by the shapeless lump in the sleeping bag. But he had been misled before. He was reassured by Devin's soft snore.

Noel woke up and checked his watch. It was three AM. He turned to look at Devin. The sleeping bag was empty. The jungle was peculiarly quiet. No nocturnal jungle noises; no serenade by the howlers. He put on a pair of gym shorts and slipped on his boots. Grabbing the flashlight, he stepped into the night glimpsing Devin entering the trail. He thought about waiting until daylight but decided against it. His problem had reached critical mass.

With the cone of light from the flashlight guiding his steps, Noel wondered how hard it would be to persuade Devin to leave the relic and depart the island. The nearby rustling of the vegetation beside the trail caused him no concern. He reached the relic. Devin was not there. He shone the beam on the thing. He ran back down the trail to the camp. Only a small lingering flame rose from the fire pit, but it was enough to see Devin was not here either. He glanced into the tent; the amorphous lump had returned. Reassured, Noel sat by the fire to collect his wits.

Noel was startled by the sudden rustle of a stampeding animal. Devin slammed through the trees at full charge, the machete above his head like a samurai. Noel bolted to his feet and turned. He felt the swift wind of the blade pass his face. Devin's forward momentum caused him to trip and fall to the sand. Quickly regaining his footing, he held the machete behind his shoulder cocked like a bat. Noel knew in the time it took his brain to process it that if Devin connected, he would instantly be decapitated or hacked to death.

He backed away and shouted for Devin to come to his senses and that he would get them off the island any minute.

Devin panted heavily and gave out a guttural, barely perceptible grunt.

"Devin, you're going to hurt yourself with that thing! Put it down, for Christ's sake!"

Devin grunted again and pushed his feet against the sand in a lunge but only managed to push the sand away and fell short. Noel easily avoided the swinging blade. Noel grabbed some rocks and hurled them at Devin. One hit him in the chest and only managed to elevate his fury.

Lifting the machete once more, Devin lunged. Noel dodged the blade again and tripped him as he went by. Devin fell to the sand and lost his hold on the machete. As he reached for it, just barely beyond the extent of his grip, Noel fell on him and pushed his left hand down onto Devin's throat, screaming at him to knock it off. Devin, teeth bared in a sardonic grin, tried to push away the hand locked on his throat.

Fearing he would break loose, Devin's eyes bulging with rage, Noel hit Devin's skull with a rock. It was not the fearsome blow he had hoped for. It was almost a timid strike. It only served to enhance Devin's seething rage and strength even as his forehead streamed with blood.

His grip tightening on his friend's throat, Noel mustered all his might and brought the rock down on his head hoping it might knock some sense into him. Instead, the blow, fueled by adrenalin, made a muffled cracking noise and Devin fell limp.

In an uncontrolled instant Noel struck a third blow and felt the brain yield underneath the crunching skull.

If Devin was not dead, he soon would be. He slowly released his grip on his friend's throat and sat back on his legs. Devin's eyes were fixed on the tent. They reflected the faint glimmer of the fire.

"Jesus, what have I done? Oh, God. I'm so sorry, Dev. Forgive me."

After an hour of staring at the calamity before him, he tried to figure out what to do. It was self-defense surely.

As the first rays of daylight arrived, he pulled back the mangled scalp and cut away a portion of it. He scooped out some brains with a spoon and removed a shard of skull. He took them to a rock outcropping in the woods and doled out the brains like a dollop of pudding and placed the scalp and skull fragment on a rock suitable for the scene of the accident. He tossed the spoon into the dark pond below.

Scavengers would consume it before dusk, but it was his best evidentiary effort.

He retrieved Devin's sleeping bag; the formless lump had been two pillows. With great difficulty, he shoved the body into the sleeping bag. As he zipped it shut, he caught a last glimpse of Devin's reddish-blond hair and started crying. He wept uncontrollably. Gathering himself, he sealed it with duct tape and started digging a hole. He was about five feet down into the moist, compact sand when he pushed the sleeping bag into the grave and refilled it. That way the animals would not seek it out. If somebody needed the body for any purpose, they could dig it up. He piled as many large rocks as he could find onto the grave.

"Here lies Devin Coates, PhD. Mad scientist. God bless him. May he rest in peace."

He gathered the notes and tossed them into the fire along with all the camera chips.

...

For three days, he sat on the beach and watched the horizon awaiting *Miasma's* arrival. Mackenzie accepted his explanation of the accident and saw no purpose in digging up the corpse. Noel told them where the accident had occurred and offered to show them, but the Captain declined. He also told them the little expedition had been a complete bust. They saw nothing of interest.

As he boarded the tramp steamer, he looked back at the camp and the summit. He could not see the relic from this vantage. He asked if he could have something for his headache. As they sailed away, he stood by the railing staring at the island until he could no longer see it.

The Swansong of Perphrobisher Barbash, III

It started out just another call. The ghastly had become ordinary. I know I speak for all of us. They say I should smile more. I ask why. I do not know how I can.

It was hot and rainy when I stepped out the door sliding open with indifferent electric precision. I usually don't go out to greet our guests, but tonight the lightning and thunder echoing through the city intrigued me. In the distance, I can hear the approach of the familiar singsong wailing against the concrete walls, walls that when erected held so much promise. They turn a corner and the red, twirling light sabers slash at the moisture. I turn and go in. The adrenalin rush of each arrival has long since passed.

The bay is ready. Everyone knows their place and mission. It is a ritualized preparation that has become grotesquely and pathetically routine.

His name is Perphrobisher Barbash, III. Twenty-nine-year-old white male. Multiple gunshot wounds. Odd, I thought. What kind of destiny did your parents expect for you when they chose your name? The continuation of the bloodline? Instant social acceptance? Inheritance by preordination?

They roll him in. I stand aside. I take in whole gigabytes of information in a second. Tube in his throat. IV in his arm. Pale. Sweaty. Expensive suit slashed apart by eager scissors. Expensive loafers only the one tenth of one percent can afford.

Three holes. One in each chest. One in the abdomen. One in the right thigh. For once it is no sullen, defeated gangbanger but, instead, someone whose life had meaning. Mr. Barbash, you are different. Maybe my skill honed on the savages will save you.

I don't care to know, but they tell me anyway. He was out with his young bride. A stroll after a dinner no one within my range of vision could afford. Waking up this morning, you thought you might live forever. You are an innocent caught in the crossfire of savages. For this I feel sadness in my heart as my hands start to move about you. My survey is complete. Plugging holes. Trying to restore some semblance of continuity.

A resident shoves a line as big as a knitting needle under the skin of your collar bone. He has done this a thousand times. He is expert. He never misses. He has had lots of practice.

I pull down your underwear so I can run my fingers over your groin. Other expert hands grab your penis. For the uninitiated it is a rape. You are stripped naked for all to see. I can feel a fleeting pulse. Your bladder contains clear urine. The color of the sauvignon blanc you so recently savored. I look at the monitor. The bouncing point of light tells me your life force is still strong. You have not given up. Nor do you struggle. You just lay there.

A splash of brown paint on your chest and I take a knife. I find a convenient rib. I cut deeply. I am disappointed by the meager volume of blood released by my blade. I take a clamp and drive it with great effort into the chest cavity. I feel the satisfying pop at the release of tissues and am greeted by a spurt of dark blood horizontally over my gloved hand and naked forearm. This is bad; very bad.

I take a tube the size of a garden hose and drive it into the opening. I take the hand of a med student and tell him to hold it. Do not let it move in time or space, I say, for I cannot spare a single moment to sew the wire in place to secure it.

I move to the other side and repeat the act. I use tape to hold it as there is not another med student handy.

Red blood seeps from the hole in his belly like lava lifting from the depths of molten earth, red rivulets directed by impartial gravity. Mr. Barbash's belly is as tense as a watermelon.

They tell me his pressure is dropping fast. It is a redundant statement. I do not need to be told.

I tell everyone to stand back. It is the last great maneuver of desperation. They have seen it before, and no one wants to get cut. I again take the knife and slash at the skin of his left chest. It would appear a most violent act were it not performed so expertly and with such focused desperation. I reach in and push the distended lung aside so I can feel my target. I touch his aorta, the wellspring of life. Instead of firm and tense with delivery, it is soft with empty defeat. I put a clamp on it anyway. I have nothing left to offer. If we can keep his upper half alive maybe we can save him. But I have been down this road before. The bouncing light goes haywire and, my hand still in his chest, I reach in to touch his heart. It is quivering. I squeeze it. I shock it. I beseech it. It does not listen. It becomes flaccid at the moment of surrender. It cannot hear me.

Alas, Mr. Barbash, I cannot save you. Too much of you has spilled from the holes. I do not have enough fingers to plug your punctured dikes. Death, once so clearly committed, cannot be staunched.

Silently, I curse you Mr. Barbash because things have happened inside you that I cannot fix before your last particle of life departs. You are the victim of a barbarity even Orwell could not have imagined.

I feel I owe you an apology as you lie naked and lifeless. I am sorry we so thoroughly brutalized you in an effort stop the flood. We stripped you so completely of your dignity. Sorry, man, it comes with the territory.

One day before the end I will write "Tales of a Cutter." In it I will state that God guides my hand; all I do is hold the knife. I will also state all lives have worth. Sadly, some more so than others.

I clean up and wait for the next one.

Task Force Boston

An excerpt from the forthcoming novel

Prologue: The Truck Driver Who Wanted to Be a Soldier

2230 15 Dec 44

I sat on an old wooden chair in front of a delightful, hypnotizing fire. My feet rested on the raised stone hearth, warm, dry and toasty. A rare treat. I wiggled my toes. Above the fire on a telephone wire strung between two nails driven into a mantel the size of a railroad tie, hung my other socks, three pair of thick woolen ones recently acquired. They were drying after washing them with my last sliver of Ivory soap. Sally had sent me the soap, along with cookies packed in popcorn, stationary, pipe tobacco and a birthday card, after we had cleared the Hurtgen. Three bars had lasted me through the past month. I was sipping some scotch out of a canteen left over from the Colonel's liquor ration. The soft sound of Armed Forces Network was playing Christmas carols emanating from a little box radio in the corner.

Third Battalion headquarters was billeted in a strongly constructed stone farmhouse with planked floor, a kitchen and three bedrooms on the second floor in the little Luxembourg town of Consthum on the reverse slope of a ridge running parallel to the front just a mile or so east. It was cozy and formidable. Another piece of wire was strung between the back door and the outhouse. It was a necessity in the dark, frequently foggy night. The house and the land it sat on had been untouched by the war. An oddity. A big, hay-filled barn was about twenty yards beyond the outhouse. The battalion headquarters staff, cooks, clerks and Signals crew were shacked up in it not realizing they were a ripe target for a well-placed artillery round. It was surrounded by a large stone wall that acted as a small corral.

I pulled Sally's most recent letter out of my breast pocket. It was written the week after Thanksgiving. I received it a few days ago and had read it at least a dozen times. Replacing the letter into my pocket, I started darning my fifth pair of socks. A hole had developed over the big toe. Ever since I was a kid, the idea of wearing a sock with a hole in it was anathema and new socks were difficult to come by.

In the corner, near the large table on which was spread several layers of maps, overlays and papers, sat the communications corporal in front of the battalion switchboard. The coziness must have gotten to him because he kept nodding off. It was mildly amusing to watch his chin bounce off his chest and his head spring back again.

As I studied him, I again lamented that, with increasing rank and position, the value of the life of each individual soldier became less in the economy of war. Sad that I did not even know his name.

The phone rang startling both of us. The corporal answered, and after an exchange of words, turned to me.

"Major, it's Sergeant Mayo, Love Company. He wants to talk to Colonel Speith."

He didn't need to tell me which company Sergeant Mayo was in. Everybody in the Battalion knew who he was. And if Mayo was calling to speak to Speith, bypassing the entire chain of command to discuss something with the 3rd Battalion commander, there was something serious on his mind.

"Here, I'll take it." I walked over and answered the phone. "Mayo. What's up?"

"Good evening, Major. Where's the Colonel?"

"He's at Division. He has a toothache."

"Don't you think he oughta get that damned tooth pulled?"

"Too chicken."

First Sergeant Mayo laughed.

"What can I do for you?" I wondered if he could sense the annoyance.

"Well, I hate to bother you, but a couple of outposts have reported some noises beyond the wire. Maybe it's just jitters by some of the new guys, but Klayman says he heard it too. He's pretty insistent."

Klayman had been a private under me in Love Company. By the time we left the Forest, he was a platoon leader. The annoyance had evaporated. At least partially. I sighed involuntarily saying, "OK, I tell you what. Let me run up there and have a look."

"Sorry to put you out, Major, but I did not want this to go unreported. Rookies."

"Yeah, rookies."

"Thanks, Runt." I hated that nickname. It offended both my short stature and my rank.

I put on a second pair of socks. They had warmed by the fire. I bloused my pants and laced up my prized jump boots, pulled on a sweater and wrapped the woolen muffler around my neck. I slipped my boots into the three-buckle galoshes and snapped them up. I pulled on my tan mackinaw and zipped it up until the muffler was tight around my neck. The Signals corporal studied me as I flung my shoulder holster over my head, resting the .45 over my heart. I put on my web belt and stuffed the canteen with the scotch into its pouch. I slipped on my gloves and grabbed the carbine. I turned to look at the corporal. He smiled wanly; no doubt glad it was me instead of him.

"This better be good."

He nodded.

"You know where I'll be."

"Yes sir."

I stepped into the cold, foggy night and climbed into a jeep. But not before running my hand over the wire cutting post welded to the front bumper. I refused to ride in or drive a jeep that did not have one. German infiltrators have been known to string stout piano wire between two trees across a road at about the level of your neck. You can't put up the windshield this close to the front for fear of having some stray light reflect off it and give yourself away to some enemy observer who would only be happy enough to drop in a mortar round or two just to say hello.

The warmth I had accumulated while nesting in the farmhouse rapidly dissipated and the cold moist air on my face made me shiver. I couldn't be pissed at Mayo. Whatever attention from me, or more properly Speith, he requested, must have been important, but I was still more annoyed than worried.

The nearly worthless cat's eye lights guided me up the twisting, muddy road that snaked across the hills and draws that lead forward through the little Luxembourg town of Holzthum, Love Company's HQ, without stopping to converse with anybody, they were all probably asleep anyway. I continued up the muddy path to within a few hundred yards of the sector of outposts, foxholes and slit trenches, that made up our forward line astride the dominant ridge known as The Skyline Drive. I had been up and down this road so many times in the past several weeks I could make the journey in my sleep.

I parked the jeep atop the road and left my carbine on the front seat. I did not plan to stay long. I started down the reverse slope, my overshoes making sucking noises in the partially frozen mud.

"Halt! Who goes there?"

"Crumb."

"Cake," the sentry responded.

"Where's Beach or Mayo?" I said in a low voice.

"They're down the hill a piece in one of the slit trenches straight ahead. I can run you down there, if you want."

"No, I know where it is."

"Good evening, Major."

I continued the descending path to the line. One of the Company's runners, who I recognized by voice, PFC Rabinowitz or "Rabbi," challenged me then led me to the slit trench where I was to meet Mayo; or Beach, if he was there.

Captain Beach was new. A replacement for the recently decimated Company L. In essence, *my* replacement. It gave me a selfish and proprietary interest in the man. He was yet to see combat other than some shellings and a few recon patrols beyond the wire. He was still an untested commodity which was why Mayo did not give him much latitude. Yet. He did not give me much latitude either when I took over 1st platoon of L Company in the Forest. Even though it was just a month ago, it seemed like years of time had passed. I caught on quickly.

First Sergeant Achilles Mayo was tall, over six feet, and towered above me. He had Hollywood good looks. Piercing blue eyes, dark hair and perfect teeth that were so impeccable that he was forbidden to smile on the line for fear light might glint off an incisor. In an unguarded moment of disgust as we charged through the brush and trees towards

Simonskall amidst a hailstorm of lead, he grabbed me by the arm, threw me to the ground and said "You're gonna get yourself killed, you little runt. Stay back where you belong."

From that point on, when it was just the two of us he referred to me as Runt. Not out of disrespect, but as a term of endearment, much as I would refer to Sally as 'Hon' or 'Babe' or 'Sweetheart'

Mayo met me at the end of the line. I was a little pissed off. If Mayo thought the situation warranted a phone call to the Battalion CO and now a visit from the Battalion XO, then Beach, the company commander, should have been present, if for no other reason than professional courtesy. As company top kick, Mayo should have known better.

"Sorry to disturb your reverie, Sir, but a couple of the holes are reporting some rattling like mess kits or canteens beyond the wire. A couple heard a cough. There were no flares tonight either. The Krauts have set off flares every night since we got here."

If Mayo thought he had piqued my interest he had not.

"OK, let's go have a look. Probably just a lost patrol."

I often asked him how he had come by the given name Achilles and every time I did he gave me a different, equally implausible answer.

He guided me to the forward CP and then to the dugout at the end of an even smaller path. This was a quiet sector where the 28th Infantry Division, a former Pennsylvania National Guard unit, had been sent to regroup, recoup and refit after essentially being destroyed a month earlier in the Hurtgen Forest, the result of bad generalship and criminal, poisonous hubris.

The holes were only manned during the day. They were vacated at dusk which comes around 1600 this time of year. This saved the men from enduring a cold, often soaked, lonely night. Instead, they would cuddle together in their sleeping holes several hundred yards behind the line.

Very little happened. We would spot an occasional patrol and take pot shots at them and they would return the favor. From time to time, when the fog lifted, they would see some activity across the river. We would send over some howitzer or mortar fire and they would reciprocate. S2 had passed on some rumors from time to time, but nothing came of them. It was a perfect case for creeping complacency; something the ever-cautious Speith fought hard to prevent.

Recently, on their own initiative, the three company commanders had started manning the forward outpost and fox holes at night. Much to the chagrin and protest of the soldiers doing the manning. I thought it was a good idea. Speith thought it would just erode morale especially while trying to recover from the debacle in the Forest. A week earlier, I had told the company commanders to have the troops improve their holes. Speith also had the engineers improve the trip wires and flares across the broad sloping plain in front of us. They also laid mines before the ground froze solid.

"So, what's going on?"

"A couple of the guys thought they heard the tinkling of mess gear and some coughing. I would not have thought much of it, but when I checked with King and Item's forward platoon, they said some of their guys heard the same thing.

"Even so, we've been running nightly patrols on a rotating basis and they've reported nothing. Although, someone up the line in King reported mechanical noises one night last week.

"A week ago, some Signals guys were listening to the BBC kinda loud one night and we caught some Heinies sneaking up in the bushes to listen. Looked like kids. They ran off when we got close. We figured they were trying to surrender and got scared. Two nights ago, they came back. We trapped 'em and sent 'em back to let the S2 guys have a crack at 'em. Just kids. They didn't tell us much except they were cold and hungry and that soon we would get what's coming to us."

Frequently, it was worth more to capture these strays than just kill them outright. Most of the time they didn't know shit from Shinola. But from time to time they were a wealth of intelligence. A good hot meal, some cognac and they would spill their guts. Occasionally, a German patrol would proceed unarmed, that way if they got caught they could just claim they were surrendering.

"Was the Signals idiot listening to Harry James too loud?"

"No sir. There was no radio on tonight."

"Okay." None of this was suspicious enough to alarm me. Krauts were walking into our lines with their hands up all the time. But sometimes they would send over a patrol to infiltrate behind the line and hit some mess tent or supply depot and kill the occupants or plant some mines or string heavy wire across a road. They even hit a battalion HQ once and shot up the place. Equally unsettling was in recent weeks there was a steady stream of civilians from the other side of the Our headed west. All they would say is that the Germans were up to something. A report came in that an F Company patrol from the 112th Infantry, our compatriots on our left flank, had trouble making it back the other night. They kept running into Germans. Battalion S2 was always demanding we send out aggressive patrols and nab prisoners. Also disturbing was that recent captives were intelligent, above average in their military bearing and seemed motivated. Not your typical conquered conscript or transfer from the *Kriegsmarine*. There were rumors, unsubstantiated, I might add, of many horse-drawn wagons and artillery pieces, pontoons and small boats. The Our River was only forty feet across in most places and fordable. It was flowing swiftly because of recent heavy rains and melting snows. Over and above all of this, it was not uncommon for the Germans to launch an attack at a freshly dug-in, repositioned unit. These thoughts were on my mind.

If Battalion S2 and Divisional or Corps G2 were not alarmed why should I? This front-line stuff could be tricky business. Really, though, not much of any import had happened in the month we were here. It was easy to become complacent. I worked against that, exhorting the troops to stay alert, rest up. But don't let your guard down.

We finally arrived at the dugout; our conversation reduced to whispers. I had visited this one just the other day. It was one of the best I had ever seen. It was about six feet long by four feet wide and six deep. Perfect for a coffin. It was rimmed with sandbags two deep. It had wooden step that observers could stand on to look over the sandbags. They had a pallet of thick longs that could be pulled up and over the slit trench on a moment's notice. It had a floor of straw covered with a couple shelter-halves for added comfort for the guy whose turn it was to sleep.

Tonight, all three men normally manning it were awake including the guy who should have been asleep waiting his turn. This did not give me pause but should have.

The outpost sat on the top of a plain that fell off the ridge in a gentle slope toward the Our River Valley which marked the boundary between Germany and Luxembourg. It had a commanding view of the hills beyond the valley in a 180-degree arc. In a few places, you could glimpse the river. There were many wooded draws that blocked the view. During a sunny day, you could see for miles, but in the fog and mist or during any variety of precipitation you couldn't make out anything beyond a couple dozen yards, if that. To each side of the pit there was a large copse of fir trees into which had been placed the platoon's .30 caliber machine gun and three 60 mm mortars. They had a clear field of fire to anything in front of them—provided they could see it. Tonight, and on most days, there could be a thousand grazing buffalo covering the ground to the river's edge and, except for the looing and the farting, we would have no idea of their presence. In any event, at this point in the war no one was expecting a tidal wave of Germans racing up the hill.

Further down the line were fifty caliber machine guns from the Weapons Company and closer to the apex of the ridge near the road were some 81millimeter mortars also manned by the Weapons guys.

The 28th was in a precarious situation covering a huge 25-mile gap in the front facing Germany. This was frontage that would normally be covered by three infantry divisions not one. The vaunted Siegfried Line had been punctured in numerous locations and units were walking around on German soil in several places. We could see dragon's teeth, concrete tank obstacles, stretch across our entire horizon.

The situation was made even more unsettling by the fact that the 110th's front was the largest of the three regiments, Measuring sixteen kilometers. The 112th was on our left flank and the 109th on our right. In addition, and equally distressing, was the front our Division was responsible to protect was held by only two of the 110th's three battalions, the First Battalion to our north and the Second Battalion in Divisional reserve in the village of Donnange, four miles behind the wire.

"Coming in." I climbed down into the slit trench to greet the three soldiers stationed there, a sergeant and two privates. One was resting but stirred up quickly. The last thing they probably thought they would see this night was the Battalion XO. They looked surprised. Very surprised. I was equally surprised by the fact there were four soldiers in the hole not three. The fourth one was black.

"How's the leg LaValle?" He had been wounded by a shot through the fleshy part of his thigh at Kommerscheidt—in and out hitting nothing important. He had been evacuated. He was lucky. His wounding had probably saved his life; he was evacuated before the collapse. Few left Kommerscheidt alive. Fewer walked out. I was one of the lucky ones. For his troubles, they made LaValle platoon sergeant upon his return.

"Fine, Captain."

"I made Major."

"I heard." He extended his hand and I shook it. "Good to see you again, Major."

"You too, Pierre. Thank God it wasn't worse."

"I thank God every time I open my eyes each morning."

I smiled at him.

In the distance, we could hear the muffled thump-thump of harassing artillery fire accompanied by the occasional flash. Ours or theirs? I'm not sure anybody really heard it anymore.

I pointed to the Colored soldier. "Who's this?"

LaValle started to speak, but Mayo cut him off.

"He's Private First-Class Moses Jackson, a driver with the Service Company. He was delivering a load of ammo to Company HQ when his truck broke down. He asked if he could get some supper while they fixed it then volunteered to help bring up hot chow if he was allowed to spend the night in a foxhole. Seems he wants to win a Combat Infantryman's Badge."

I looked at him for a moment and he smiled so brightly I was afraid his perfect, Mayo-esque white teeth might also draw fire.

Mayo turned to Jackson and said, "You stay as close to me as my shadow. I don't want you out of my sight."

"Can I keep the Tommy Gun?"

Mayo must have failed to notice in the dark that Jackson was holding a sub-machine gun. Mayo took the gun from his hands and removed the magazine, sticking it into his pocket. He clicked on the safety and handed the weapon back to the boy.

"I'll give it back to you when you need it."

Perhaps they could tell I was a little annoyed by the disruption of having this stranger in a firing pit. "Well, okay," I said speaking as if the Negro wasn't there. "But tell him to be careful. He doesn't belong to us. His momma gonna be real pissed off at us if anything happens to him. That's a burden I'm not willing to bear. LaValle, keep an eye on him." I turned to Jackson. "Don't touch anything, people might get hurt."

Jackson seemed conflicted about whether to smile or salute and say 'Yessir.' So, he did both.

Mayo leaned in close so only Jackson and I could hear, "Behave yourself, Nigger. Don't do anything stupid or that might get yourself hurt."

Jackson moved in close to Mayo's ear, "You call me that again and I'll slit your throat so fast you'll be dead before you even know I done it."

LaValle said, "I'll keep an eye on him. I doubt anything will happen. He'll be alright. They'll fix his truck in the morning and he'll be off."

I stepped onto the bench and took the binoculars and scanned the horizon. I didn't expect to see anything for the fog, but it seemed like the right thing to do. I handed the binoculars to the Colored kid and he started scanning the horizon. I bent down and lifted a shelter half over LaValle, one of the privates, then Mayo and myself lit cigarettes. I sat against the wall of the slit trench and pulled out the canteen. The one with the scotch. I passed it around and everyone took a swig except Mayo. He waited for me. I took a sip and then he took his. The black kid grinned so brightly after his swallow I was afraid he would get giddy.

"Seen anything?"

One of the privates, whose name I did not know, said he had heard tanks in the distance when he was out of the pit taking a piss.

"Relax," LaValle said. "You're hearing things. You been here all of–what–three days? Take it easy. Eat a candy bar. Take a nap. First we hear Germans whispering, coughing, now we hear tanks."

"No sir," the other private whispered to me as he stood nearby. "I heard 'em too."

"I haven't seen so much as a lit match or a fart the whole time I been in this hole, Major," LaValle piped up.

"Kinda spooky. People keep hearing things," the first private said.

"Coming in," spoken as a whisper.

It was the Company CO, Captain Beach. He was out of breath. Probably heard the XO was in the pit and came at a dead run. When he saw me sitting in the corner of the trench, he saluted.

"God-damnit, Beach, don't salute me. You want to get us both killed?"

Mayo chimed in, "What did I tell you? You do it again and I'll break your arm." Mayo was probably the only non-com in the whole battalion who could address an officer that way and get away with it.

Properly chastened, Beach whispered, "Good evening, Major. I was just checking with the other outposts. All is quiet on the Western Front."

I told myself I was going to choke the neck of the next man who said that. Here was my chance.

He rested his M-1 against the back wall and gave me the scoop on his situation. Earlier in the day, he had tried to register his mortars on the slope. But the exercise had been useless because of the fog. He could only tell where they were dropping by the sound. Otherwise, he said, everything was okay. They had checked the trip wires and put a few more mines out under cover of this morning's fog. He was anxious to please. This was his first command; sent direct from the States to the front line, skipping a stay at the Replacement Depot.

I knew all four of my company commanders well. Three of the four had replaced the others killed in the Forest. Not one had arrived with any experience leading a rifle company. I had spent the last three weeks giving them the benefit of my Georgia training curriculum and limited experience in deadly combat, I had joined the Battalion only six weeks earlier as a captain barely worth of the rank. I had survived only by the good graces of the Almighty and the generous assistance of one Achilles Mayo. I was a quick study.

Of the three new ones, Beach concerned me most. He seemed clumsy not just in the physical sense, but in his ability to react and think on his feet. In a jam, I was not sure he could be counted on. He was my weakest link. I also had a personal stake in Beach's leadership. Love Company had originally been mine

Kennedy of Mike, the Heavy Weapons company, and Lanier, Item's commander, seemed steady enough and I felt they would be fine. Sachetti, King Company's CO, had been with the company since they strutted down the Champs Elysee in July. Speith said he was within a cunt hair of being a Section Eight. I believed him. Sachetti gave me some sleepless moments. He was wound pretty tight. I was surprised he hadn't berserked himself right out of action in the Forest.

After another cigarette and some whispered small talk, I decided to go. I asked Beach if he needed anything and he said, "No sir, I'm fine."

"Call me if anything changes."

"Yes sir. Thanks for stopping by."

I shook their hands. Despite his skinny stature and child-like appearance, the Negro private had a strong grip. He smiled again. I tapped Beach on the shoulder and left. I turned to Mayo as he escorted me back down the trail.

"Settle everybody down and get some sleep. They act like they're seeing ghosts."

He touched my arm and peeled off toward L Company's forward CP.

Within half an hour, I was back in the farmhouse. Speith was in my seat.

"Where were you?"

"Making the rounds. How's the tooth?"

"Dentist at Division said he should pull it. I'll go back tomorrow. He gave me a shot of penicillin and told me he'd see me in the morning."

I recalled the 26th Volksgrenadier, the *Wehrmacht* division facing us across the river, would send outpost units across from dusk till dawn. They had been there at least as long as we had. Except for the occasional collision of patrols in 'no man's land,' they never caused any trouble and I assumed they were there more as sentries than an offensive threat. Perhaps this was what they heard; the sound magnified over the slope by some acoustic aberration. Perhaps a tank or halftrack in need of lubrication was shifting position afraid to get caught in the daylight by fighter-bombers or a well-placed artillery round.

Earlier in the month the Germans had undertaken what appeared to be routine rotation and relief. The 112th Infantry to our north had reported the sounds of horse-drawn vehicles and motors moving in low gear. It was mentioned in the morning intelligence briefing last week. Speith and everyone above him dismissed it out of hand. Even so, I rang up the Regimental Cannon Company and the Fire Control Center of the Divisional arty units to make sure they had registered the sloping plain before us and the hills beyond the Our. Matter-of-factly, they assured me they had.

I had to remind myself yet again that the Intelligence people were there to tell us of the enemy's capabilities and distribution not their intentions.

"Something I should know about?" I could tell in the dim light of the fire that the side of his face was slightly swollen.

"No, just the usual rookie jitters. Every once in a while, they need their hands held."

Speith stared into the fire and took a swallow of his scotch, undoubtedly for medicinal purposes. He lit a cigarette. The old chair creaked in protest as he leaned back lost in thought then sleep. I climbed into my sleeping bag on the floor.

I stared up at Speith as he dozed off, his chin resting on his chest.

I did not like Speith, practically from the minute I laid eyes on him. He was one of those officers that, in the peacetime Army, would never rise above the level of captain and spend his entire career fighting nothing more threatening than lassitude, ennui and federal indifference. How they could now trust him with a whole battalion of soldiers escaped me. Silly of me. I knew exactly why.

Now here he was a lieutenant colonel, a man about equally concerned about his liquor ration as he was about the sounds that came in the night.

I always tried to avoid making snap judgments of people, students, colleagues. Make them prove to me their worth or lack thereof. In the case of Speith, my snap judgment was spot-on.

Still, thinking like a company commander, I would have preferred to be closer to the troops even if the living conditions might be a bit more Spartan. But who was I to decide? This passed through my mind as I tucked the open end of my sleeping bag up under my chin.

My last waking thoughts were of Sally.

Around 0430 the phone rang.

The Dead of Night

A gun shot. Then another. I waited, pulling the blankets over my head. Nothing. Then another.

The Season

It was the season. I knew the time had come. Those waiting, who bided their time would see a final opportunity. Their patience rewarded. They would first have to win a proper challenge. For me this was the last one. I would win or be forced to yield, my fate sealed for all time. I stood no chance of winning. I faced three opponents. Young aggressors, each the master of his own destiny. It was not long before I was attacked. The one left standing would be the new owner. I fought hard. I had my honor. I also had a destiny. I was slashed. But I would not go down. I had my honor and my pride. I fought with all I had. But it was too much. Attacked from all sides, I was forced to slink away, bleeding from a mangled lip, flesh flayed from me by the sharp edges. Defeated. It was only natural it would come to this. I still had my dignity. I walked away to find a cool place to die. I found a small, low tree, a cool place to lie down. I would rest here until it was over. My reign had come to an end, death near.

I felt the rough wetness on my torn mouth. It was a scent I did not recognize. I opened my eyes. A young mother and her cub. Her tongue was a comfort. The cub was smiling at me. He wanted to play.

Shelter from the Storm

It was snowing hard, as if you could see it growing up from the ground. The bus pulled up to the stop, nothing more than a small wooden shelter with a bench and light.

"Here you are, son. The next bus to Ephrata should be along directly."

I gathered my B-4 bag and stepped off the bus into the soft, ankle-deep snow. Its brakes let out a hiss, and it lumbered off into the night. The last thing I saw were the two red taillights disappearing into the gray darkness. I cleared off some snow, took the bench and waited. I accepted his word as genuine that the bus to Ephrata would be by soon. Once there, I would be home. I snuggled myself further into the trench coat and tightened my scarf around my neck, concerned if the bus did not come soon I might freeze to death.

An hour passed and my teeth were chattering. I could not feel my feet. The storm was unrelenting. Every few minutes, I had to shake off a new inch of snow. What an ignominious way to die, I thought. A combat pilot freezing to death on a wooden bench detached from civilization except for a naked light bulb, never having confronted an enemy. I could seize the initiative and walk home, but it was twenty miles; likely they would not discover my body until the thaw, and by then I would be declared a deserter. More ignominy.

I was so sleepy and numb I did not hear the approach.

"Hey, Son! How long you been sittin' here?"

Minutes. Hours? I was so frozen words would not form.

"Where you headed?"

I looked up. The truck stood on the road a few feet away, steam from the exhaust made a dense cloud behind it.

I gathered what warm strength I had left and said, "Waiting for the bus to Ephrata, sir."

The dark figure in the truck said, "I doubt it will be by in this. You want to come in out of the cold? We'll get you warmed up and wait for the one in the morning."

It was an offer impossible to decline. I gathered my bag, and with stiff, barely responsive legs walked around the truck and climbed it. I met his dog, obviously glad to see me. He happily gave up his space.

"How long you been sittin' there?"

"I don't know."

"Well, come with us, and we'll get you warmed up 'til the next one comes along."

...

I don't remember how long we rode into the snow, great cascades of the stuff. It filled his headlights like the backside of a waterfall.

He pulled up to a small bungalow perched in a dark, frozen wood. By the time we arrived some of the cold had left me, and I started to think clearly. A large barn stood nearby, indifferent to the storm. The lights were on inside the house; smoke rose from the chimney, and I could see a small, humble Christmas tree in the window.

The fire roared and popped as if the wood was angry at such a fate. He sat me down and made me undress down to my uniform. I loosened my tie and kicked off my shoes to allow my feet to unfreeze.

He offered me a drink. Bourbon. It went down smooth and warmed my insides just like the fire warmed my toes.

"I appreciate your kindness, sir. I'm glad you came along."

"You're welcome, son. Can't allow a serviceman to be stranded on a night like this. Where was you headed?"

"Ephrata. To see my folks. Last furlough before shipping out."

"Air Corps?"

"Yes sir. I'm a copilot on a Liberator."

"I 'spect you're hungry. Can I fix you a sandwich and heat up some soup to wash down your bourbon?"

"That would be great, sir, but I don't want you to go to any trouble. It's late."

"No worries. I'll be back in a jiffy."

The dog, I could not tell the breed, sat on his haunches staring at me. He seemed to be smiling. Every time he caught my glance his tail would wag. I wondered what he was thinking.

Between the bourbon, the fireplace, and the Christmas tree, I warmed up quickly.

The man returned with dinner on a wooden tray. I placed it on my lap and ate. The dog licked his chops shifting from one side to the other in anticipation of a morsel. I did not disappoint.

"What is your name, sir? If you said it, I did not catch it."

"My name Caleb Fincastle and this is Bocephus. He just wandered up one day and I took him in. Kinda like you."

"Thank you, Mr. Fincastle. You are most kind." I finished my sandwich. "You are most kind. Bocephus. What a funny name."

"Don't go makin' fun of his name. He thinks you're makin' fun of him he's liable to piss on your leg. I seen him do it. He's got sensibilities."

The bourbon, the fire, and the meal forced me to drift off. I suspect it was mostly the bourbon. I pulled my legs back for fear of giving some unintended slight.

A rap on the door startled me awake.

Mr. Fincastle was gone. I sat up. No doubt Bocephus was with him. Maybe I imagined it. I found myself covered with a blanket, so I settled back trying to regain the warm spot.

The noise at the door repeated. This time there was urgency to it.

I went to the door. Through the frosted window, I could see a figure moving. I hesitated answering it. I opened the door exceeding my authority. It was not my door to open.

A wet, disheveled man stood on the porch. Snow covered the bill of his cap and shoulders, the look of desperation etched on his face. An arm was missing.

"I seen your light was on. I need help."

He suddenly took note of my uniform.

"Please, mister. I need help."

I turned hoping to see Mr. Fincastle.

"What's the matter?" I asked.

"My wife's having a baby. We was on the way to the hospital, and I slid off the road in my haste and got stuck in the snow. I seen your light."

"Where is she?"

I would have preferred Mr. Fincastle's assistance.

The man turned and left the porch. I followed him into the night. He trudged through the knee-deep snow, I followed close so as not to lose him. It would be spring before they found my body.

After I guessed a hundred yards, we found the car. It had impacted a drift; the embedded left headlight shone in the snow like neon. The engine was running yielding billowing steam that seemed to hang in the air. He ran to the side, opened the door, reached across the amorphous lump in the front seat and turned off the engine. I was beside him as he helped his wife out of the car. I could hear her moaning over the soft whisper of the snow.

He took one arm, and I took the other. Guided by the light, we returned to the cabin. It was a struggle. My pant legs were wet to the knee, but I had no sensation of the cold. All I could think about was not losing my grip. Without warning, she crumbled between us as a burst of pain overtook her. Jesus, I thought, what if she had the baby out here in the snow?

Finally arriving on the porch, Mr. Fincastle and the dog were there to greet us. As if he saw this thing every day, he calmly guided the couple into the parlor. He led the woman, her face contorted with an unremitting pain, to the chair I had so recently vacated. I stood to one side. He seemed to know what he was doing. He glanced my way and told me to boil water. Lots of it. I went to the kitchen to do what I was told. I could hear screaming from the parlor. It made me grieve. Clearly, the woman was dying. Nobody made that sound and lived.

When I returned with a kettle of hot water, she was on the floor panting, struggling to catch her breath. She grabbed her knees trying to sit up, her legs spread apart, a pool of blood under her bottom. Her husband sat on the floor by her side, stroking her beaded forehead with his one hand.

"What happened to your arm?"

"Burnt off when the *Wasp* went down."

I was stunned by the amount of blood that spilled out of her at the delivery of her child.

Mr. Fincastle must have taken notice of my distress. He turned to me and said, "Rest easy, son. I birthed a lot of cows and spent time opposite the Hun. This ain't nothin.' She's fine."

The baby's lusty cry filled the room. A boy. I did not know who I was happier for: the mother, the baby or me. The father, on the floor beside his wife, looked up at me and smiled as I tried to orient myself to what I had just witnessed. I knew I was smiling; I even laughed once.

Mr. Fincastle bared the mother's breast and placed the slick, pink child on it then covered them with a blanket he had warmed by the fire. Not once did he touch my kettle of boiled water.

Bocephus walked to the mother's side, licked the baby's wet head once, laid down beside her and went to sleep, his body in contact with hers. The baby boy had been baptized. Through the night, the dog, sleeping soundly, never left her side.

About an hour after the birth, as the baby suckled the teat, there was another knock on the door.

Now what? I thought. Another displaced person. Another fool stuck in a drift.

I opened the door suddenly confronting three men, about the same age as Mr. Fincastle, each covered with snow.

"Who the hell are you?" the soberest one asked.

"I might ask the same question, sir."

They pushed me aside eyeing the bloody rug, the nursing mother, and the one-armed man without apparent surprise as if this was regular fare around these parts.

One of the men had a weathered wooden box under his arm.

"Where's Fincastle? It's Christmas Eve. Time for all night checkers."

The third one lifted up two bottles of what I took to be whiskey.

I did not know if the birth of a child is regularly followed by a party, but this one was.

Through the night, we took turns holding the baby, congratulating the parents and drinking. We also played checkers. Every time the new son cried it just added more joy to the room.

The next morning, blinded by the sun against the snow, I caught my bus and headed east.

Mr. Fincastle and I exchanged some letters. The subject always returned to that night. I loved hearing from him even if it was repetitious. I asked after Bocephus. I inquired if he had anointed any legs lately. I told him of my adventures at the airfield in Italy conducting my little sliver of the war as best I could. He should see it someday. Despite the war, Italy is a beautiful place.

Not long after rotating home, I returned to Mr. Fincastle's bungalow in the woods. I wanted to offer him my thanks; catch up on old times. All I found were the remains of the shack demolished years ago by the weight of weather and abandonment. By the way it looked, no one had lived in it for many years. Only the stone chimney was still standing. I inquired at the nearest Post Office about Mr. Caleb Fincastle. I wanted to track him down so I could thank him. Perhaps reminisce.

They were sorry they could not help me. No one had ever heard of a Mr. Fincastle. Or his dog.

Flight of the Valkyries

She woke up. Empty spot in the bed to her left. She found him at his desk sitting in his chair; his head flopped back in an unintended angle, mouth agape, stale drool on his chin. He was wearing his expensive Amazon headphones. She wondered what he had been listening to that had killed him so thoroughly. Flight of the Valkyries was his favorite. Then, of course, there would be funeral arrangements

The Songs of My Father

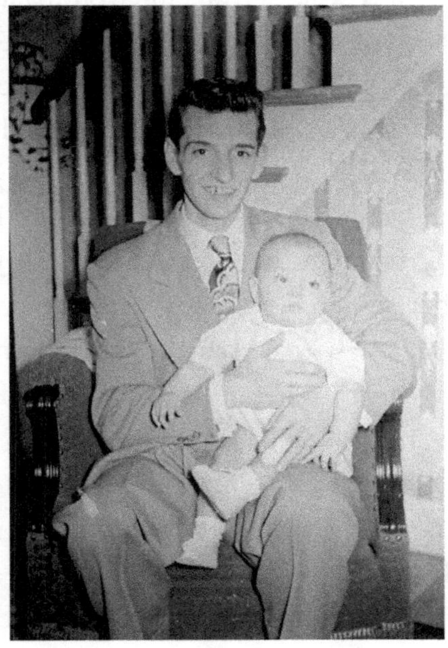

One day a few weeks ago, I was listening to Pandora. Over Christmas I found a channel that played nice, less frequented Christmas music and fell in love with the station. Beegie Adair Radio. She is a noted pianist known for playing the classics from the '50s and '60s. Soft, relaxing music, easy to listen to. It provided familiar background noise for a hectic office.

Then it happened. "Dreamsville." It was a song Henri Mancini wrote for the soundtrack of the Peter Gunn TV series. I was the first time I heard it since, well, I can't remember. My dad bought all of Mancini's albums, playing them endlessly. Thirty-three and a third. After work, he listened to his records as he drank his beer and smoked until the grooves wore down on the plastic.

When I heard that song it was as if I was teleported back to my mom and dad's middle-class, suburbanite living room half a century ago; the sudden, intrusive memory made a pain in my chest. All I could think of was my father, in his easy chair, beer in one hand, cigarette in the other.

He had his favorites besides Mancini. Mantovani. Jackie Gleason. Johnnie Mathis. Songs of romance, happiness and peace. Perhaps, they took him to a happier place. Every time I hear "Someone to Watch over Me" in any rendition, I think of him. He played it repeatedly. But then I heard "Dreamsville."

A child of the Depression, he worked hard and kept his promises. His reward was three sons, each a college graduate, each successful in his own right. What more could be expected of a father who never finished high school? He worked hard at the papermill rising to shift supervisor. If a snowstorm was predicted for the morning, he would spend the night in the plant's locker room so he would not miss his shift.

I inherited his strong will, industriousness and his belief that tomorrow always held a better future. We failed to agree on a few of things. That is, I believe, as it always will be between father and son. He was of one mind and I another. On two occasions, a combination of too much beer and irreconcilable positions had nearly led us to blows. Each instant is a compelling recollection I regret to this day.

He was intensely proud I became a heart surgeon. His greatest pride, though, was seeing me as an officer in Naval uniform.

I moved frequently, my medical training and eventual practice took me away. My mother developed Alzheimer's Disease and it became an increasing struggle to look after her as he was not well either. Finally, he became very ill and was placed in intensive care. It was unlikely he would ever leave. After consultation with the doctors and the concurrence of my brothers, I told them to take him off life support. I held his hand holding his wedding band between my thumb and fingers until he was gone.

My mother did not attend the funeral. She would not understand the nature of the event and it might frighten her. She lost him a long time ago.

He was given a military funeral. His casket was covered with an American flag and several members from a local American Legion post served as an honor guard firing a volley at the end to signify his honored departure.

So, I would like to sing two songs to my father:

The Spirit of Christmas

This was a terrific Christmas. I was surrounded by family and friends. Made out well in the gift department. Drank some wine, a little bourbon. I made a big fuss as I always do trying to achieve perfection for my family. That's the way I remembered Christmas growing up. Mom and Dad always made a big deal of the holiday, with a Griswold-sized tree, spending more than they could afford on their three boys. But every time the gifts were opened, and the excitement had settled, my dad would invariably become withdrawn. I never understood why. I asked but he would not tell me. Then one Christmas, when he figured I was old enough to understand he told me his Christmas story. It was the winter of 1944-45. His outfit raced north to relieve the siege of Bastogne. He was an infantryman in the 26th Infantry Division of Patton's Army.

Not long after arriving at their point of engagement, he and two other soldiers were placed in a foxhole atop a snow-covered hill. Their sergeant told them to hold this position at all costs. Don't let anybody get past here, the outcome of the war in the balance. Cold and scared, it wasn't long before three Germans in snow-capes, appeared out of the fog and ran up the hill. My father and his two buddies fired as they approached and quickly killed them. The GIs ran down the hill and rifled through the bodies looking for personal items as souvenirs. They took wallets, identity tags, Lugers. They were young kids. They returned to their pillbox and waited until relieved.

Dad looked at me, tears in his eyes and said, "And some German mother never knew what happened to her son." He never had a happy Christmas. I have never spent a Christmas without thinking of that German mother.

Bennie

Dad told me another story of the War. John Benson was my dad's best friend growing up in a hardscrabble neighborhood outside Chester, Pennsylvania. Bennie was drafted into the Combat Engineers with the First Army. (He claims to have been at the wheel of the first 2 1/2-ton truck onto Omaha Beach but who knows?) They were inseparable, a trial and a joy for my dad's mom. After he left for the war, Bennie was a constant concern for her. How was he making out in the war? Was he well? Was he getting enough to eat? Trying to allay her fears, my dad told her in every letter he wrote home that he had seen or ran into Bennie the other day and he was doing fine as if the war in Europe was nothing more than a colossal Boy Scout Jamboree. Whenever they stopped to rest, Dad would always ask if there were any engineers around. If there were, he would charge off looking for Bennie but it invariable it was not Benny's outfit. On a cold, wet, fall day, my dad's convoy stopped briefly outside Metz and dad found some engineers resting for a few moments beside a blown-out building. Dad made his usual inquiry. Yeah, he was told, there are a bunch of 'em up there. Dad ran up the stairs. Bennie was sitting against the wall staring across the room at a GI eating limburger cheese. Unfortunately, it was a brief reunion. Dad's unit was pulling out in a few minutes. It was the only time he saw Bennie until after they were discharged. For the rest of their lives they talked about the smell of that cheese. My grandmother passed away never knowing they saw each other only once and then for about ten minutes.

When We Were Young

An excerpt from the forthcoming novel
The Examination

Then, as England clung to life, the Congress of the United States passed the Selective Training and Service Act of 1940. It was duly noted that this was the first peacetime draft in American history requiring all males between the ages of eighteen and sixty-five to register for Selective Service. Inductees had to serve twelve months in the Army. Probably just enough time to get the hang of it before mustering out.

So, in compliance with the law, I went down to the Front Royal post office and signed the necessary forms. It was then I realized that I was a pacifist. I had no penchant for war. Especially combat. I amused myself with the reality that I was chicken and intellectually superior to those ranks required to do the fighting. It was ignoble to concede oneself to be yellow, but it did make the choices easier. Screw the Southern tradition of derring-do for a lost cause.

December, FDR declared the U.S. to be the Arsenal of Democracy. Lofty words, I thought. Sometimes it was difficult to push back cynicism.

Then, as 1941 matured, the situation stabilized. Against all odds, England held on and, for the moment, disaster had been averted. I thought summer was good invasion season. But the Nazis hesitated. Meanwhile, conscription was extended to eighteen months.

I worked hard on a series of short stories with the theme of romance denied but had not gotten anything published. I took this as an omen.

In April, I received my draft notice and had to report for induction. It was painful, tragic, to contemplate that my Bohemian life had come to an end. I did not have enough self-respect to declare myself a conscientious objector for, in doing so, I would have declared my hide special and above the ordinary rank and file who would defend freedom and the way of life we so comfortably took for granted. I did not think myself a genuine coward. I also knew I would never be able to look into the eye of someone who had taken my place and suffered for it. Still, this sense of nobility was not foreign to me, disguised in great tales of Confederate gallantry and sacrifice in the face of a blizzard of Federal musketry.

Standing in line, a mere towel wrapped around me to shield my privates from prying eyes, eventually it was my turn. My wild imagination had me bringing down a charging tank single-handed, drowning in a flaming, oil-covered sea or falling from a fiery, disintegrating aeroplane as it hurtled downward to rejoin earth. I broke out in a sweat. I felt ill. I wondered if those around me would notice. Or care. Fucking college kid.

I stepped behind a curtain, a feeble concession to modesty, and stood in front of the doctor. He made me drop the towel and proceeded to shove a finger, which felt as big as a rolling pin, up my testicle telling me to turn my head in the opposite direction and cough. Turn my head the other way and cough again as the rolling pin impaled my other nut. I did not know the purpose of the maneuver. Satisfied, he took my penis in his hands with the same detachment and roughness a mason might display examining the next brick. He directed me to pull back my foreskin and swiveled my retracted, little member one way then the other. No trace of VD. He inspected my eyes and ears, felt my neck, and listened to my heart, no doubt seeing if he could find one. He had me cough again. He poked my belly as if he were looking for some trace of backbone and then, making me stand up, pushed back his stool staring down at my feet.

"Ok," he murmured. "I see."

"See what?"

"That."

"I don't understand." I thought maybe the crack of my ass was not truly vertical.

"You have flat feet."

The implication was lost on me.

He snatched the clip board from my hand, scribbled something totally illegible and told me to precede to the last station in the line. I did as I was told and stood behind three other guys, also discretely covered with towels. Each stepped up to the clerk in turn and was told to get dressed and go home

When they told me the same thing, I asked what this meant.

Flat feet. You can't be in the Army with flat feet.

Deliverance. Even though they didn't look flat to me. I climbed all over the Shenandoah Valley with these feet, how much harder could a jungle be?

I returned home with mixed emotions, conflicted by the fact that I had been found defective but happy that I would not be storming some God-forsaken beach.

I wondered how many members of the Army of Northern Virginia had marched to Chancellorsville on flat feet.

The war news, as April turned to May, was mixed. Throughout the winter and spring England had been hammered by bombing raids. Casualties were high and the destruction significant. But the Royal Air Force gave back in kind. If they kept this up the United Kingdom would not succumb. I was no military genius, but I knew the opportunity for the Germans to invade England would soon be lost.

On May 21, the U.S. freighter *Robin Moor* was sunk by a Nazi sub. The country was shocked. Our neutrality had been violated like some virgin in a hidden garden. FDR was sufficiently outraged to declare a national, unlimited state of emergency. I am not sure what that meant. I was slightly bemused at the charade of our neutrality as we had been openly assisting the Brits with Lend-Lease for months if not surreptitiously for years. It all seemed a *fait accompli* as Roosevelt had announced that one could not reason with incendiary bombs. It was the moral, if not entirely legal, thing to do. No one should have been surprised when torpedoes punctured the little merchantman.

Then a few days later, Hitler, in a fleeting moment of insanity, attacked the Soviet Union. England was saved. Once and for all. It was, by all accounts, a cataclysmic, if illogical and strategically stupid, turn of events yet entirely within character.

I received letters from Marcus and Artemus Bell. Both letters came within days of each other not having heard from them in months. The coincidence was striking.

Marcus was a mess boy on the U.S.S. *California*. He was very pleased. He missed Virginia and his family of course, but his heart had found a home on the dreadnought. Sailing around the Pacific was a delight, he wrote. The sunsets were magnificent. Hawaii was beautiful beyond description and the Hawaiians didn't seem to mind his skin color.

Artemus Bell was working in Chester, Pennsylvania, content teaching fourth grade math and history. He was happy and about to be married. Her name was Ruth.

I wrote each a long letter congratulating them on their new-found happiness and the advancement of their careers. I told them of the situation on the plantation but withheld mention my 4-F status. Flat feet. An anatomic embarrassment. It would probably make them laugh. 'Hey Duck, Massa got flat feet.' I could hear them guffawing all the way down the mule path.

...

It was a warm, summer afternoon when I got the news that Russia had been invaded by the Nazis. Everyone who understood the implication was jubilant. They saw it for what it was: a catastrophic blunder. They said for Germany the war was lost. The Germans wanted to turn Russia into something akin to the British Raj. Limitless resources, natural and human. Most said it was a political decision, the antithesis of National Socialism was communism. I never quite understood that. It was really about race and resources.

In the beginning, I did not share the view that Russia, its vastness geographically and ruthlessness politically, would prevail. The centralized government could be quickly decapitated, and the masses subdued by uncompromising brutality. Bonaparte had tried it and failed although, to be honest, I do not think Napoleon was as indiscriminately murderous. The Russian winter would be the great neutralizer. I was glad it was the Russians and not us. The enemy of my enemy is my friend.

Summer progressed into a sultry August that was punctuated with violent thunderstorms and the Atlantic Charter which codified once and for all our allegiance to the British.

In September, the U.S.S. *Greer*, a destroyer on convoy duty in the North Atlantic, belonging to a neutral nation flying a neutral flag, was fired on by a Nazi submarine. It was only a matter of time before a stupid act, a mistake or brazen demonstration and the US would be drawn into the European war.

I reached the point where I withdrew and chose to remain ignorant of evolving history. I had flat feet. So what did it matter to me anyway?

Mid-month, I got a brief letter from Artemus Bell saying he had joined a Negro Army Air Corps squadron to become a pilot. He was on his way to Tuskegee, Alabama. He had Ruth's reluctant blessing. They married quickly, he said. Wish me luck, he asked.

On Halloween, a U-boat sent the U.S. destroyer *Reuben James* to the bottom. A hundred sailors were blown to pieces or drowned. War was unavoidable. It would be a matter of months. Perhaps weeks. Maybe no more than a few days.

Longing

I long for the Fifties and early Sixties when the people trusted their government, virginity counted for something, ideology was a little-known concept and a man's word was his bond. And no one had touched the moon.

The Hammer of God

An excerpt from a forthcoming novel

Covered with Our Glory

A memoir:

There are times during the course of human history when an event presents itself to the unwary that will change the course of that history only to be lost because of failure of recognition, opportunity or will. Even more tragically, the failure of all three.

Prologue: Covered with Our Glory

April 23, 1945

The image, the reality of what until that instant had been an abstract horror yet unseen was penetrating and painful beyond his imagining. It was a vision, a smell that would remain with him every waking moment until he died. The guilt seized his soul in its grip as if he alone could have stopped this.

Van Patten continued his memoir:

In retrospect, it seemed inevitable, a foregone conclusion, that it would work out this way. It had worked exactly as we said it would. Germany had been pummeled from the sky for sixty-four months in an unstoppable crescendo until now, caught in the crushing vice of two great armies, there was, quite simply, nothing left to bomb. The pain, anguish and doubt we all felt in the beginning were gone. We were right: vindicated and victorious beyond even our most extravagant predictions. The destruction we unleashed exceeded anything we could have imagined.

If it hadn't worked, and in the beginning, there was no way of knowing it would, it had to be somebody else's fault. The wrong plane. The wrong people. Failure to stick to the theory we had come to espouse with our very blood. The blood of disciples.

The Germans had failed at bombing. Why? It was, we said, because they took a good idea and failed the execution. They were impatient. Perhaps even inept. It was patently unthinkable that the idea itself, The Great Premise, was untenable. They switched target priorities. They failed to defeat the fighter force, RAF radar. They had the wrong planes, they switched from day to night. They didn't have the

Norden Bombsight. They were unlucky. They were not Americans. It was an endless litany of excuses.

We had waited all our professional lives for the opportunity to pulverize a country with bombs and end a war. It was the reason we woke up in the morning. We were not about to be deterred by friend or foe or cost. The cost...

So, we rolled into Germany covered with our glory, advancing behind tanks a mile or so from the ever-advancing front lines. A party to survey the damage we had wrought, to account that which we had laid waste. Learn to do better next time. If there was a next time.

As we grew closer, we could smell it. The sickeningly sweet stench. It quickly became overpowering. Putrefaction. The concentration camp. A small one, a slave labor camp, where the bodies were stacked like cord wood rotting in the afternoon sun. Then I knew we had made a monumental mistake. Perhaps one of the greatest mistakes of human history.

Van Patten was part of what came to be known as the United States Strategic Bomb Survey. His strength in economics and the fact that he had, among other things, helped with targeting, made him an ideal candidate to go in with the Army as an advanced guard to sort through the damage, make an accounting. The fact that he had bombed some of these very places gave him an added perspective that abstract economics and bomb damage assessments simply could not. For nearly two months he had led the Spartan life of an infantryman, riding with an armored infantry column through Karlsruhe, Stuttgart and numerous smaller towns as each was conquered by the ever-advancing juggernaut of the American Seventh Army. Assigned to the 12th Armored Division, they were on their way toward Munich when one of the Combat Commands was diverted toward Landsberg-am-Lech to liberate a work camp and eliminate isolated pockets of resistance.

They drove practically unmolested through the German countryside past homes, farms and villages that seemed picaresque, virtually untouched by the war. They were headed over a short rise through some woods toward a crossroads. Van Patten was dozing in the passenger seat of a jeep in the van. He slouched down to lower his center of gravity so a sudden lurch of the jeep would not toss his sleeping hulk onto the road. He awakened with a start when shots rang out. The driver of the lead jeep was hit in the throat when a bullet ricocheted off the wire-cutting post mounted on the front of the vehicle. The hapless corporal gurgled and sputtered until he died a few minutes later. *Waffen SS* troops had been reported still active in the area and the infantry boys were wary, even so they drove into an ambush as they emerged from the woods. They dismounted from their halftracks and deployed along the treeline. The major in charge was about to call up the Shermans to destroy the farmhouse where the fire had originated. Then he thought better of it. Not wanting to risk any more lives to a lucky hit from a *panzerfaust* this close to capitulation, he had the forward air observer call in a flight of Thunderbolts who were stooging around aching for something to shoot up.

The major grabbed Van Patten by his jacket, oblivious to the difference in their rank and pulled him aside so they could sit under cover and wait.

"Keep your eye on that farmhouse," the major said. "I love this part."

Van Patten stared at the quaint, stone farmhouse that probably dated back two hundred years. Suddenly the ground before it erupted with geysers of dirt and turf and disappeared beneath a cloud of thousands of shell hits. An instant later, a silver P-47 hurtled overhead and banked sharply away, its brutish hulk banking for another run the sun glinting off its silvery wings. Van Patten returned his gaze to the house and the cloud of dirt and pulverized stone that swirled around it. Just as suddenly four smoke trails streaked overhead and exploded against the farmhouse. Rockets from a second Thunderbolt.

It was hard to imagine anyone remaining alive, but he spotted a lone figure running from the back of the rubble. The pilot walked a line of tracers expertly across the back yard and cut the man into pieces.

Before the dust had settled, the major turned to the forward air observer and said, "Thank Top Hat for us. Tell him his work here is done." He then turned to a lieutenant, "Let's move 'em out." The soldiers climbed back onto their vehicles and the convoy resumed its snake-like advance deeper into Germany. Perhaps a bit more cautious than they had been earlier, thanks to the unfortunate demise of the corporal.

It was later they came upon the smell. At first Van Patten, sitting in an open jeep, did not understand what it was. The major said, "We're close."

They rounded a bend and crossed a narrow stone bridge across the Lech. The major muttered something about whether the bridge would support the weight of the tanks, so he ordered them to be sent over one at a time. The sun was hot for late April, Van Patten thought. He could feel it on his face, the sweat under his helmet leaving droplets on his forehead. The sky was blue, devoid of clouds. It would have been a perfect day for bombing, one they had wished for countless times over the past two years.

Then he saw the camp. It was surrounded by a thick barrier of barbed wire and a tall fence also festooned with barbed wire. Watch towers were placed at each corner. There were long, single story wooden barracks. Dozens of them in a perfect row, evenly spaced with typical German precision. Outside the stockade were several larger, more carefully constructed buildings. Headquarters, Van Patten surmised. He could hear dogs barking from a kennel nearby. As the jeeps approached the front gate several prisoners emerged from the shadows between the barracks. They were barely alive, barely human. Staggering, stumbling skeletons on which hung loose skin. Their eyes were dark, vacant, retracted into their sockets. First a few dozen then hundreds. It was surreal. For a moment the soldiers stared through the barbed wire at the inmates and no one moved. Each man on either side of the fence sharing the same expression of disbelief. Those behind the fence would not raise their eyes to look at their liberators.

The major stepped from his jeep and strode briskly to the gate. It had been padlocked. He drew his .45 and shot of the lock with a single, precisely placed round that shattered the silence. He kicked the gate with his boot, and it clanged loudly against the fence. One prisoner watching this dropped to his knees and fell onto his side. Not fainting. Dead. The strain, the surprise, was more than he could take.

They soon discovered the origin of the smell. A huge pit had been dug behind the compound and hundreds of bodies had been thrown into it, their emaciated arms and legs intertwined, heads cocked at impossible angles. Flies in their thousands buzzed around the pit. Nearby a pile of naked corpses lay stacked like cord wood, limbs askew, covered with dirt and feces. Maggots in sheer delight danced in their mouths and eye sockets and raced into and out of their nostrils.

Midway through the journey of our life I found myself in a dark wood, for the correct path had been lost. Van Patten had arrived at the *Inferno.*

Several soldiers, all hardened veterans started vomiting. Four shots rang out and the barking stopped.

You have the Hammer of God in your hands, she said. *Use it.*

Van Patten said aloud, "We should have bombed this place."

The major turned to him and asked, "Why?"

A Rock in the Sun

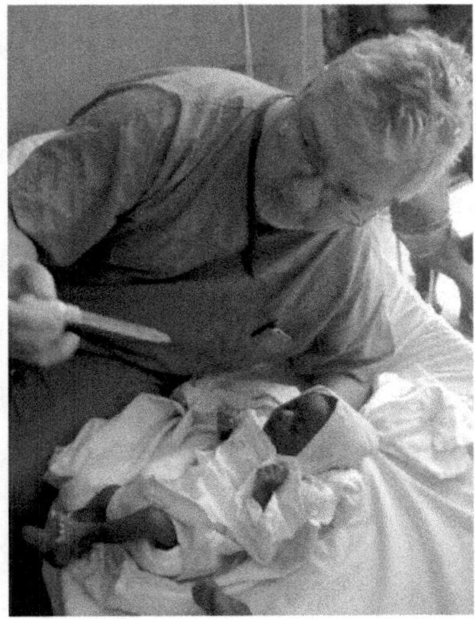

Will Durant once said, Civilization exists by geological consent, subject to change without notice.

At 4:53 pm ET, Tuesday, January 12, 2010, an earthquake of 7.0 magnitude on the Richter Scale occurred approximately 10 miles southwest of Port-au-Prince, Haiti. It lasted about 35 seconds to a minute.

Geologically speaking, it was the result of the release of energy 6.2 miles below earth's surface from the Enriquillo-Plaintain Garden fault system, the subduction zone between the Caribbean tectonic plate and the North American. This same fault system produced the major earthquakes of 1751 and 1771, both of which destroyed Port-au-Prince.

At least 200,000 people were killed, 196,595 were injured and 800,000 to a million displaced with extreme damage suffered at Port-au-Prince. The good news, if any, was that the earthquake occurred on land and not the ocean which might have resulted in a tsunami. (The Indian Ocean earthquake and resulting tsunami was of 9.0 to 9.3 magnitude. Also, by way of reference, the 1906 San Francisco earthquake was 7.8 magnitude and the Alaska earthquake of 1964 recorded a magnitude of 9.2, the second strongest earthquake ever recorded in the world.)

As I had done in the past for 9-11 and Katrina, I got online and volunteered my services as a general, thoracic and trauma surgeon with several agencies, private and governmental. I was well suited by my military training and experience in addition to civilian trauma work. After several days without response, I gave up the pursuit, assured that somewhere my name was on a list and they knew where to find me. Tuesday, one week after the earthquake, my operating room circulating nurse, Mike Vandervort, told me, in the middle of a hernia repair I was doing, that he along his wife Dawn, also and RN, told me they were leaving for Haiti in three days. They were old hands at Mission work there. I told him I would like to join him and within a matter of an hour or two I was on the roster to go. This would be at the behest of OMS, One Mission Society. To my surprise, the next day my wife, Debbie, also with extensive medical background, said she would like to go. We spent the rest of the week gathering supplies and donated equipment, everything from aspirin to amputation knives. AirTran offered to fly our supplies from BWI to Fort Lauderdale free of charge. After we landed in Fort Lauderdale, one of the luggage porters asked where we were going with all our supplies, 23 boxes and packed luggage. I told him we were headed to Haiti. In broken English, he explained that he was from Haiti also and his wife lived in Port-au-Prince and he had not heard from her since the earthquake. He did not know if she was dead or alive. He gave us his contact information as well as information about his wife. Dawn noticed the address was the same street as the mission's villa which would be our station. I reassured him we would find out what had happened to his wife. Mike pulled me aside and admonishing that the chaos in Port-au-Prince would make my promise impossible to fulfill.

We landed in Cap Haitian, on the north side of the island. It was unaffected by the earthquake except for the huge influx of displaced persons, surviving family members and refugees that streamed north from the earthquake zone. This placed a nearly insurmountable burden on the resources of Cap Haitian. Importantly, however, it afforded my wife and I an opportunity to see what Haiti was like before the earthquake. As my first trip to a Third World country, I found Haiti numbingly destitute and impoverished. It is hot, crowded, dirty and smells. But it is also a place of raw, almost primitive beauty where people make do, live for today and smile a lot. It is a country devoid of any semblance of modern infrastructure.

Saturday, we spent a pleasant day with missionaries, the same mission Mike and Dawn had lived at for eight years. Later, other members of our contingent arrived. While there, we had to fill out insurance forms required by the mission to underwrite the risks incurred by those of us entering the earthquake zone. In addition to contact information, there was the disquieting request to name the place where we would want to be interred. Mike wrote "where I drop". Debbie and I wrote a more realistic location. The next day we climbed onto a truck and left Cap Haitian before sunrise. It was a long, bumpy, dusty eight-hour trip to Port-au-Prince. It is the main north-south highway, their I-95, connecting Port-au-Prince and the north coast of Haiti. The only resemblance to a highway is that there are occasional sections which are paved. For most of the trip we rode over a bone-jarring combination of ruts, potholes, craters and foot-high speed bumps. How the axle was not ripped from the chassis remains a mystery. Debbie, because of her bad back and me, presumably because I was the oldest member of the party were afforded the luxury of riding in the cab. The folks in the back, sitting on narrow benches and on luggage and boxes of supplies were quickly covered with a choking, tenacious dust. We passed many small towns and villages. They were identical to each other. One- or two-room cinder block and cement hovels. Invariably, there were small, scantily clad children, old women, chickens, goats and the occasional prized cow or hog tethered to a bush or tree trunk. The women swept dirt off the dirt. Laundry was strung between tree limbs or simply flung over bushes to drying. We waved, they waved back. They knew where we were headed.

As we approached the suburbs of Port-au-Prince, we began to see toppled shacks with fallen walls. Initially, we thought this was evidence of earthquake damage. No, we were told, this is how Haiti normally looks. People milled around looking distracted for the most part, going about the activities of daily life.

We arrived at the mission's villa in Carrefour, a western suburb of Port-au-Prince, on Sunday afternoon. After a hasty dinner, we loaded our truck with equipment, supplies, and Haitian translators and drove up the mountain to Daquini as small town on a hill above Port-au-Prince. We took over an abandoned plantation house with an expansive lawn under huge shade trees. It was nothing more than an ordinary ranch-style home one might see in the States. We pitched five tents donated by The International Rotary Club, one of which served as my operating room, and arranged the place for business Monday morning.

Curiously, on the way to dinner that evening, we saw some young Haitian men who resided in the mission surfing the net on their laptops. I asked Mike if he thought they might be able to locate the porter's wife and family or perhaps contact them by cell phone. They took her phone number and were able contact her immediately. It turns out that after the earthquake Haiti had changed its international exchange. It was a simple matter to correct and after we advised his wife of her husband's concern, she promptly called him. This was our first miracle.

The home had a commanding view of the Bay where we could easily see a small flotilla of naval vessels swinging at anchor and of course, the USNS *Comfort*. I found it reassuring to have a completely self-contained tertiary medical center a short helicopter ride away. I asked Gavin McClintock, an emergency room physician from Northern Ireland and the head of the mission's activities on the hill, what contingency plans he had to evacuate a critically ill patient off the hill. "None," he replied. This was not reassuring. We set up a primitive pharmacy in a shed used for lawn care materials and mowers.

Monday morning, as we drove up the hill, both sides of the dirt road were lined with people. Seeing us putting together the clinic the evening before, word of our arrival must have traveled quickly. They parted ways as we drove into the hacienda. No rush, no disorder. Patience is the Haitian way.

In the meantime, I went to the Adventiste Hospital to offer my services as a surgeon. I met with the ostensible chief and he said the place was crawling with surgeons. Coming to Haiti was suddenly, as he put it, the 'sexy' thing to do and, while he appreciated my offer, there was little for me to contribute. Abundance of medical help was available as teams from the States and all over Europe were mobilized. Getting patients to it and it to the patients was the problem. Therefore, our little tent clinic on the hill was sorely needed.

We started seeing patients within minutes of our arrival. Each had a story to tell. Many were refugees from Port-au-Prince, displaced by the devastation to their homes and neighborhoods. They lived in a tent city that grew by the hour on the side of our dusty hill. Most had simple problems like belly aches, often related to intestinal parasites, headaches, aches and pains, scabies and general anxiety manifesting as somatic complaints. Virtually all got treatment for worms. Most left with acetaminophen, ibuprophen and an oral cephalosporin. All of them were given reassurance they would be fine and an opportunity to convert from voodoo and black magic to Christianity. It was not long before the ER docs were convinced many of the patients were suffering from post-traumatic stress disorder. This was entirely understandable considering what had happened. Many people related the loss of a child, spouse, or parent. They shared a collective grief.

I immediately started seeing neglected wounds on arms and

especially legs. Some were infected and required debridement of necrotic tissue. Many people who saw us off figured I would be doing a lot of amputations from crushed and badly mangled extremities. This was not the case. By the time we arrived all the limbs requiring amputation had been removed or the patient had expired.

Other issues requiring surgical attention started to appear. A two-year-old boy was brought to us by his mother who had suffered first and deep second degree burns over his right arm, shoulder and chest. This had occurred when he fell into the family campfire. Before arriving at the clinic someone, probably a voodoo doctor, had covered the burns with gentian violet. He was covered with a thick, dried, purple crust. I gently picked this off as he lay there patiently. The burns were already healing nicely. We gave him a tetanus shot and some antibiotics and pediatric analgesics and advised him to return daily. I saw him the next day, picked at the gentian violet crust again and was pleased with his progress. We never saw him again.

The next memorable case was that of a two-week old little boy who appeared dead when his mother handed him to me. He was critically dehydrated, his chest barely moving with short shallow breaths. His mother had tossed him out the window when the earthquake started for fear he would be trapped under the collapsing building. She and the rest of her family got out before it fell apart. From what we gathered in the translation from creole to English was that she was advised by a voodoo doctor not to breast-feed baby if it was crying because of a possible head injury. This admonition resulted in the rapid dehydration of the infant. His eyes were sunken, and glazed over, he had virtually no skin turgor, and his anterior fontanelle was hollow enough to touch his brain. We had no intravenous fluids available, so I started to feed the baby a solution of water and brown sugar we used to sweeten our morning coffee. I took a medicine dropper and placed the liquid on his tongue. This triggered a reflex for him to swallow. The baby wasted little time sucking down the fluids. Eventually, one of our nurses gave us her Propel powder which we also mixed in water and I fed this to him.

Several hours later we convinced the mother to resume breast-feeding and he took to the breast with great abandon. She brought the child back every day until we left and each day he showed improvement. He was a survivor. His name was Daniel. He was miracle number two.

Once word passed there was a surgeon in the clinic, all manner of minor surgical issues appeared. It wasn't long before I was removing numerous lipomas, sebaceous cysts and a large congenital nevus that had disfigured his face his entire life. I removed a chondroma from behind a man's head that had made his ear stick out for ten years. These procedures were performed under in a makeshift operating room with one case done in a lounge chair on the patio because I needed extra light afforded by the sun. We sterilized our instruments between cases with bleach and rubbing alcohol. Each patient marveled at the miraculous change in their appearance.

There were several reasons why the damage was so severe and widespread. The cinderblocks were poorly made and were not allowed to cure sufficiently to acquire strength, barely a step above mudbricks. The cement mix was diluted by excessive amounts of sand to make it go further. Minimal re-bar was used to support the structure and foundations were practically non-existent. There are no building codes in Haiti. No one could afford to build proper home, no matter how austere or primitive, if they had to comply with building codes.

Haitians are very proud, resourceful and resilient people. Their gratitude for our services was overwhelming. One elderly woman after having a large, bulbous sebaceous cyst removed from her chest wall walked through the camp and hugged every white person she saw. Cell phones were ubiquitous. There was the occasional mp3 player. Motorbikes laced in and out of traffic with suicidal abandon often carrying several people at once. One occasion, I counted five adults hugging each other on a motors-scooter like slices of bread in a loaf. I rarely saw anybody smoking. For them, seeing a doctor was a privilege and they came to us in their finest clothes.

As we left Port-au-Prince, we had the chance to drive through the earthquake zone. The damage was staggering. Buildings collapsed and knocked down like dominoes. Some of the wreckage had not been touched and no doubt still contained bodies. Bodies were still lying in the street as we passed. The Presidential Palace had simply collapsed on itself leaving the once elegant rotundas cocked on the green lawn and everyone in it dead.

Lastly, at the end of our stay, Mike and Dawn stayed another week, my wife and I tried to leave Haiti. The first day we were placed on a standby list and none of the little trans-Caribbean airlines that service Cap Haitian had room. So many people were trying to get out. Discouraged, we got up at 5 AM Sunday morning and went to the airport to be first on standby. After waiting around for several hours, it was increasingly clear we would not get out then either. Late morning, a Navy helicopter landed to off-load some supplies. I ran out to the crewman and asked if it were possible to get a lift to Port-au-Prince airport to get a flight out. He checked with his superiors and we were taken aboard. What had taken over eight dusty hours by truck took us about 45 minutes by chopper. We refueled on the back end of the frigate USS *Underwood* before finally arriving at the airport. We were taken into custody by State Department officials and waited in a tent. We were given two choices. Fly to Miami in an Air Force C-17 cargo plane without certainty when we might leave, or we could get on a United 767 that had been chartered to bring in supplies. It would be deadheading back to Chicago. If we wanted to go along, we could then make our own arrangements to get home once we got there. It was a no brainer. We boarded the 767 and the crew treated us like heroes, which of course we were not. It felt good to be heading back to the US. We caught a late flight from O'Hare to Dulles and finally got home at 3 AM, nearly 22 hours after leaving the mission. Our third miracle.

It is difficult to image poverty at the level seen everywhere in Haiti. People in our country living at or below the poverty level would live like royalty in Haiti. The politics of Haiti is complex and not easily understood or explained. The place has a tortured history. Everyone with whom I discussed Haiti said it ran better when it was under the control of the Duvalier's. The roads were paved and there was a semblance of order. Democracy was a dismal failure under Aristide. The extent of corruption is mind-numbing. There is no controlling authority. That was quite apparent.

There is a Haitian saying: A rock in the cool water knows not the pain of a rock in the sun.

The Patient with Bad Taste

"Doctor," he said, "I don't taste good lately."

He immediately thought of a brain tumor affecting the olfactory center. He would order a CAT scan and maybe an MRI of the brain. It was a very rare presentation.

As the permutations and diagnoses zinged around in his brain, he grew more intrigued. He turned to look at the wife seated quietly in the corner of the exam room to gauge her degree of concern. When he exchanged glances with her, she smiled slightly and turned red. She looked down at her shoes.

When he turned to examine the patient, he was red-faced as well.

"Before we proceed, let me ask you if you have been eating a lot of garlic recently."

They laughed and laughed.

For the Glory of France

AN EXCERPT FROM
When We Were Young

I swore the next time I found The Corsican in my room unannounced I would kill him. Or it would kill me. Finding the man sitting calmly in a chair, legs crossed, arms resting in his lap, as if he was watching a baby sleep when I opened my eyes in the morning scared me enough times that I vowed the next would be his last.

Of course, that did not happen.

"Jesus Christ," I muttered, "will you please knock."

"Good morning, my friend. I have some news for you."

"Unless the war is over and we won, I do not want to hear it."

"Your army is so pleased with your clandestine activities you have been promoted to major in the OSS."

I rolled onto my back and looked up at him.

"Even as a joke that's not funny."

"I am quite serious. You have done everything that has been asked of you. Expertly, I might add. You blew up the train, you helped with the assassination of a very important SS general, you have provided intelligence for us on these rocket bombs. Your army has noticed."

"Listen, you fool, I have been a bit player in every drama you guys have cast me in. Instead of promoting me two jumps in grade, why don't we do the Allies a favor and send me to Dover in a rowboat and call it a day."

"That's not what Snake said. He said you were cool under fire and an asset despite your handicap."

"I knew that man was a poor judge of character, but I had no idea."

"We want you to do a job."

"You really are crazy. You went from a tail gunner on a Stirling to king pin in the Resistance. It is time you people started to think in terms more consistent with reality."

"I understand you are a very good shot with a rifle."

"I can pick the eyes out of a chipmunk at fifty yards."

"Have you ever used a telescopic sight?"

...

I sat up in bed. I knew I had to kill him and dispose of the body where no one, even after the war, would ever find it.

I chuckled. I told him the last time I had fired a rifle, other than a skeet shotgun for gunnery practice, was over two years ago. I told him I had no experience with a telescopic sight and if he wanted me to be a sniper they were putting all their eggs in a basket with no bottom. Whatever they had in mind now was doomed to fail.

It took no more than a second to notice he had the rifle with sight across his lap. I instantly recognized it as a Winchester .30-06.

"I'm not doing it. Whatever it is. I renounce the war. Tell the OSS or Isabella or whoever is pulling the strings that I have become a conscientious objector."

"Your army might take back your promotion."

"Fuck the promotion. I am a one-legged, retired bombardier of little value to anyone. I will not do it."

I must confess my heart raced at the mention of her name.

"The collaborationist security forces are getting desperate. Despite the fact the Allies are taking their time trying to get out of Normandy." He paused for no apparent reason. Perhaps he was caught in some deep thought or pining for Isabella. My hope was that he had come to his senses over this folly and/or saw the wisdom in abandoning it.

No.

"We know of a meeting between a high-ranking officer of the *Milice* named François Robineau. A particularly despicable and sadistic gentleman. He is looking for a way out. We think he has made an arrangement with a fascist element in Sweden. He knows what will happen to him when the tide of war changes as it inevitably will. He has been betrayed by one of his bodyguards, a faggot who is also particularly sadistic and violent named Patrick duMond. Once he was involved in the round up of Jews in Nancy and shot two old ladies in the back because they weren't moving fast enough.

"I don't know if duMond has turned on his boss because Robineau has decided to flee the *Milice* and is thus betrayed or duMond has had a sudden change of heart concerning his vicious maleficence. Regardless, he contacted us through the Isabella and has offered Robineau for the taking. We want you to kill him."

"Why not take him prisoner and give him a bit of his own medicine?"

"A rapid assessment has suggested he would rather die than be tortured. More than I can say for his victims."

"Why doesn't duMond just kill him himself?"

"I will ask him next time we chat. But we believe he wants to give himself up to us in exchange for us doing his dirty work. He lives, Robineau dies and vice versa."

"Seems like a fair exchange."

"Trust me we would just as soon kill all of them. But we believe duMond can be useful to us and we want him spared."

"Not that I have agreed to do this but when and where do you expect this to happen?"

"Day after tomorrow. Two pm at the customs office in Calais. There is a three-story flat across the street, opposite the customs office. It has an excellent perch from which to fire a shot or two. Robineau is very punctual and he needs this escape badly. He has eluded the maquis for months. duMond knows if the maquis gets Robineau no one around him will be spared. So, he chose us."

"Fortuitous."

"*Oui.* This is not an operation against the Nazis so once you have completed the mission you can calmly just walk away. No manhunt, no reprisals. All France will be grateful. You can keep the rifle if you like. The flat is easy to find. It is the only one with a small Swedish flag in the window."

"How will I get there?"

"Ride your bicycle. It is not far. You can go tomorrow night and be there well before dawn."

"And the rifle? How do I stow that?"

He reached down to the floor and pulled up a battered, stained, medium-sized valise of no distinction, placed it at my foot on the bed and broke down the rifle to its four component parts and dropped them into pre-cut slots. I had never seen anything like it.

"How will I know him?" I paused, "Not that I have agreed to do it."

"Robineau wears a bowler like the one that funny movie star wears."

I had to think for a minute.

"Oliver Hardy?"

"No. the skinny one."

"Stan Laurel."

"Yes, that is him. He will be accompanied by two bodyguards, duMond and another. For your efforts we will deposit a quarter million francs in your bank in Front Royal."

"You are kidding?"

"I never joke about money."

"Two sharp."

"Yes, Major. duMond will take two steps back after they arrive outside the customs office."

"I'm no fucking major."

"Well, according to your high command you are." He looked at me thoughtfully and continued, "I have thirty rounds for you. That should be plenty to learn how the gun and sight work. After you have done the deed you may return here at your leisure."

"And if I fail?"

"We trust you will not but if you do, he will be lost. Unfortunate in terms of justice but you will still get the money for the attempt. We have every confidence in you. The Customs Office is in the northern part of town. Near the port. It is easy to locate. Unfortunately, much of the place is in ruins and it is in a group of buildings that remain standing close to the docks."

"Why did you pick me? Surely you must have others in the organization more capable and willing than I?"

"Unfortunately, no. We are at a disadvantage as to experienced hands. Attrition. But mostly, now that the Allies have managed to finally break out of the Normandy lodgment, many of our people have been sent west to lay the groundwork for their advances. Sabotage. Foment civil unrest. Tear down road signs. Break up railroads." He grew suddenly pensive. "When the landings finally came, all those too, shall we say, reluctant to resist now see their fortunes changing and have found the courage to put on the uniform if even only figuratively and help us. Their sense of guilt at four years of passivity and acceptance of occupation, whether they have collaborated building German aircraft in Renault factories or looked the other way as their neighbors were murdered or just accepted their fate under the Germans, has caught up with them. No one can blame them. They were more preoccupied about their next meal than they were for their country. For the few of us who would not stand still for it there were many more who lacked the desire to risk their lives in what all thought would be a losing proposition. An empty stomach trumps humiliation.

"Nor did they know how to go about resisting. Competing organizations with conflicting interests. They saw the occupation of France turn into a rape of the country while its men, crops, coal and production went east. Their violence and methods of reprisal would cower any man. Anyone who wanted to take care of his family and put food, meager as it is, on the table could not risk becoming a resistant. Patriotism and the Glory of France had nothing to do with it, if only to make their guilt worse. They saw their countrymen, the Jews, carted away in industrial fashion and did very little to stop it. This only made them feel even more guilt.

"They should not be judged. They all thought the Reich would last a thousand years and we would be just a French-speaking colony.

"The ones who found the guilt and dislocation unbearable resisted. After four years there are not many of them left."

I hated this man. If I still harbored any reluctance to participate in this little escapade, it quickly evaporated. He knew it as soon as I sat up in bed bare-chested and studied the disassembled rifle neatly resting in the valise.

He fell silent once more. He looked like he had the fate of France resting on his shoulders.

"Where are the bullets?"

He lifted up a bag of rifle shells.

"Thirty rounds. The magazine holds eight rounds. You should have plenty to practice."

"Thanks."

"No, thank you." He stood and left.

...

I started my journey as an assassin by taking account of my skills as a marksman. I was very good with a small rifle against rabbits and such. I was also very good hunting deer on the plantation. So my ability to hit something as small as a human head at fifty yards was not in question. I was more concerned about being caught with the rifle and my subsequent getaway.

Nonetheless, I needed some familiarity with the weapon. The most isolated place I could think of to test the rifle was an open area with a small copse of trees in the middle of a wheat field half a mile from the nearest road. It was an hour's bike ride south and west of town. I wanted to go out early enough for good light but late enough in the afternoon so there would be little activity that would arouse local suspicion.

I opened the bag of shells and found two thousand francs, enough at current prices for a couple weeks' worth of meals and other necessities. I cooked an egg and melted some cheese on it and put it on a slice of bread to serve as my breakfast. The coffee was not as lavish. It was made of chicory and barely drinkable. When the war was over the thing I would savor the most was a good, rich cup of coffee. And maybe getting laid.

I waited until after two and got on the bike with the valise around my shoulder much as I had done with the crutches. I pedaled across the canal below the town and then rode down on the west side of the waterway. I saw nothing. Not a truck or plane or farmer. I took a white page and a hammer and nail and when I arrived near the copse, I put the bike into the tall grass and took the valise to a small group of rocks in the field and assembled the rifle. I walked to the trees and nailed the piece of paper at about shoulder height. I walked back and took the rifle and loaded the rounds into the weapon. I trained the cross hairs of the scope on the white piece of paper. It fluttered slightly in the breeze.

I took careful aim and squeezed the trigger with the gentle touch of an angel. The rifle gave me a healthy kick in the shoulder. It had been a long time since I had felt the recoil of a big gun. I fired two more rounds and pulled myself to my foot and walked back to the tree. Two hits. Not good enough. I took lipstick I had found in Isabella's drawer and marked my two hits. I walked back and adjusted my aim through the scope and fired three more shots. Walked back. Two out of three hits. I marked them with lipstick. Four out of six. I would not feel satisfied until I was three for three. I repeated the shooting. I was always concerned about the report of the rifle, but it was windy and I doubted there was anyone close enough to hear it.

Another cluster of three. This time I had all three hits. I repeated the exercise and three for three. Six for six. The last time I fired as fast as I could work the bolt. I was satisfied. I had the scope zeroed in and felt comfortable with the rifle. I packed it away, rode home and cleaned the weapon as best I could with what I had available. Early the next morning I rode off to Calais.

The terrain from Watten to Calais was flat and featureless. Some woods cultivated fields and pastures separated by hedges or split rail fences. There was a scattered assortment of villages, some no more than a few houses clustered around an intersection, some so small as to be nameless. The main road to the coast was a good two-lane highway. I wanted to avoid that, so I used the old tourist map and plotted a course away from the more heavily traveled routes. The journey would take about twelve or fourteen miles. Nothing more than a lazy afternoon bicycle ride. I should have plenty of time to find the customs office, get situated in the small flat across the street and set up the firing position. I also needed to find an escape route.

I had packed a lunch of cheese and bread and put it into my knapsack. I cleaned the rifle as best I could with some old underwear; I had no oils or fluids to do a proper job, reassembled and then disassembled the weapon and placed it in the molded pockets in the valise. To maintain the ruse, I packed the valise with dirty clothes and particularly offensive, soiled underwear and closed it. I had used a piece of cardboard to create a false bottom. I took the rest of the rounds, about fifteen by quick count after loading the magazine, and placed them in the pockets of an old jacket after carefully wrapping each in some old newspaper.

I set out for the journey. It was a little before noon. The sun was up and it was hot. I pedaled north and looked for crossroads that might connect close to the outskirts of the city. It was a pleasant, uneventful trip.

I saw scattered evidence of German army units. There were a few positions with quad 40 antiaircraft guns. There was an attempt to conceal them with branches and tree limbs but from the ground their presence was unmistakable.

As I approached the outskirts of town, I saw a solitary German soldier, rifle slung over his shoulder, standing in the middle of the road. He held up his hands and I coasted to a stop.

He held out his hand and said, "Papers."

I said nothing but reached into my shirt pocket and pulled out the identity card and handed it to him. He spoke a German variant of French.

"It says here you live in Valmy. Where is that?"

"South of here. In the Champagne-Ardennes region. I live with my sister. We received word our mother has fallen ill, and I am on my way to care for her."

He perused the card but did not hand it back.

"What is in the case?"

"Dirty underwear. Would you like to see?"

He walked around me as if he was looking for something.

"Are you looking for something?"

"We have had rumors of saboteurs infiltrating to the coast. You fit the description."

"Monsieur, I fit the description of half the grown men left in France. Listen, I have worked with your army on more than one occasion. In fact, I have worked with SS Major Rattzenberger in Vitry. Maybe you know him? He helped get me this."

I pulled up the pant leg high enough for the German script to be clearly visible. He bent down to read it.

When he became erect again, he returned the identity card to me and stepped to one side and nodded. Poor bastard no more wanted to be here than I did.

I resumed my journey. I had decided not to bring the .45. Had he made any attempt to search me I would have be caught. I looked back and waved. The human reflex is to wave back and he did.

Poor fellow. Standing in the hot afternoon, he smelled and looked like he had spent the night sleeping in a dusty foxhole.

Finding the customs office was surprisingly easy. I went to the area near the harbor and looked for the cluster of buildings still standing. I was appalled at the magnitude of the destruction of this famous town. Whole blocks were gone. Shells of buildings remained. Some were smudged with soot. Others had burned to the ground. Very sad.

I could not understand quite how the Customs House and the few surrounding buildings had escaped the annihilation. It could not have been that they were intentionally spared, no one bombs that well. Perhaps there was nothing of genuine military value worth destroying. Perhaps it was just luck. Oddly, I could see activity at the port. There were small vessels plying the harbor. A small packet freighter. A couple of dockside cranes continued their work as if it were just another day in peacetime.

There was activity around the town. People were moving about as if in ordinary times.

I rode the bike around the block twice both to see who was about and find the window of the flat with the Swedish flag in it. It was actually one of the first things I saw. I also checked where to stow the bike and how to quickly depart when the time came.

I was quite hungry. I took the valise and knapsack up to the room. The door was unlocked, and I went in and closed the door. The room was not inhabited. There was a bed with a mattress and a table and two chairs but nothing else to signify someone had lived here recently. The window was open and a hot breeze, smelling of the corrupted water of the harbor wafted into the room ruffling two dirty lace curtains that hung beside it. I took the lunch out of the knap sack and ate the cheese and bread. It was a meager lunch. I had brought along two dime novels, the last two remaining unread works in Isabella's collection. One was about betrayal in marriage; the other was about professional jealousy among thieves. I would read them later.

When I was done eating, I moved over to the window and sat down on one of the chairs. I was far enough away so no one on the street could see my face. I could clearly see the customs house. It had a sign and a large wooden door. The buildings on either side were intact and looked like offices. From this vantage point I had a shot downward and to the right. I figured about 35 to 40 degrees down and about 45 degrees to the right. It would be easy. I looked around and tried to figure out how to position myself for a steadied shot without being too close to the window. I did not want the barrel of the rifle visible, so I had to stand back from the opening.

No mattered how hard I worked on the problem the only solution I could figure out was to put one of the chairs close to the window, rest the gun on a rung and stoop over. This would not work.

So, I assembled the gun and tried aiming it from various positions. I had a clear shot, no question about it. It was just more difficult to do it, be accurate, yet remain concealed. I was a clever fellow. I would figure it out. I still had nearly a day to think it over.

It was hot. The sea breeze stopped, and the room was still and stifling. No air moved. Not even the lace curtains twitched. I stripped naked and lay down on the bed for a nap.

When I woke up several hours later, I was covered with perspiration and the mattress was soaked. During my sleep I had dreams. I thought of all the deer I had killed. I thought of the sound a pumpkin makes when it is smashed to the ground. I thought of exploding heads.

I drank a gallon of water out of the faucet. It was tepid. I redressed. When it was close to suppertime, I left the flat and ventured out. There was a key by the door suspended on a nail. It locked the place.

No one noticed me. I was just another Frenchman with a limp. I had to walk three blocks to find a restaurant. It had a sidewalk café. I sat down outside, ordered a glass of wine and smoked a cigarette. I watched people go by. I had never seen people who looked so downtrodden and defeated. Whatever hope had been kindled by the invasion had not touched them.

I ordered supper and a bottle of wine. When I asked for the best bottle he had he stared at me with uncertainty. Just get it, I said.

A moment or two later, he returned with a bottle, opened it expertly and decanted a glass. I waited, letting it breathe for a moment and took a sip. I gave him a nod. He turned and left. I could not help wondering what he was thinking. Here was a slightly disheveled appearing countryman with long hair, in need of a shave and a long hot bath ordering a fine bottle of cabernet sauvignon in his little restaurant. Maybe he wondered if I intended to pay for it. I was only mildly surprised he did not request payment in advance. I assumed my most arrogant pose, good leg crossed over bad one, as I watched people walk by as if I was annoyed at having to share the same air with them. I must have been a sight. Haughty as the Sultan of Persia. Dirty as a hobo.

I laugh even as I type this.

When I finished my meal, fresh breaded sole, potatoes and fried turnips, I paid for it peeling off the franc notes from a wad in my hand. The waiter was impressed and bowed as he took the money and left. He asked me to come again before he parted.

In retrospect, perhaps this worked against my desire to avoid attracting attention, but I was hungry and had partaken in one of the best meals I had eaten in months. I probably only had one more day to live. I wanted my last meal to be memorable as I approached the Pearly Gates with a smile.

I went directly back to the room and read until the light would no longer permit it. I went to sleep but slept fitfully. Mostly because it was hot but, also because I did not want to fail. I was more concerned Robineau would not show than whether I would hit him.

...

I was awake when the sun came up. I was pleasantly surprised that the tub in the bathroom had running water. The building, for some reason not apparent, was abandoned. I was the only one in it. I sat in the tub and luxuriated in the cool water. My fingers and toes were wrinkled like prunes when I got up. I trotted back to the room naked and sat on the bed, a cool breeze coming in from the sea. I checked my watch for the first time. It seemed to be around six am and I was correct. 0605.

I waited. I did not want to leave the flat for fear of missing Robineau in case, aware or unaware of the plan as the case may be, he showed up early. I sat by the window in the shadows. I carefully checked the rifle for the dozenth time and watched the morning yield to the afternoon.

I had the rifle across my lap.

I waited.

I watched people go in and out of the customs office. No one wore a bowler.

I waited.

1:55 pm.

...

It should not have been a surprise, but it was. A big black sedan pulled up to the front of the Customs Office and two men, one I assumed was duMond stepped out. They were in suits. One ran around to the door and opened it as if he were a doorman at the Ritz. A man with a bowler on his head stepped out and stopped momentarily looking one way then the other. François Robineau.

I had the rifle to my shoulder, my eye on the sight.

The bowler looked too small for his head. He should be shot just for looking ridiculous.

The sedan pulled away.

His head filled my sight. He took two steps forward and stopped waiting for the door to be opened. DuMond, on his right took two steps back and crossed his hands in from of him like an usher at a funereal.

I let my breath out.

In the time it took for the impulse to leave my brain and order my right index finger to begin its calculated squeeze, Robineau moved slightly and the bullet struck him in the neck not his left ear. I knew I should have practiced more.

He grabbed his throat and went to the ground. I worked the bolt. The man on his left turned to look in my direction and the bullet caught him square in the face. His head exploded in a pink mist.

Bolt.

I waited a second as duMond stood perfectly still shocked perhaps by what had just happened. Paralyzed maybe by the suddenness or the enormity of it or the simplicity of it. The shell I fired entered his chest. I hoped it hit his heart. That way in its last beat it would know pain too.

I was prepared to put another round in the first one who twitched. None moved. Each lying over an expanding puddle of blood. I put down the rifle, picked up the three shells and put them in my pocket. I broke down the smoking rifle and quickly stowed it, replaced the false bottom and filthy underwear. Whoever was supposed to snatch up duMond did not show. There was nothing to snatch up.

Milice or not, the place would be crawling with *gendarmes* any second. It was time to go. Before I did, I made sure there was no trace of my presence except for the lingering smell of gunpowder and the stain of sweat on the mattress.

I went down to the back door of the building and got on the bike. But once I started, I was in no big hurry, pedaling at a leisurely pace.

I went down alleys and through a park keeping my southerly course by the sun to my west.

I took a different course to Isabella's and was not stopped.

The Irresistible Urge to Tinkle

I was standing before the urinal. I could hear the sudden roar of the crowd. Dumchek must have scored again. Inconsiderate beer. I would be a while. I looked down to make sure I wasn't pissing on my penny loafers. I saw a pool of blood slowly edging toward my shoe. It came from under the stall. I thought I was the only one in here.

The Speed of Light

Barlow pulled himself to his knees and rested his elbows on the windowsill. It was cool with a nice breeze for the middle of July on the prairie. The moon had not yet risen, and the stars were beyond counting in the cloudless sky. He turned to look at the mobile that hung from the ceiling by fishing line and thumbtack. It was of the solar system. He had made it out of paper mâché, thin wire and more fishing line. The sun was about the size of a softball painted yellow with a few dark sunspots. The planets, each in corresponding orbit, were also of paper mâché and appropriately painted. Mars was red, complete with white *canali*, which he knew, of course, to be an illusion; earth green and blue; all seven continents and oceans painted just so. Even Australia and the white poles. Jupiter had its spot. Construction the rings for Saturn had been tricky. The furthest planet was tiny, inconsequential Pluto. It had not yet lost its standing. Uranus always made him chuckle.

The arms were perfectly balanced. He had taken more pride in that accomplishment than any other part of the sixth-grade science project. He had received an A. He had painted the canals as a joke to see if the teacher would catch the error. She did not.

By now space travel was almost routine. Men, mostly Americans had flown in space, driven on the moon and the Russians had even taken pictures from a space craft on Mars. There was talk of one day putting a permanent space station orbiting the earth. It was all very thrilling.

He lay back down and stared at the mobile. Soon he was asleep.

Earlier that evening, he and his little sister, Jenny, spread a blanket on the grass and lay down to watch a meteor shower. This was not new to them. They often watched the night sky together and Barlow would draw the outlines of the constellations and the bold smudge of the Milky Way with his finger.

"So many stars," she whispered.

"Yep."

"Do you think people live on them?"

"Sure. Why not? If every star has an earth, then there must be a million of them."

"Wow."

"Think about it. There are probably a billion suns in the Milky Way alone. If each one has an earth just like ours there are probably kids up there layin' on blankets lookin' down at us askin' the same thing."

Jenny was young and impressionable and always deferred to her older brother. He thought about correcting himself saying alien children lying on their blankets were looking up at us, not down. But he was afraid it might confuse her. 'Wow' was her universal expression of amazement, understanding or satisfaction.

He loved his little sister. He felt the obligation of an older brother to impart any wisdom and knowledge available to him to help her along the way. Sometimes she followed him around like a little puppy.

...

Two nights later he saw the light. It was in the freshly furrowed field beyond the house. It was quite bright. Odd, Barlow thought. It was not very big. A flashlight at about one hundred yards, he figured. His dad must have dropped it while he was surveying the field. He would remember to go fetch it in the morning.

Distracted by breakfast and morning chores, he failed to recall the wayward flashlight. That night his star gazing was spoiled by heavy rain. Good for the fields. Bad for astronomy.

The next day, he worked hard for his father and mother. He was so tired after his bath he fell fast asleep; no thought of constellations or nebulae entered his head.

The next evening, it was a Sunday, he returned to his perch on the bed and looked out at the window. There again, in the exact location was the light. He had completely forgotten about the flashlight. He would certainly get it in the morning. He lay back and looked at the mobile gently turning in the breeze created by the noisy, little fan that sat patiently oscillating on his dresser. But he was puzzled. How could a flashlight still shine after four days? Impossible. Perhaps it was moonlight reflected off foil, like from a Jiffy Pop cooker, "as fun to make as it is to eat." Except there was no moon.

He gave thought to putting on his sneakers and running out into the field to see exactly the origin of the light. But the field was still muddy and anything that persistent could wait until daylight for a proper investigation. He had little doubt he would find the source of the light.

Before breakfast he dressed, pulled on his boots and stood outside the house directly below his second-floor window. He looked up to be sure and gathered his bearings. Taking long strides, triangulating his exact course by keeping the windows of the three bedrooms behind him, he set out across the muddy field.

He found nothing. He could not possibly have missed it.

When he stopped, going well beyond the place where the light should be, he looked back all he could see were the furrows and his boot prints in the mud. He was pleased the line was perfectly straight back to the house. He could not possibly have missed it.

He suspected Nature was playing some trick on him. Some optical quirk, like the illusion of an oasis in the desert. Regardless of what it was in nature, the light was unsettling in his mind.

The light returned almost every night of the summer and fall. He always checked for it. He went out to see if he could find it once or twice more but gave up on the explanation. But he always looked. It was the last thing he did after saying his prayers. It was not a constant but close.

His father never planted a crop there that summer. He was giving that field an agricultural rest.

Finally, he let it go; he had more pressing matters. School resumed.

He thought about telling his father or teacher about the light but did not. How could he explain it? Who would believe him?

After Labor Day, several days passed without the light. It never returned. Instead of missing it every night it was not there he would be thankful that perhaps he was rid of it.

Sadly, six months later, Jenny was dead of a rare childhood cancer.

Green Bank

Had it not been for his exceptional grades and perfect scores, the only way he would have gone to Princeton was as a tourist. At first, walking in halls Einstein had travelled was humbling, especially for a scholarship student, and exciting. As time passed, the novelty wore off and he became absorbed in his studies. His field was narrow and competitive. Everyone wanted to be as smart as Sheldon. Employment opportunities were few and the higher you went the more you became a member of an elite, isolated fraternity into which you had to discover or explain to survive. DeGrasse Tysons, Sagans and Michio Kakus notwithstanding, there was not a glut of popular science opportunities. Besides, his lean stature, unruly hair, oversized sweatshirts, sockless penny-loafers and slightly crooked teeth provided no photogenic advantage. He looked less an astrophysicist and more a beach bum on Duval Street.

So the task was to find a niche, answer the previously unanswerable, reveal the heretofore unknown or be consigned to the dustbin of teaching undergraduates at some mid-level university competing, like a school of intellectual piranha, for an ever-dwindling supply of grant money.

He counted himself lucky, then, to be taken on by the faculty at Princeton after being awarded his PhD in Astrophysics and Cosmology. His thesis was "The Molecular Diversity of Narrow Band Near-infrared Ejecta in Hyper novae." It was not spectacular, and his defense of the thesis was underwhelming but still sufficient enough to get him a job, under the auspices of Princeton, at the National Radio Observatory in Green Bank, West Virginia. a real cherry gig, he said. He was given a low-level faculty position and told to have at it.

...

Barlow moved into a small trailer park in Bartow, West Virginia, eschewing residence at the enclave for the staff on the Observatory grounds. Barlow in Bartow made him laugh. He had a Honda Civic but preferred to ride his bike when feasible. He settled in late August of 2010. It was a rural area, the nearest Walmart was in Harrisonburg, Virginia and the closest to anything resembling a metropolis was Charlottesville. The isolation did not bother him. For others new to the place, it might as well have been the middle of nowhere. But he was used to rural Kansas and this was not nowhere.

His chosen field of investigation was Fast Radio Bursts. No one was still quite sure what they were or what caused them. The first detected Fast Radio Burst was the "Lorimer Burst" picked up in August, 2001 by a radio telescope in Australia. It was discovered after the fact when, in 2007, radio data that had originated outside the Milky Way was being culled for something else. The whole episode lasted only five milliseconds. No further occurrences were heard in the ensuing ninety hours of recording suggesting it was a singular event, brief and unbelievably powerful, from either an atypical supernova or the collision of black holes. The mind reeled with the possibilities. Half tongue-in-cheek, Barlow speculated that it was a neutron star sucked into a black hole. It was as good a theory as any even as a scatological joke. Regardless, there was a thirst for more data, new discoveries and he was just the man to find them.

He had been to Green Bank Radio Observatory before. It was dominated by the huge, white parabolic dish listening to the random electrical noises from deep space. It was enormous nearly beyond comprehension. It was so big and appeared so fragile that it could, at any second, collapse under its own weigh and once it did. In 1988, a bolt broke and the whole thing fell to the ground like a house of cards. Its ear was sensitive enough to detect the impact energy of a fly's wing drifting onto a kitchen table in Modesto. But it didn't think. It didn't discern. It couldn't figure out where to look. It didn't even know what it was listening to or why. Humans and their little brains were required for that. Only Arecibo was bigger and that could not be pointed beyond a certain declination.

The huge antenna was nestled in a beautiful valley in West Virginia, surrounded by smaller, randomly placed dishes all eavesdropping on the Universe's most intimate secrets. The facility sat next to a national forest nestled in the Alleghany mountain range. The entire observatory was guarded, along with a Naval communications facility and an NSA listening post, by a federally imposed radio quiet zone, thirteen thousand square miles of West Virginia and Virginia. The area was actively policed for stray high energy radio emissions like microwave ovens, Wi-Fi routers and malfunctioning electrical equipment. Spark-ignited engines were prohibited within a one-mile radius of the facility.

He was anxious to get settled and observe, record, analyze and, ultimately, speculate.

The first thing Barlow did was create his study in the trailer home. It consisted of a rectangular piece of laminate counter atop two sawhorses and a swivel chair. He placed a picture of Jenny on his otherwise sparse, rudimentary desk. Moving in was easy. He completed the task in an hour.

The trailer was a Spartan, if cozy, affair. It had been very well kept by its previous occupants, a couple who had finally moved into a house up the road. His library and computer took up a large area of the living room. It had an adequate kitchen with a few pots and pans, decent shower and bedroom. They had left some furniture which was in reasonably good shape. He gave little thought to what had transpired on the couch or in the bed. They had two young children so he could have figured it out had he so desired.

The best news of all was that it had a window unit that was more than adequate to cool the entire place and enough space to bring his bike in at night. The bike, a hybrid mountain/road bicycle, his computer and headphones were the most expensive things he owned. And the most valuable. He listened to smooth jazz while he read or worked. Most of it was over the internet. He owned a TV, but he rarely watched it. The thing was a distraction at best and only served him well when they were broadcasting a baseball game. Any baseball game.

He had purchased a satellite package that allowed him to view any game he wanted but it was still early on the east coast, so when he was settled, he decided to drive over to the local store for provisions

Upon returning, he made himself a peanut butter sandwich and a cucumber salad. After cleaning up he got on his bike for an exploratory ride. He rode around the neighborhood. It was not very populated. He was surprised that for such a pleasant summer evening, there were not many people about.

When he returned, he took a shower, found the Royals game and settle in with a beer. They lost to the Yankees, five to two. He said his prayers and went to bed, the air conditioner dutifully humming.

Weekly Report

Monday morning, around five-thirty, Barlow rose spontaneously without need of alarm and fixed breakfast, Wheaties and coffee, checked his email and showered. His pace was leisurely. There were few people which whom he exchanged email. His parents were dead, and he had no close friends. Lots of acquaintances but few with any emotional attachment.

He had a meeting with the head of the Green Bank Observatory, Doctor Raquel Balestriere, in her office in the administration building at seven. He calculated the bike ride to take about half an hour but for his first day he would drive. He arrived in plenty of time.

The morning was sunny with barely a cloud in the sky. He stood outside the two-story offices and looked at the radio antennae scattered around the grounds. In the distance, he could see the huge, dominant one-hundred-meter telescope which resembled an ordinary satellite TV receiver. It was painted white, held erect by girders and weighed nearly nine thousand tons and had the distinction as being the largest land based movable object in the world. It was pointed straight up, known as the Bird Bath position, and Barlow reflexly looked up into the blue sky to see what it was listening to. Whatever it was spying on existed hundreds if not tens of thousands, even billions of light years away, well beyond the human eye, perfectly blue atmosphere or not. It was surrounded by a scattering of other telescopes which were dwarfed in comparison. It reminded Barlow of little ducklings tagging along after mother.

He easily found Doctor Balestriere's office. He knocked once and stepped into a small reception area and announced himself to the secretary behind the desk greeting her with a warm smile.

"Yes, good morning, Doctor Barlow, come in and have a seat. Doctor Rocky will be with you in a minute. She's on a call with Socorro. Can I get you coffee?"

"I'd love some. Black."

"Right away. Please have a seat." The secretary, her name plate read 'Ruth Jones,' got up from her desk and stepped into Rocky's office closing the door behind her. She was quite attractive with shapely legs extending beneath a tight skirt. She was maybe twenty-five or twenty-eight. She returned with a cup of steaming coffee. He stood up. As she handed him the Styrofoam cup, he checked for a wedding ring but found none.

Barlow looked around the room. It was a nicely appointed office with pictures of nebulae, a huge rectangular picture of the Milky Way, radio telescopes and a picture portrait of Karl Jansky, the father of radio astronomy. It was clear this was the room out of town firemen and dignitaries would come to first. Funding was always an issue and it was wise to make a good impression.

Suddenly, Doctor Balestriere burst through the door. With one long stride she reached out and shook Barlow's hand.

"Doctor Barlow, I'm Doctor Balestriere. Nice to meet you." She had a strong grip.

"Nice to be here."

"Call me Rocky. We don't stand on formality here unless you

capture a Nobel Prize for something. Good to have a Princeton man here. These Cal Tech and MIT men are driving me nuts. Come on in."

Without saying another word, she swept him into her office. The contrast with the outer office was striking. There were stacks of papers, books floor to ceiling, some on metal, hardware store shelves and some not. It could only be described as a fire hazard. It also reflected an impatient, inquisitive mind.

Rocky was medium height and build, not unattractive, with silver hair that she wore short and pulled back behind her ears. She had reading glasses laying against her chest, suspended by a bejeweled chain around her neck, the kind one might purchase for five bucks at Walmart. She moved quickly again reflecting her impatience.

Barlow took one of the seats in front of her desk. He had no choice, the other one was covered with printouts.

"No, no, no. No sitting, we have to go to the Monday morning conference. We talk about the work, update the status of observations and discuss staff problems. It's the only time I can get everybody in one place at one time. It's mandatory. They hate it. Almost as much as I do. Come on."

Barlow rose suddenly to his feet in an effort to keep up with her. She gave a wave to Ruth and walked briskly into the hall. The hall was lines on both sides with framed pictures of celestial objects, photos from Hubble and a copy of the Wow! Signal signed by Jerry Ehman himself. It had a small inscription: "To my friends at Green Bank. Keep your ears to the ground."

"Will you come on?"

Over the door into the conference room was a sign with another pithy statement: "Ignorance is questions not asked."

The conference room was filled. A half dozen young men and women sat on chairs that ringed three of the walls. Likely the undergrads or post-docs. They all looked up and smiled when Rocky entered the room. They were all sitting in less comfortable seats. They were not meant to be comfortable. They were meant to sit quietly and absorb.

They dressed in cut-off sweat shirts, Birkenstocks (who wore those anymore?) or Crocs and tee-shirts with some sort of cartoon or phrase as if their eccentricity and disregard of any dress code might validate their intellect. It looked familiar.

The room was dominated by a large white rectangular desk around which sat various older men and women who Barlow took immediately to be the scientific staff. Only a few of them looked up, only one, the Sikh, smiled. In the center of the table was a telephone speaker that could allow conference calls to astronomers anywhere in the world. All four walls were covered by white boards on which were haphazardly scribbled formulae, notations and rudimentary drawings of solar systems and pinwheel galaxies in red, blue, green and black dry marker. There was no common theme to the colors.

Rocky stood at the head of the table behind a vacant chair. She pointed to the other empty seat to her immediate left. Both remained standing while she began the introductions.

"This is Doctor Barlow. I emailed his CV to all of you. He will be joining our staff. He will be working on Fast Radio Transients."

There was a snort from the end of the table, "Yeah, good luck with that. It's like trying to spot a flashbulb on an iPhone through a wrapping paper tube in the Los Angeles Coliseum."

"In the dead of night," added one of the astronomers.

"In a fog," added the Sikh. There were scattered chuckles.

Barlow smiled. At this point no one had seen a fast radio burst in real time.

Ignoring the banter, Rocky turned to the man to his right. "This is Doctor Clemmons. He is working on hypervelocity stars." Clemmons leaned across the table and shook Barlow's hand. It was a weak handshake. Nothing to be proud of.

"This is Doctor Emily Parkes. She is working on binary systems in near-field galactic dispersion." Barlow had been taught etiquette by his mother. In fact, she had been a stickler for it. A man never offers his hand in greeting to a woman unless she offers hers first. Parkes did not so he did not and wondered if he had committed a *faux pas* in the process as the others were none-the-wiser of the finer points of long-forgotten etiquette. Parkes was overweight and otherwise ordinary. She quickly turned her gaze to the man to her right.

"Next, we have Doctor Cadwallader." She mentioned his field of study, but it was lost on Barlow as he took in Cadwallader. He had a pipe tersely clamped between his closed lips. Barlow thought nobody smoked a pipe anymore that didn't have cannabis in it. The building was smoke-free so, of course, the pipe was unlit.

She might have said 'magnetars' but, so overwhelmed was Barlow by Cadwallader's persona, he could not be sure.

Cadwallader was his own caricature. He wore a short-sleeved white button-down shirt with a thin, dark tie and tie clip. He had several pens in a pocket-protector and black horn-rimmed glasses. He could have been teleported from the control room when the first Vanguard blew up on the pad. He looked up from a paper he was reading and nodded to Barlow his pipe bobbing. But Barlow knew of Cadwallader by reputation. He was not just a brilliant astrophysicist he was also an accomplished engineer. And rather full of himself as a result.

Next was Doctor Ramesh Patel. He wore a baby-blue turban and had a full beard. He immediately stood up and walked briskly around the table to give Barlow a warm, firm handshake. He was the only one to do so. He had a bright, very engaging smile surrounded by his beard. His interest was pulsars.

At the end of the table opposite Rocky was Burt Simmons. He was the chief engineer. MIT trained. He gave Barlow a wave and 'hello.'

The three PhDs on Barlow's side of the table were Debbie Grayson, a pretty, recent addition to the staff from Penn State. Her field of interest was growth and evolution of galaxies and star nurseries. She leaned forward and said hello as well. She had a nice smile. Nicest of the bunch.

"Next, we have Doctor Tyrone Williams who is interested in black holes." Rocky said it with all sincerity but some of the members of the scientific staff, Cadwallader especially, snickered. For a moment the rudeness was lost on Barlow until he realized Williams was African American. He and Barlow leaned in together and exchanged grins. Williams winked and gave him a 'thumbs up.' He was from Cal Tech.

The person beside Barlow was Doctor Chessie Goldsmith from Harvard. He wore a yarmulke. He stood, shook Barlow's hand warmly and told him if he needed anything to let him know. His field of investigation was interstellar chemistry.

"OK," Rocky said finally. "Let's get started." The Monday morning report commenced. It took an hour.

There was clearly a pecking order amongst this critical mass of egos. It seemed reflected in the arrangement of seating. The closest to Rocky sat the one who had made the most recent or critical discovery.

On the far wall, above the white board was a sign. It read: *Proficimus More Irretenti* – "We Make Progress Unhindered by Custom." That explained a lot.

This place looked like the bar scene in Star Wars.

Even so, Barlow knew he was no slouch. He was not intimidated. After all, the two most important recent discoveries in all of astronomy were made at Bell Labs in an effort to make radio and telephone transmissions free of atmospheric interference. One was that of Karl Jansky who first discovered extraterrestrial radio sources in the thirties and Arno Penzias and Robert Wilson who, by process of elimination, found the faint residual afterglow of the Big Bang in the mid-sixties. They were right up there with Copernicus, Galileo Galilei and Hubble.

Betsy

Barlow went to his lab. It housed computers, spectrographs and receivers. It was cooled to counteract the heat generated by the electronics. That's why Betsy, the observatory's techie wore a sweatshirt. She was there when Barlow arrived and introduced herself. Her reputation preceded her, known for her ability to make things work, craft workarounds and design equipment that would help the less technologically gifted extract what they wanted from raw data be it light, sound, radio, x-ray or anything in between. Betsy and Simmons were the real brains of the outfit.

Betsy went over a few things making the assumption Doctor Barlow knew his way around these instruments which, of course, he did. She showed him the sweeping receiver which scanned hundreds of radio channels twenty times a second. All he had to do was pick a target, aim the telescope and bingo. Data.

At the end, she showed him where the Keurig was and the small fridge for the Coffee Mate. She had taken the liberty of stretching out several printouts on the long white table in the center of the room, a smaller version of the one in the conference room.

Barlow looked over them eagerly.

"So, what are you looking for?"

"Fast Radio Bursts."

"Huh. Ever found one?"

"No. But they're out there somewhere."

"Where are you going to look?"

"The Canis Major Overdensity."

"Why there?" she asked with enough disdain to suggest she didn't care what the answer was.

"The Overdensity is a dwarf galaxy on the periphery of the Milky Way and it is being dragged apart and consumed by the outer arms of our galaxy forming the Monoceros Ring. The Ring circles the Milky Way three times. The Overdensity has about a billion stars and a large percentage of red giants. It's twenty-five thousand light years from earth and about forty-two thousand light years from the center of the Milky Way. I think it is an active place and might yield a reliable source of bursts."

"Really?"

Barlow couldn't tell if she was just being obtuse or cynical.

This did not damper his enthusiasm.

"The first FRB was found in 2007 in archived data that was being examined for something else. They last about a few milliseconds. They emit in one millisecond as much energy as the sun emits in ten thousand years. I'm going to try and find one in real time."

"How long are you going to have to wait?"

"Well, it is estimated about ten thousand strike earth every day. But they are rarely observed. Less than a dozen have been found so far and none in real time. I plan to be patient."

"Do they repeat?"

"Not that we are aware of."

"Aliens?"

"No. Why does everybody think every new transient emission is somehow a text message from ET?"

Betsy shrugged her shoulder and said, "Because it's the Holy Grail." As she closed the door behind her, she said over her shoulder, "Call me if you need anything. Let me know what you find."

It was well after dark when Barlow left the lab. This was his moment. Here. In this lab. He would finish work on an algorithm that would sift through thousands, if not millions of hours of data trying to find more bursts. All the while looking through a soda straw for the pinpoint, millisecond flash of light.

The Big Dog

The algorithm, which was finally finished, was similar but not identical to others already being used at the Sternberg Astronomical Institute at the Moscow State University, Cambridge and at Swinburne in Australia. It would be even easier if he could get time on a supercomputer but that was impossible.

These were his thoughts as he drove home.

It was well past eleven when he pulled into the small lot in front of the trailer. He entered quickly and made a bowl of Cheerios. He got on the internet to check the ball scores. The Royals beat the White Sox. He paused to look at Jenny's picture. He smiled and told her he had made it. He was too pumped up to go to bed, so he took a bottle of beer and went out to sit on the lawn chair and stare at the stars. He had a good view as there was little light pollution. He thought of all the people he had met earlier. Rocky. Ruth. Betsy. Cadwallader. Ramesh. His thoughts returned to Ruth. Very pretty. Shapely butt. Nice legs. He chuckled out loud thinking she was the for-better-or-worse girlfriend of some local who rolled up a pack of Luckies in his tee-shirt sleeve and drove around in a noisy, black pickup truck with huge wheels and a gun rack.

He finished his beer and got another. He could feel the approach of the dew point but was drawn to the stars and his thoughts which kept him in his seat.

Canis Major, The Greater Dog and its little smudge of a galaxy, would not be up until November. It would last until March. He would not be able to directly observe it until then but, in the interim, he would look elsewhere for FRBs in what he considered promising galaxies especially those few that had yielded bursts in the past. He would also plug archived data into the algorithm and see what he could find. He would start with Sagittarius A*, a hot bed of all spectra of emissions at the center of the Milky Way, the very place Jansky found the first astronomical radio waves. By the third beer he was getting sleepy and had to pee. He went to bed.

The Irresistible Hum of Deep Space

Barlow made himself scrambled eggs and microwaved some sausage. He drank coffee but sparingly. He took what was important and placed them into a backpack and at exactly seven AM mounted his bicycle and rode off to the lab. He was excited to get to work and there was an irresistible impetus to go fast but, he was unfamiliar with the route and its hazards and thought it best to go slow or at least reasonably.

It was a good road. Blacktop with freshly painted double yellow lines and a white line at the edge. There were sections where it wove down through some tall, wooded hills and others where the drop off beyond a shoulder too narrow to fix a flat was deep. These places were protected by a guard rail. He would remember them.

He arrived at the main building and checked his watch. The ride down took him forty minutes. Traffic was light. He went to his office, emptied his backpack and headed for the lab. He stopped off at the snack bar, more or less a room on the main floor separate from the larger cafeteria, where he picked up an apple. The shapely Ruth was there fixing tea.

"Good morning," Barlow said cheerfully.

"Good morning, Doctor Barlow. Getting settled in?"

"Yes. Thank you."

This close Barlow thought she was in her early thirties not twenties as he first surmised. That made her older than Barlow by a half dozen years at least. She was gentle on the make-up. She had a natural smile and pretty teeth.

She must have felt his scrutiny because she shifted her stance and looked directly at him. It was a pre-emptive strike.

"Doctor Barlow, I do not date scientists. I don't go out for drinks with the staff. And I make it a rule not to socialize with people outside the observatory except at Christmas and the annual company picnic."

"Gee. All I said was 'good morning.'"

She finished dipping the tea bag and lifted it into the trash. "Yes, well. Stop by the office when you get the chance, I have some paperwork for you to sign."

"Sure." The first defense of attraction is to deny its existence.

...

At the lab, Barlow pulled the archived data from the last ten years of observation, examining the wavelengths of radio bursts that had been detected in the past. The targets had been galaxies in the Local Group, super novae and strong radio sources all scrutinized for specific information that had nothing to do fast radio bursts and, in fact, had been obtained before Lorimer ever discovered them. There had been a flurry of excitement about gamma ray bursts and NASA had even launched a satellite, called Swift, to examine for them. They were, like FRBs, unbelievably short, very powerful and ancient, red-shifted back to the early, prodromal days of the forming universe measured in the first hundreds of millions of years after the Big Bang.

There were several strong spikes and, initially, Barlow was hopeful but the dispersion measure, a validation of the amount of intergalactic and interstellar detritus, electrons and dust mostly, the beam had to pass through from source to antenna, was zero, indicating they were local and not very powerful. Probably the sign at the Piggly-Wiggly shorted out or some kid put a knife into a wall socket.

These minor humps did not discourage Barlow. There were terabytes of information to sift through and even with the fastest computer and algorithm he would still have plenty to stay occupied.

Barlow settled into his new life. He made friends and would occasionally go out for beers. After-work pilgrimage to Chili's became a regular Friday night event. Even the increasing receptiveness Ruth exhibited toward his flirtations could not salve his oppressive loneliness.

Barlow would put on his headphones and listen to recordings of space noise. Then he started listening to it live. He sat on the lounger, closed his eyes and listen for Jovian whistles, the timid beep of passing satellites and space roar, the static in his ears coming from deep within the Universe. He would occasionally hear an odd sound or squeak and think of someone trying to say hello from the other side of the Milky Way. He had to intermittently remind himself that he was listening to sounds generated millions or even billions of years before but was only just now reaching his ears. There was a natural human tendency to think of everything that happened in space was occurring in real time or at most a second or two delay like a called third strike on the radio. Sometimes that tendency had to be resisted, even for Barlow. After all, the photons striking the petals of a buttercup were already eight minutes and twenty seconds old. Light that's already stale. Even one of his early astronomy professors quipped that if you want a nice tan in a hurry move to Mercury. Three minutes is all the time you need.

He dreamt of Jenny. Wondering what she was up to in Heaven. When he awakened at two AM his incredibly expensive earphones were cocked half off his head. He removed them, turned off the radio and went to bed.

In a few hours he was pedaling madly down the winding road

arriving at the lab a little before seven-thirty oddly refreshed. As he parked the bike, he gave a desultory wave of the hand to Ruth as she emerged from her car. She returned the smile with a little more enthusiasm than his deserved. He held the door for her but said nothing. She thanked him.

OK, You Win

A short time later he went for his morning apple. Ruth was there, as was often the case, brewing tea.

"OK, you win," she said.

"Huh?"

"You win. If you want to go out with me, pick me up at five Saturday afternoons. We'll pick a place." She handed him a small slip of paper. "Here's the address. Google it."

"Five Saturday it is."

Barlow returned to the lab not sure quite what to think. Either way, today was Tuesday, he would have to wait until Saturday to find out. She lived in Marlinton. It was the Pocahontas County seat. He would need to research the town and find a place to eat worthy of the woman. It would be his first genuine date in months. He got on the internet, found her home and perused the town from satellite images on a maps app, certain he would have no trouble finding it.

He started reviewing recent data from the center of the Milky Way. He had figured it would be alive with radio bursts from its gigantic black hole. But it yielded nothing exciting. No stars being ripped apart and sucked into the dark, voracious maw of the black hole. No new pulsars whipping around their axes at speeds impossible to imagine. Surely, if earth was zapped with ten thousand fast radio bursts a day, they should be easy to find. Instead, there was only silence or the occasional clatter of other things. One could massage the data of the seven or eight known FRBs for days on end and be no nearer to an explanation of the phenomena as the Neanderthals had been. His frustration chipped away at his patience as it must have for all the other astronomers around the globe looking for the same thing. Surely, somebody should hear something somewhere out there.

Barlow had his own theories on the matter. They had all been elegantly thought of before by others buttressed by the weight of mathematics but that was a matter of finding the explanation that fit one's prejudice. He was convinced it was the sudden disintegration of rapidly spinning neutron stars. Somehow the reactive centrifugal force overcomes the centripetal force and the mutual attraction of its constituents causing the thing to fly and it flies apart with a massive release of energy of incomprehensible proportions. Unless it was proven otherwise, it was his theory and he was adhering to it.

...

Shortly after five on Saturday, he pulled into her driveway. The place was a nicely maintained bungalow. To his surprise there was a bottle of wine in an iced chiller on a table between two wicker chairs. The screen door was open, and she immediately knew of his presence.

"Hi," she said. "I thought we'd have some wine on the porch before we went out. Its's such a pleasant evening."

"Sure. I love wine."

"Good. Then have a seat."

She always wore her blond hair up and pulled into a wrap that sat on the back of her head. Until now he hadn't been aware of how long her hair was. This afternoon it fell to her shoulders in long, shiny curls. How, delightful, Barlow thought.

"Here," he said. "Allow me."

With all the grace and etiquette his mother had told him, he poured two glasses of wine, handed one to Ruth and clinked them.

"To a pleasant evening."

"Cheers," she replied.

They sat and sipped the wine.

He held the glass up as if to sort out exactly what kind it was. White, was his best guess.

"It's a Riesling."

"As opposed to red and pink," he said and they both smiled.

She asked how things were going in the lab. "Mind you," she added, "what is said on the porch stays on the porch."

He sipped the wine, of a gulp size usually reserved for a cold Bud.

"Well, slow."

"Yes, we all felt it would be slow."

"We?"

"Yes, when you submitted the proposal, we all thought you were looking for a needle in an infinite hay-stack."

"We?"

"Yes. The committee is made up of Rocky, of course, Cadwallader, Ramesh and Chessie Goldsmith. I was there of course as executive secretary of the outfit. They looked at your algorithm and your qualifications and found you quite acceptable."

"You added your two cents?"

"Oh, yes, of course. I got my B.S. in astronomy from Penn State. Which, of course, is as useful for employment as gender studies in of the early Cro-Magnons. Then I got my MBA from Mount Saint Mary's at the insistence of Rosalyn Balestriere. In addition to being Rocky's personal secretary, I help with grant applications and expenditures."

"Gee."

"Good scientists come and go. Great ones are forever."

Barlow wondered which category he was in. She asked his story. He told her in detail but did not mention the light in the field. It was the only thing he left out. She looked visibly moved when he recounted Jenny's illness and slow, heart-rending demise.

"So, you have no one now?"

"I have a cousin in Seattle but never met him. There are a couple uncles, but I recall them only from my childhood."

"That's sad. The bloodline ends with you."

"The bloodline ends with me."

By now the bottle was empty.

After a wistful few minutes he asked if she was ready to go.

"No, whadoyasay we skip dinner and get another bottle of wine and order a pizza?"

"But you got all dolled up."

"You calling me a doll?" She seemed to have taken offense.

Stammering slightly, he said, "No, of course not. I just meant you look great. Shame to waste the effort."

She said sternly, "Did you skip the sensitivity and sexual harassment lectures. They were mandatory."

She really had Barlow rattled. He knew of no such lectures.

"Relax, I was kidding. Wait here while I get another bottle and order the pizza."

He tried to smile at the little joke she played but at the moment it wasn't funny.

She went into the house and a few minutes later returned with a fresh bottle of wine.

"Pizza will be here in fifteen minutes." She placed a small speaker and her iPod on the table. She turned it on and soon music filled the porch.

"I guess we're not going out."

"Nope, I think we are doing fine right here."

Barlow instantly recognized the music.

"Brian Culbertson."

"Yep."

They sipped the wine and listened to the music.

After they finished the pizza and most of the wine, the conversation renewed.

"So what do you think is causing the radio bursts. ET?"

"Not really. It seems every new astronomical discovery or cosmological observation requires quick explanation. With the passing of each plausible explanation consistent with physics and mathematics the discussion inevitably turns to intelligent extraterrestrial sources. It gets old. Oh, don't get me wrong, I think life is abundant in the Universe. It's kind of a big deal given that until 1995, the only planets astronomers and scientists had any real knowledge of were the ones in our solar system, the ones we already knew about. As if somehow the solar system was unique in all the Universe. Now they've spotted thousands. I bet most every star has a planetary system, at least the ones that have not already destroyed them, and there are hundreds of billion stars in the Milky Way alone. Drake equation and the Fermi Paradox notwithstanding, the statistics are overwhelmingly in favor of life everywhere." He reflected for a moment. "Shame about Pluto, though."

"You've thought this through."

"We all have. It's almost like a parlor game. SETI papers have achieved scientific legitimacy. Somehow it is considered wrong not to eventually insert extraterrestrials into the discussion. Not to demonstrates the singular absence of imagination. As far as the bursts are concerned, I think they are one-offs. Some cataclysmic event; a collision or explosion. Or the collapse of a supermassive star into a black hole. No two bursts, what few there have been, are similar or have been repeated. Besides there is no message we can discern, they are in a part of the spectrum we would consider a broadcast unlikely if they think the way we do and the amount of energy in the bursts is so unbelievably powerful it would be prohibitively expensive just to send a text message. Like Sagan said, 'extraordinary claims require extraordinary proof.'"

She said, "Absence of evidence is not evidence of absence."

"Methane and water found on Mars. Haldane and Oparin made organic sludge in a flask using nothing more than sparks. Throw in a little Darwinism and the next thing you know you have Flava-flave or Donald Trump.

"I think Von Neumann probes come whizzing past us all the time. Using nanotechnology, they are cheap, and they can shoot them out into interstellar and intergalactic space like confetti out of a cannon. Poor Drake. He left out the possible number of galaxies in his equation."

Ruth started talking about her journey. She was quite attractive and when she stood up to and bent over to pour more wine, she revealed an enticing microburst of unrestrained décolletage. She seemed quite at ease with him, he thought. Maybe it was the wine.

Finally, it was dark, and Barlow told her he should go. Any more wine and he'd be in no shape to drive home. He judged himself capable of driving home. She agreed.

"Well," he stood, "thank you for a pleasant evening. This was the most conversation I've had since I moved in."

"Good. I had fun, too. We will have to do it again sometime." She leaned in and gave him a kiss on the cheek.

The Algorithm

His algorithm was designed to filter through large volumes of data spanning many years at very high speed yet with the precision to catch the indentation of the bullet into the balloon or the muscles moving in a single flap of a hummingbird's wing. By using multiplex input, he could look through nearly the entire radio spectrum. After sifting through three months of data he had nothing to report; a few possible squeaks but nothing with the dispersion measure or intensity to qualify.

Some around the table seemed sympathetic others projected an 'I told you so.' Some, like Rosalyn appeared both understanding and disappointed. No one more so than Ruth who Barlow knew was pulling for him.

"Maybe the problem is your algorithm." All eyes turned to Ramesh. "If these things are as common as everyone seems to think, your program should have picked one up by now. Using the lower bandwidth makes detection weaker and may eliminate those from detection. Also, you need to adjust for scattering and intrachannel smearing"

Cadwallader pulled the pipe from his mouth and looked at it. Barlow was aware of Doctor Cadwallader's skepticism from the beginning.

"Maybe it's a software problem. Let me stop by this afternoon and have a look. Possibly the FRBs are outside your detection threshold. Also, the FRBs may have multiple components and you are looking for single spikes."

"Thanks. I would appreciate that."

Cadwallader nodded.

"Well, Doctor Barlow, I have some news for you," Rosalyn said.

Barlow's heart sank.

"Since you are low man on the totem pole you have the distinct pleasure of presenting a brief lecture to the eleventh-grade science class at the Powhatan High School in Durbin. It's part of our outreach program designed to get the little urchins interested in science. Public relations. That sort of thing. It's this Friday at ten. A colorful PowerPoint would be nice."

Barlow was both relieved and annoyed. He could detect a subtle smile on Ruth's lips as she shifted in her seat. She refrained from allowing their eyes to meet.

By Thursday, Ramesh and Cadwallader had found nothing wrong with the algorithm. They were surprised Barlow had come up so empty. Maybe, they said, the fast bursts were much rarer that had been predicted. After going algorithmically through archived data encompassing three consecutive years of Green Bank data and nearly two years of Arecibo data, he hadn't turned up a single specimen that fit. He picked the wrong horse for the race.

Ask the Astronomer

Every citizen *for miles around was aware of the enormous, white, dish-shaped antennae. They* drove past it frequently and probably gave it hardly a thought. So, when Barlow turned up to give a colorful one-hour PowerPoint presentation on radio astronomy and the importance of continued public support through tax dollars it fell on interested ears. Never really trained in the art of public speaking, Barlow, nonetheless, put his best effort into making it compelling. One girl in the front row was absolutely rapt with interest. When the session was over, she approached him and asked, not about ET as he expected, but whether the radio bursts could be related to gamma ray bursts since both species, she said, were short, hard to capture and so powerful.

Yes, he replied. That was a possibility except they were at opposite ends of the electromagnetic spectrum. But that doesn't mean they are not elated. They seem never to have occurred in temporal proximity, however. Then she asked if it was coincidental that they were near the cosmic water hole. He was stunned. The water hole was the nickname for the terrestrial microwave window between the hydrogen and hydroxyl lines of frequency, a relatively quiet EM zone between one and ten Gigahertz through which, most experts agreed, would likely be the portal through which an extraterrestrial intelligence might reach out.

"That's not entirely correct but, I take your point. There are also others that dispute whether the water hole would be the EM gateway they would use. Instead of a continuous broadcast, they would send out messages at intervals some speculating that the interval might be as long as a year."

"Why would they do that?"

"Cost mostly."

"I figured they would rest a phonebook on the telegraph key and wait. Anybody that advanced could probably afford it."

"How come you know so much about all of this?"

"Internet."

The more she spoke the more she reminded him of Jenny.

"Maybe you should stop by the lab sometime."

"Wow. I'd love to."

"What's your name?"

"Cora. Cora Jenkins."

"Cora, have your mommy or daddy drop you off at the lab Saturday morning with a permission slip and I'll show you around."

"I can drive."

"Permission slip. Don't forget."

"I'm sixteen."

It was pouring. He leaned out the front door and waved. She leapt from the car and ran in.

"Hi," she said.

"Good morning, Cora. How are you today?"

"Good. Got the slip?"

She reached into her pocket and produced the note. It read, "Cora has my permission to spend the day in the lab. (signed) Her Mom."

It was counterfeit and they both knew it.

"OK, come with me."

She followed him. As they climbed the stairs to the second floor, Barlow could hear her footsteps and thought he might turn and see Jenny, pigtails bouncing with her steps, a few feet behind. It took his breath away. As he approached the last steps near the top, he gave thought to calling her on the bogus permission slip and telling her she couldn't spend the day just so he could avoid the sadness her presence would incur.

"This is very exciting, you know. I appreciate your inviting me."

"Sure, just don't touch any of the buttons."

They entered the lab.

"Wow. This is so cool."

"They have to keep the temp down for the computers."

"No, I meant"--

"Yeah, I know what you meant."

She dropped her bag and coat on the table and looked around.

"These are the multichannel receivers. They are connected to the big one out back. It operates at meter to millimeter wavelengths. The 100-meter diameter collecting area, unblocked aperture, and good surface accuracy give it unparalleled sensitivity across the telescope's full 0.1–116 GHz operating range."

"What are you trying to do sell it to me?"

He ignored her. Jenny had her few faults. This Cora might end up a pain in the ass. A very smart pain in the ass but one, nonetheless.

"Here are the instruments that analyze the radio input depending on the wavelengths to be examined. This is called a waterfall display showing the frequencies we are looking at with drift based on the velocities of sender and receiver. Each dot represents an empty data point. This is in real time. We then have printouts which we can assess at our leisure. All this is archived, and I have spent the last three months going over the archives."

"Found one yet?"

"Sadly, no. There are supposed to be ten thousand a day but since

2007 there have only been seven detected. The first one was found by the Parkes radio-telescope and so far they have found the majority of them."

"Sounds like something is wrong down under."

"What do you mean?"

"A non-recurring phenomenon sounds like a fluke. Like the 'Wow!' They figured *that* out yet?"

"Sadly, no."

"Boy, Doc. You must find this stuff a real downer."

"Sadly, yes." They both laughed.

"If it finds something it will alert you, right?"

"Yes. It will send out a text message. That way we can let everyone know one has happened. The last time one occurred it was found in close to real time and observatories around the globe were alerted and a six-day afterglow of radiation was detected from the source."

"Huh. How much data have you looked through?"

"I'm up to June of last year."

"Anything I can help with?"

"Not really, It gets fed into the computer, lets my trusty algorithm look at it and it gives me what it finds in this compressed printout with any anomalies marked."

"So, you just look at computer print outs all day. Find anything interesting?"

"Oh, yeah. I get a near-miss quite often and then analyze it for dispersion and red shift. It's never panned out like I hoped though but, I am patient."

She leaned over his shoulder and pointed at a spike, a large one.

"What about this one here?"

"No, that's lightning somewhere."

"Oh." There was disappointment in her voice.

"Sorry to disappoint."

They went over the computer printouts for most of the afternoon and decided to call it a day.

She parted by telling him not to give up. It's out there somewhere.

Barlow went home to the trailer, the rain still drumming on the metal roof. Ruth had made other plans. He drank a beer and thought of Cora and how much she reminded him of Jenny.

The Cora Burst

He ate dinner, a microwavable pasta meal he later regretted. He listened to smooth jazz on his ancient iPod and closed his eyes. The first inkling something was amiss was the sudden cessation of the rain. He could feel the soporific vibration on the thin-skinned trailer and suddenly it stopped. He was nearly asleep but came awake and fully alert in a moment. He took the headphones off and sat up. What had he forgotten? Did he fail to lock the lab? Was he so taken by Cora's resemblance to Jenny had the better part of his brain misted over? He put the headphones on and tried to suppress his disquiet when suddenly it hit him. There was something about the spike Cora, in her sweet ignorance, had noticed what he had been too quick to dismiss. That had to be it.

No, he was thinking clearly now and there was nothing atypical about it. He had seen similar spikes, and none were powerful enough to conform to a fast radio burst. At least any that had occurred before. He chalked them up to something ordinary and casually wrote each off; his objectivity had been restricted by his prejudice of knowledge. At initial glance it lasted longer, too. Much longer than would be accounted for by wavelength delay in FRBs everybody had seen previously. Instead of a few milliseconds it had lasted several dozen. Maybe he had uncovered something new. His 'Lorimer Burst.' Or, more correctly, Cora had.

He could not suppress his excitement. The music became instantly annoying. Quickly he was out the door on his way to the lab. It was nearly midnight. He was oblivious to the cloudless, moon-filled sky. The night sky would have been teaming with stars were it not for the contamination by the moon. The roads were still shiny from the rain. Pondering what he had found, the possibilities flitted around his brain like moths around a bulb.

If it was not a fast burst, what was it? Had he dismissed previous examples as not significant because they did not qualify as fast bursts: extremely brief, extremely powerful and extremely distant?

He negotiated the turns on the rain-slick road at speeds even he considered dangerous. When he arrived at the lab, he used his code on the keypad to let himself in. He could not remember who had the 'watch' this night. Might be one of the post-grads. Either way their presence was irrelevant.

Barlow opened the door to the lab and was greeted by the dozens of lights, some white, some red, a green one or two, some blinking, others steady: the beacons of modern science. He flipped on the overheads. There, stretched out on the table was the long, unfolded computer printout just as he and Cora had left them. He went right to the anomaly. But, suddenly, he did not know where to begin. But his most prevalent emotion was concern for why he had missed it in the first place.

His mind cleared and he began to focus on certain questions: was it real or some stray artifact? If real, where in the sky did it originate? How far away? Jansky flux? Were there more than just this one? Dispersion measure and red shift. That would score the thing as extraterrestrial.

Quick calculation showed it to be a 112 Gigahertz radio flash from 3 million light years away. Astronomically speaking, that was the equivalent of the house next door. Most FRBs had been from the next state. Barlow's heart pounded inside his chest.

No. This was too good to be true. Red-shifting, with the longer blue wavelengths arriving ahead of the red ones, confirmed the distance: 3 million light years. Give or take. There was always a give or take with astronomical measurements. He was beside himself. He failed to realize it was already Sunday afternoon.

He checked the coordinates of the antenna when this anomaly had been observed. That was easy. The thing had arisen in the Triangulum galaxy, M-33, a pinwheel galaxy, the abused little sister of Andromeda. A rather ordinary place.

Now he dissected the radio signal itself. He splayed out the signal because it was broad based: a single, sharp spike initially then dropping down to a shoulder of longer duration. But there was a roughness to the shoulder and further lengthening revealed it to consist of a dozen or so smaller similar amplitude spikes all compressed together like multiple, off-pitch musical instruments all letting go at the same moment, some slightly louder than others. If it was a fast radio burst there were three things that didn't fit. It was not as 'bright' as, and therefore, less powerful by a factor of ten, than all the others previously observed. It was not a single, narrow spike or incredibly powerful. Instead it was a family of spikes, like a chaotic picket fence, heralded by one large sentinel spike. And it was very close. Not the billions of light years distant he expected. Finally, it lasted more than 50 milliseconds. Unheard of in the universe of FRBs, all seven of them.

His first thought was that a medium-sized stellar object, perhaps a dozen solar masses, part of a binary system with a black hole as the silent partner had finally cannibalized its orbiting mate by reaching some critical threshold in physics and coming apart with a flash and the residual debris spiraled in trail creating the shoulder.

Jesus Christ. What had he found? Or, more correctly, what had the little smart ass discovered?

By now it was dark outside.

He pulled out more archived data. There were no recurrences.

Huh.

By now he was late for the Monday morning conference.

...

"Still looking," Barlow said. He knew he looked like hell. Disheveled. He hadn't showered in nearly 48 hours and wondered if he gave off an aroma. Ruth smiled at him. Rocky acted as if he wasn't there.

Cadwallader and Ramesh had reviewed his software and algorithms, and both stated it was without flaw.

"I appreciate your help. I have nothing to report. Just like last week." He did not dare be wrong.

At the end of the meeting, Ruth smiled at him from across the table and winked. Then she took her index finger and tapped the side of her nose twice.

There was a locker room in the basement with a shower. It would be his next stop.

His time in the shower gave him time to think. It was almost too good to be true. He had discovered something. He just wasn't sure what. His shower was thorough but brief. He was back in the lab with water still dripping from his small ponytail.

He went online and checked the date of Cora's Burst. It came in at almost exactly 1:10 pm February 11, 2011, a few months before he had joined the Observatory. He checked all the astronomical catalogs and bulletins that report this sort of thing: a new planet, nova or threatening asteroid. Nothing. The data base was nearly clean except for a few random, minor events in some galaxy far, far away. All were trivial. Why had no one noticed this at that time? It did not matter. She found it.

He spent the rest of the day programming a new set of parameters to alert him to a recurrence. He expanded the bandwidth and adjusted the frequency amplitude. If one happened again, he was ready for it.

Ruth opened the door and came in.

"Morning, Buckaroo. You seemed a little preoccupied this morning.

Metzger told me you were in the lab all weekend. Find something?"

"Oh, hi Ruth. No, thought I had a bite, but it turned out to be an old tire somebody tossed in the river."

"OK, well, come by the office later. I have some papers for you to sign."

"Will do."

With that, she closed the door behind her.

He worked most of the day, setting a plan for further study of this radio signal, or signals, and left having forgotten to report to Ruth's office.

...

Before he turned in he gave some thought to telling Cora but decided he would show her instead. He fell asleep quickly, mentally, emotionally and physically exhausted.

...

Tuesday morning, Barlow was in the lab by six am. The siren song of Cora's Burst could not be ignored, and he analyzed the shoulder more intensely. There were actually 52 separate, smaller spikes. The last one was the largest after the sentinel spike. Then the trace returned to baseline noise. Fifty-three milliseconds. All previous FRBs were at or less than 5 milliseconds. Jansky spectral flux suggested it was quite powerful. And whatever it was occurred 3 million years ago when the first man worthy of the name, *Homo habilis*, first walked the earth, the Piacenzian epoch and the Great American Interchange of species across the newly formed Panamanian Isthmus.

Barlow went back over a year's data prior to Cora's Burst and the search revealed nothing even remotely resembling it. He had examined this data before. He then started a computer search of data subsequent to Cora's Burst. He adjusted the parameters of the search to include anything above the baseline noise.

He was speechless when, within an hour, burst number two was revealed. He dove into it quickly. Number 2 was forty-nine milliseconds long, had a large initial spike and was less powerful. But the redshift, dispersion measure and signal drift were identical. He could barely contain himself. He wanted to run out into the hall and bang on every door to tell them of his discovery. But he did not. He did not want to be wrong.

He checked the dish's line of sight. It was at the Triangulum galaxy and had occurred 91days after the first. The blink of an eye in astronomical terms. It had an initial spike, a small, short shoulder and a terminal spike. Quick check showed no reports of astronomical events worthy of mention. Had to be the same source. Not only had he found a new fast radio burst, it had repeated. After accounting for different positions of earth in a three-month span, and possible movement of the source galaxy which was too small to be noted at this distance in just three months, Barlow had no doubt they were the same source. Like a monstrous, sucking whirlpool in space, the black hole had taken another victim.

The third radio burst surprised Barlow only slightly less than the first. It was 93 days after the second. The initial spike was identical to Cora's; the shoulder and terminal were not. It was longer than the two previously, 71 milliseconds. He easily imagined a trail of debris from a shattered white dwarf or neutron star falling into the black maw piece by piece. Not only was he convinced he had found the source for these atypical fast radio bursts, he had found a voracious black hole. The period orbit around the black hole was 92 days, plus or minus, with more breaking off and spilling in with each pass.

Then he noticed something peculiar, as if all of this was not peculiar enough, something he had overlooked when comparing it to the first. The Jansky flux, the power of the burst, was absolutely identical. He expected the dispersion and red shift to be the same but not the clatter and crunch of the debris. Perhaps it was so far away small differences in measurements would be expected but nothing should be identical. Nothing. The Jansky flux was less in the second. He wasn't sure what to make of that.

Barlow started a spreadsheet with a column for each piece of data. The parameters of the first and third bursts were nearly the same. a few percentage points off but not by much. The third didn't fit at all. Except for the fact that it came from the same point in space, it was different.

He was about to leap ahead in the recordings when the door opened. He was startled.

"Hi, cowboy."

"Oh, hi Ruth."

"Am I interrupting something?"

"No, not really." Inwardly, he was pissed at the sudden interruption.

"I was hoping you would swing by the office so I could invite you for supper tonight."

Barlow realized that if he did not force himself to take a break, he might not leave the lab for the next several days.

"Come on. Take a break. The stars will still shine tomorrow."

"OK. Let me run home and shower and change and I'll be by in a bit."

"No. If you need a shower that bad, you can take one at my place. I'll make us a nice peanut butter and jelly sandwich."

"Ok. Let me finish up here and I'll be by in an hour or so." He looked at his watch. It was after four in the afternoon. He wanted to quickly jump ahead 90 days to see if there was a fourth repetition of the burst.

Ninety-two days after the last burst was number four. By the time he finished his analysis it was nine o'clock. The fourth burst was similar to the second and identical in Jansky flux. It was totally different than number one and number three.

Jesus Christ, he muttered, what have I found?

He had to quit. He was so mentally spent he could no longer focus on the numbers and, to his dread; he realized he had stood up Ruth and her sandwiches.

He called Ruth but there was no answer.

He tried to settle down with a beer. He wanted his head clear, so he played no music and listened to no ballgame even though it was playoff season.

He needed a working theory as to what he had found. There were known luminous Cepheids in the Triangulum galaxy and binary stars with strict periodicity. Instead of light perhaps they were radio Cepheids. If this were the case, why had no one found them before? Perhaps, he thought, no one was looking.

Cora

"Hello, is Cora there?"

"She's not here. Who's calling?"

"I'm Doctor Barlow."

"Doctor Barlow?"

"Is something wrong? Did something happen to Cora?"

"Oh, no. She's fine far as I know."

"Did she get an abortion?"

"Heavens, no." He had trouble suppressing a slight giggle. "I'm with the Observatory. She came by Saturday. Didn't she tell you?" He kept the counterfeit note to himself.

"No. She told me she was at Becky's. She and I will have a talk when she gets home."

Barlow was about to explain when the phone went dead.

...

There was a slight tap on the door. It was the light rap of knuckles on aluminum.

Cora entered the trailer as if she lived there.

"Jenny, you found it. The burst. The one you found Saturday."

She started snooping around the small trailer without touching or disturbing anything, as if looking at a fresh crime scene. He thought she was so distracted she might not have heard.

"I think I might have gotten you in trouble with your mom."

"That's OK. She drinks a lot. She'll be fine."

Cora continued poking around as if on an uninvited surveillance.

"You like baseball?"

"Yes. I do. Besides track and field and crew, it's the purest sport there is. You throw the ball, you hit the ball, you catch the ball, and throw the ball. Simple. Although I still haven't figured out the infield fly rule."

"Who is Jenny?"

"My baby sister. Why?"

"Jenny?"

"Yes. She passed away a while ago."

"Pity."

She sat down on his recliner as easily is if she lived there.

"So, tell me about my burst."

Barlow could not contain his excitement. He dove into the details without regard to what she might or might not understand. She listened intently until he was finished.

"So, what do you think?"

"Certainly sounds like you're on to something. Let's hear it."

"No, it is not something you listen to. You could make a wav. out of it, I guess but why would you want to?

"I think you eavesdropped on a conversation."

"No, this is much too powerful to be a chat. This amount of energy just to gossip? Not hardly. Do you know what the Dan Goldsmith Rule is?"

"Uh-uh."

"Goldsmith states earth receives about one billionth of the sun's energy. And we consume one million billionth of the sun's total energy. Do you have any idea how much power would be required to send just a single millisecond of that intensity radio wave? Who would do that?"

"How far away is it?"

"Three million light years away. In M-33, the Triangulum galaxy."

"Close. And how long was the interval again?"

"Three months give or take a few days."

"That's three light months."

"Yes."

"How far?"

"About 1.4 trillion miles."

"That's from here to the Oort Cloud."

"Yeah, that's some long-distance call, alright."

Cora grew pensive for a few moments. "I set up a small radio telescope. I found out how to do it online. You know almost the same time every night I would pick up a six to twenty-minute burst of interference. Not every night, but most nights. For the life of me I had no idea what it was. I figured a pulsar or quasar or something. Whatever it was, I was thrilled. Turns out it was from next door. I was able to correlate it with the subsequent bathroom light going on and off a short time later. Extraordinary claims require extraordinary proof. I got it when they moved away. The interference never came back.

"I'm pretty sure I know what caused it."

"Me too. So, Doc, what is it?"

"I have several thoughts. I think it could be a neutron star spinning so fast centrifugal force is overcoming gravity and it is ejecting its crust.

"No. Don't like that one. What else you got?"

"Two stars rotating around a black hole, like a trinary system and pieces are coming off each and their consumption is giving rise to the radio bursts."

"I like that one better."

"I haven't precisely localized the origin yet, but I think it's close to an H II region near NGC 604: an unformed fiery mist."

"So, it could be part of a stellar nursery."

"Could."

"How did Jenny die?"

"She had cancer."

"How old was she?"

"Twelve."

"You miss her."

"Very much."

"You gonna cry?"

"I might."

"I want you to convert the burst to sound so we can hear it."

"They only last a couple dozen milliseconds. It would be less than a beep."

"Use slow-mo."

"It could be tidal activity with Andromeda. It is leaching hydrogen from Triangulum."

She got up, walked to the refrigerator and opened a bottle of beer. She took a sip and gave the bottle to Barlow.

"What the hell are you doing?"

"I had a swig of beer. No big deal."

"How old did you say you were?"

"Sixteen."

"Knock it off or you'll have me arrested for contributing to the delinquency of a minor. I promise to convert the bursts to music. Just don't do that again. Deal?"

She snatched the bottle from his hand and took another swig, saying, "Deal."

She got up again and said she would check in tomorrow after softball practice.

"You throw the ball, you hit the ball." With that she was out the door.

A moment later the car door slammed, the engine caught, and she peeled away with a blast of gravel.

Light You Can Hear

Barlow was in the lab by six-thirty. He rode his bike since the sky was clear and when he left the stars were bright. There was no moon. The ride allowed him to think. By the time he arrived the sun was up above the ridges to the east. It was going to be a beautiful day. There was a crispness of burgeoning autumn in the air. Even some of the trees had started to turn.

As soon as he realized the origin of Cora's bursts, he used his available time on the big dish to stare at NGC 604 in the Triangulum. Each morning he would look at the printout of the night's whispers from deep space. Nothing had turned up so he went after more data and told himself after lunch he would make a wav. recording on the computer to satisfy Cora and her curiosity and the emotional need to put noise to electromagnetic emissions. It was a waste as nothing useful could come from the application of sound to the bursts except her pledge to forgo beer.

Nearly six months of data yielded nothing. No repeat bursts. Dead air. Then a small blip which was far more consistent with a real fast burst, similar in every respect to the others from Australia and Green Bank. It lasted less than a dozen milliseconds. Reds shift and spectral flux were different. He was disappointed. He would soon be approaching "real time." Not sifting through archived data.

He was about to give up and go talk to Ruth when a new burst from NGC 604 showed up on the archived printout. It was similar to number one, short shoulder and a larger terminal signal. Then three months later a short one, same everything as the first, Cora's Burst. Exactly ninety days.

Ninety days exactly another small one. Short but unmistakable.

Then a big one, nearly identical to the most recent big one he found. Then less than a week later, another big one, longer than either of the others. Then a matter of a few days later, a big one but the shortest so far. Then dead air. By now he had reached the end of the archived data. Anything received now would be 'live.' He decided to draw out the chronology of the bursts assigning 'A' to the first one, Cora's original signal, and 'B' to the second one:

A(Cora)53ms—91d—B49ms—93d—A71ms—92d—B52ms—6mo—A74ms—90d—B30ms—90d

90d—A50ms—90d—A80ms—1w—A40ms—dead air—real time

Barlow looked at the sequence, timing of bursts and assumed that B had finally been devoured by the black hole. Three more orbits for A then *kaput*. That some of the numbers were identical did not bother him. What an incredible finding. Instead of finding answers, he had found more questions. For a scientist it was a perfect predicament.

In keeping with his promise, he recorded each burst in order and, keeping true to their intensity, shortened the interval until they appeared on the computer to be one right after the other compressing the whole affair to about two minutes of time. By lengthening the duration of the each burst from milliseconds to several seconds, he made each one audible as a smear of sound. He loaded the recording onto a thumb drive and put it in his pocket hoping his little corruption of the data would be enough to satisfy Cora's curiosity.

He gave some thought to inviting Ruth to his little debut but figured she was still mad at him for standing her up.

He rode his bike home. Some of the journey was uphill but he made it easily. He put the bike away, placed the thumb drive on the table and nuked his dinner.

At seven, she knocked on the door and let herself in. For all her precociousness, she was short on manners.

"Hi. You eat?"

"Yes," Barlow replied. "I microwaved a ravioli dinner."

"She dropped a small paper bag on the kitchen counter. "OK, well I wasn't sure, so I made you some tuna sandwiches."

"OK, thanks and put them in the fridge."

She complied.

"OK, so let's hear it."

He handed her three spreadsheets: one for 'A,' one for 'B' and one with both listed in the order in which they were encountered.

"Tell me what you see."

Cora's eyes darted back and forth over and between the three sheets.

"Two sources, three light months apart in a galaxy three million light years away. Then nothing. Let's hear it."

"I've lengthened the signals and shortened the interval."

"Have you listened to it?"

"No. I thought we'd share the experience."

Barlow had loaded up the audio file and played it through a cheap set of speakers as he normally listened to everything through his headphones. The sound was purer and more intimate that way.

He played it at normal speed with the three-month gaps abbreviated. The sounds went by quickly like the clatter of a baseball card on bicycle spokes.

She looked at him as if to say 'WTF.'

"OK, let me slow it down."

He set the pulses to about one second duration each. It was more screeches just a little longer. The silent parts were also slightly longer.

"OK, now slow it down and let me hear the component parts."

He manipulated the file again. This time the bursts were fast like a multi-toned squeal.

"Very interesting. Slower and change the pitch."

Barlow adjusted and started the file.

This time the component parts of each burst were clearly audible. The sharp, loud initial spike and the following blips in rapid succession then a louder terminal beep.

"OK, leave it there and run the whole sequence from first to last."

He complied.

She stiffened. Barlow was taken aback as well.

"Let me try something." Barlow slowed the speed way down and lowered the tone into the bass range.

"There," she said after the first listening. Barlow was disturbed. He had manipulated the soundtrack to the point where it was so artificially distorted, so it bore no resemblance to the original recording. They were making a minnow stretch out until it looked like a tiger shark.

"Play it again," she implored.

He did so. Now he was losing interest in the exercise.

"Again."

He was getting annoyed when she asked him to play it a fourth time.

"This is—"

She put up her hand to silence him as if she knew he was about to say, 'a waste of time.'

"Oh my God, Barlow. It's a conversation. They are talking to each other.

Barlow played it again. This time even slower.

"Jesus Christ."

"A is saying something. B is listening and then replying. Repeating the cycle over and over until B stops and is never heard again."

Barlow thought she had lost her mind.

"There is the natural anthropomorphic imperative to impart a human energy to everything."

"For Christ's sake, Barlow. *Listen to it!*"

He played it again.

"The message is not meant for us. They are talking to someone 3 months away. That would be six months between A asking a question of B and A's receipt of B's response. The first big part of each burst is 'Hey. Listen up.'"

"I wish I had your imagination."

"I'm dead serious."

Barlow listened yet again. He could see how that might be interpreted. But he was not remotely suspicious or even open to the idea that this was anything but a naturally occurring event. He decided to play along.

"OK, I can see where the first message is a negotiation or an ultimatum. No one would use that much energy just to give the report on the closing bell."

"It might be an ultimatum. They argue. They plead. a final demand. Then poof."

"Poof? You've watched too many Star Wars movies."

"Or it's a plea for help."

There was silence in the trailer for nearly ten minutes as they stared into middle distance.

"What else could it be?" Barlow asked.

Cora said, "It could be a perfectly reasonable, perfectly cosmological event. As you say, it could be a black hole sucking down binary stars. It could be, as you said earlier, a neutron star disintegrating like a CD at 100,000 rpm."

"Two of them?"

"Or something totally unknown. And you are about to discover it." She softened her voice, "I still think it's a cry for help."

For the first time Barlow noticed the bruises on Cora's arms. They were from the rough grip of two hands.

He could not decide whether to ask or not. He was overwhelmed by a sudden sadness.

Oh, this poor girl, he thought. So bright, so innocent, so nosey.

"How'd you get the bruises?"

She looked at her upper arms and became embarrassed.

"They're nothing. Not your concern. I have things under control."

She was humiliated and he chose not to pursue the issue lest he regret doing so.

Poor kid. Mother a drunk. No father. It was amazing she was as well put together as she was.

"I think it was a warning." There was the combination of urgency and sadness in her expression. "They were trying to tell them to get off."

"What?"

"A was telling B to get off. Get off quickly. Something bad was about to happen. And it did."

"I have checked everything there is to check on NGC 604 or the Triangulum galaxy for the past two years. It has been quiet. Nothing happened after the last burst. Resist the urgency to think of these things as occurring in real time. Whatever happened happened at least 3 million years ago."

Again, Cora became subdued.

"I have to go."

She stood up.

"OK. Thanks for coming. Think about what else it could be, and we'll talk again. Maybe tomorrow."

"Maybe."

Without saying another word, she walked out the door. It was 10:30. He gave not a thought to the appearance of a young teenager leaving the trailer of a reclusive older man.

"Thanks for the tuna fish," he said as she got into her car.

When she was gone, he listened to the wave file over and over. Perhaps ten more times. He could not shake Cora's notion that he had heard something more than stars ripping apart. Nor could he shake the desire to go over and punch Cora's mother right in the mouth.

Protocol of Urgency

Barlow went to work the following morning befuddled about what he should do. He wanted desperately to report what he had discovered. But without a plausible working theory of causality, he was reluctant to divulge his secret. He was certain where it came from. Had someone else found the bursts? If so, would they get the credit and he would be just an also ran. Second place is the first loser. He might stop by Rosalyn's office and bounce a few things off her. When he got there she was gone. Some meeting, Ruth said. Visiting the Very Large Array in New Mexico and wouldn't be back for two days.

Find something?

Not yet. Still looking.

He was not convinced he had witnessed something artificial. There was this headlong race to find some transmission so compelling that it would satisfy the criteria for extraterrestrial intelligence. Inevitably, it became a discussion that bordered on the paranormal and he rejected any such discussion, Holy Grail or not. Yet there were recognized international protocols established defining how to react upon the unmistakable receipt of an extra-worldly 'hello.'

But it wasn't a greeting. If Cora was right, it was an eavesdropped conversation. He had to avoid the seduction of an artificial source. ET was to be found only by rigorous process of elimination.

The last burst, a short A burst, was only a couple weeks old in relative time. His cell dinged. A text from Cora. She would be by after dinner. They needed to talk.

Barlow spent the rest of the day working the numbers again. But he also spent time contemplating the post-detection policy. The scientist Zbigniew Paptrotny made a compelling case that the protocols should be guided by three factors: society's emotional and spiritual readiness to accept the news of detection, how the news of detection is released, and the unambiguousness of the message in the signal.

He developed a strategy consisting of a three-point plan. First, he would prove beyond any reasonable doubt his observations were accurate and real. By now, he felt this was a given. Second, he would formulate an unassailable explanation consistent with all available knowledge of physics and astronomy. This would require some work. It could take months. Third, he would dismiss any argument that it was from an extraterrestrial intelligence for conclusions to the contrary would need to be equally compelling. Depending on the legitimacy of the second point, it would be very easy or very hard. Considering the age of the universe, a Kardashev I or II civilization capable of such communications was either very common in which case we would likely have seen one by now, the Fermi Paradox in reverse, or extremely rare and virtually undetectable. The Milky Way, Andromeda and Triangulum were the three most observed and studied galaxies in the universe. So far, silence. There was no reason to think something had been missed or it would be *he* destined to make the most important discover in all of science and human history. Wow.

...

The first thing Barlow noticed about Cora was her black eye. She made no effort to conceal it with concealer or make up. It would have been impossible to hide even with an elaborate moulage.

"What the fuck happened to you?"

"I tripped over the coffee table."

He touched her cheek gently with the tips of his fingers. She winced but did not pull back.

"More likely somebody *hit* you with a coffee table. Did your mother do this?"

"No." The cornerstone of abuse is denial.

"You have to tell me what happened."

"No, I don't."

Barlow could tell she was on the razor's edge of walking out and never coming back. Her humiliation was palpable. Her courage in her willingness to expose her humiliation was stunning.

"Please don't fret over this. I have things under control, and I will not speak of it again. Nor will you."

Barlow nodded.

"I want to hear the bursts again."

"OK. Try the headphones this time. The separation of tones can't be matched. Put them on and adjust the volume to your liking."

She did so and flinched when the large earpiece pressed against her cheek bone.

Perhaps, he thought, it was fractured.

Seeing Cora and her wince filled Barlow with rage, a rage he had never felt before.

He watched her as she listened to the wave file over and over. The expression on her face changed by almost imperceptible measure. Her eyes welled with tears. One slid down her bruised cheek. She removed the headphones and turned to Barlow.

"They're all dead you know."

"I know." He reached over and held her hand. She tried to

remove it but suddenly gripped it. She started crying. It was the cry for a lost relative. Someone she hardly knew but wished she had.

He knew because Cadwallader had poked his head into Barlow's lab yesterday.

"Hey, Barlow," he said as casually as if he was mocking the defeat of his favorite team. "You know that H II region you were staring at, NGC 604? A star went supernova a few weeks ago. Big blast. Even rattled my windows."

He did not want to tell Cora. In her mental state, what little he knew of such things, she might not be able to handle the calamity. Or the heartbreak.

His parents had been so stoic during the relentless, pitiful death of his sister, he did not know how to comfort someone or how to grieve. He was helpless.

There was one thing he could do. He would confront Cora's mother and tell her to quit using her daughter as a punching bag. He stood up in an emotional deliverance and told her he was going to find out what had happened to her and fix it.

She pulled away from him as she stood up, "No you won't! This is my problem to solve! You stay out of it."

"I cannot Jenny. You have touched my heart. You have changed my soul."

He took her, despite her violent protest, to her home. When she opened the door, he caught a glimpse of her mother. He saw the gun.

"So, you're the son of a bitch who has ruined my daughter's life!"

The bullet struck him square in the chest. He heard Cora's piercing scream. As great gouts of blood flowed from the hole in his chest onto the shabby carpet, his last conscious thoughts were of Jenny and the light in the furrowed field.

...

"We must not look around on the universe with awe, and on man with scorn; for man, who can comprehend the universe and its laws, is greater than the universe, which cannot comprehend itself."

William E. Channing, Thoughts

The Rental

He signed for the car. A midsized with GPS. It looked brand new. He was pleased. He threw his bag and briefcase in the back seat. As he drove further away from the airport, he noted the disturbing aroma. Expecting that new car smell, he figured it was a forgotten doggie bag. It was intolerable. He pulled off the highway and looked under the seats. He found an abandoned, half-eaten Big Mac. He tossed it over the guardrail and resumed his journey. Listening to NPR on the XM, he was well into open country when the smell returned. He cracked open the window. It had grown intolerable. He stopped on the shoulder. He opened the trunk. The body was curled into the fetal position, a bullet hole precisely placed between the eyebrows resting in a puddle of blood. He did not know who to call first: the police or the rental company.

Wrong Number

"Little girl, don't hang up." I looked at the cell phone. It was an area code I did not recognize. "Where's your mommy?"

"On the floor."

"What's wrong with her?"

"I can't wake her up."

"Is she hurt? Do you know how to dial '911'?"

"What?"

"What's wrong with your mommy, sweetheart?"

"I have to go now."

"Baby, please don't hang up! Where's your daddy?"

"He's gone."

The phone clicked in my ear.

I Googled the area code as I did not own a phone book. I could not find it.

Alone

I was born in the light. My birth was celebrated. A short time later, my masters swaddled me and cast me off to find new ways, new lands. The world I travel in is cold, dark and empty. I am naked and alone, sailing my fragile, little ship into the perpetual night lit only by the stars. I have seen fantastic sights. I am cold, so cold. I yearn for the warmth of home. With a god-like voice, my masters still talk to me. I shout back but they hear only my faintest of whispers. I am so cold.

I carry sacred greetings to all I meet. There will come a time when I will be singing songs only I can hear. I am so cold. My hope is that for as long as they last, I will forever remain alive in their hearts as I drift from their realm. When my last ember is extinguished, I will become silent, adrift on an eternal sea long after they are gone, and earth is but a cinder. I am so cold. I miss the warmth of my home. My name is Voyager. I will go on forever. I will say goodbye while you can still hear me.

Fat

Betty walked across the parking lot as the second shift was leaving. She passed beside each blue-lit security box on her way to the building entrance alert to her surroundings even though the most violent event ever to occur there was a loud lover's spat. She did not witness it, but coworkers talked about it for weeks.

Every night was the same. She worked the grave-yard shift five nights a week, six if she needed the over time. She spoke to people all over the world on the phone she manned telling the person on the other end of the line how to boot-up their new computer, how to format a hard drive or simply how to delete unsavory pictures. Apple took great pride in their 24/7/365 customer service and across the country–even the world–computers all had clocks but were incapable of understanding the implication.

Betty was happy for the anonymity of her nightly walk to the entrance. She would pass a few people and nod or say hello. Often, whoever it was kept walking without acknowledging her. She was used to it.

It had been this way for as long as she could remember. She was the two-hundred seventy-pound 'girl-Rilla' in the room.

The odd thing was her parents were skinny. They drank and smoked; ate whatever they wanted never gaining a pound. Compared to her they were emaciated. As she liked to say, she didn't inherit the skinny gene. She tried diets of every caloric combination and biochemical principal. She would fast, drink plenty of water to curb her appetite until it seemed she spent half her time sitting on the commode off-loading it. She had met several dieticians. Each more optimistic than the last. She even considered surgery, but asked why a surgeon would reroute the innards that God had worked millions of years to perfect? Besides, there were risks.

She took the elevator. She used to force herself to take the stairs as if doing so were the first steps to resolving everything. Lately, even that had become a struggle. She was self-conscious of the strap marks embedded on her cheeks from her nightly battle with sleep apnea. Sometimes they were gone by the time she reached her computer station. It didn't matter though, most people gave her no notice, like those she passed in the parking lot. It was not that she didn't have friends. They all told her she was pretty with a great personality, glowing, funny, effervescent as if that trumped all physical defects great or small. She thought they felt better about themselves by hanging out with the fat girl like it was some demonstrable sacrifice or commitment or shared *bon homie*.

For as long as she remembered, she bore the stares of strangers as if she were a carnival oddity. Fat tub of lard, fatty, beached whale. She had heard it all. Political correctness afforded no respite. Obesity is not a protected class.

She adjusted growing up, trying to fit in. People laughed at almost anything she said, but no one invited her to the prom; no one asked her to pledge a sorority. She could not remember her last real date.

Blaming herself was easy. No one forced her to eat the extra slice of pie. She was her own victim. To assuage her guilt, she would help at her church's soup kitchen on Saturdays and Sundays, Thanksgiving and Christmas morning. In a moment of pique, she got a tattoo on her right shoulder: a cute, golden bear smiling up at a blue butterfly. She saw it in a card of thanks at the Hallmark Store and fell in love with the image. Every creature, God tells us, is endowed with unique beauty, purpose and infinite worth.

She went to the coffee room to make her first cup of tea. The night-shifters milled around. Dirk and Melvin were there. Dirk was a tall man with a receding hairline even though he was only twenty-nine. Melvin was a real computer nerd, thin, painfully shy and inconsequential. He had worked there for months before Betty even learned his name. Susan, an otherwise ordinary-looking girl with facial piercings and purple-streaked, silver hair that made her look menacing, was the nicest person she had met in the two years Betty worked at the tech center.

"Hey, Kiddo," was Susan's standard greeting to Betty when they met in the coffee room. They would chat amiably for a few minutes at the start of every shift.

Occasionally, after work, they would go to a bar frequented by night-shifters from nearby plants and offices and drink beer until all their gossip was current. About once a month, Susan and her girlfriends would gather for tacos and Coronas or pizza and Yuenglings on a Saturday night. They would tell jokes, compare recent piercings and make passes at each other, real or feigned (Betty never knew which) in a show of lesbian territoriality that Betty found neither offensive, threatening or enticing.

Betty settled into her cubicle.

The first call was an email problem easily resolved. The next was a call about a critical file that seemed to vanish off the screen into interstellar space. Again, effortlessly solved. The third call was about an issue related to compatibility. This issue was more technical, and she punted the call to Dirk who seemed to live for these sorts of problems.

By three am, the calls quieted down. And by four am they had ceased. So, Betty settled back after making herself another tea. She took out her cooler bag and opened the Ziploc to nibble on some baby carrots, apple slices, and celery stalks. With each bite, she dreamt of crème-Brule or Death by Chocolate.

She quickly cleared her mouth of vegetable when the phone rang at four-thirty.

"Hello, Apple Assistance, how can we help?"

"Hi, I am having trouble restarting my MacBook Pro. I was wondering if you could help."

"Sure."

After a few attempts at easy answers that failed to resolve the problem, she decided to turn it over to Dirk, but he was gone, bathroom break or fresh coffee, so she referred the issue to Melvin. His line was busy.

"I'm sorry, can you hold. Our tech guys are tied up for the moment. Can you hold?"

"Sure, I have all night."

"What exactly is your problem?"

"I'm having trouble with my hard drive."

"Isn't that just the way. I'm sorry. Can you still hold?"

"Yep."

There was a long pause. She could hear breathing.

"Is it snowing there?" the caller asked.

"No. This is Southern California. It never snows here."

"It's coming down hard here. About an inch an hour."

"I've never seen an inch an hour."

"You should. It's beautiful. You can hear the snow hitting the trees. A kind of hiss."

"I would like that."

"It's like God whispering."

"Wow," she said softly. "You sound awful chipper for this time of night."

"I work at night."

"Oh. What do you do?"

"Communications."

"Interesting."

"Boring," he said.

"Sorry. The tech guy is still busy."

"That's perfectly OK. I don't mind waiting."

There was more breathing. He seemed to be increasingly impatient with the delay.

"What do you look like?" The question had an explosive resonance in her earpiece. "You sound pretty."

"I am."

"I could tell."

"I am also fat."

"Oh." There was a pause. "Doesn't matter. You sound pretty. Fat is a state of mind."

"No, it's more than that."

There was a pause.

"Does being fat make you sad?"

The conversation had gone on long enough, and she reached out her finger to cut him off, but before she did, he said, "You sound sad."

"I'm just low. There's a difference. Sad has more precision."

Another pause.

"Our body is just a vehicle God gave us for our journey."

"Easy for you to say."

"Inside all of us is a perfect, beautiful butterfly looking forward to flight."

"I suppose." She was not convinced.

"Are you married? Do you have a boyfriend?"

"No."

"Have you ever thought of suicide?"

She could not give an answer that would be truthful. The words were too painful to utter.

"Yes," she said barely above a whisper.

"I could tell you all the different ways to do it."

The shock of the statement made her gasp. Somehow, she figured, he would know.

"But that would be such a waste–" he said, "–of God's most precious being."

"How do you know who I am or what I am?" the tears streamed down her cheeks.

"I just know."

There was silence.

He continued, "The inflection of your voice. The way you smiled a minute ago. The little chuckle about the quantity of snow you never get in Southern California."

Silence.

"Do me a favor, will you? Just stand up."

"Why?"

"'cause I asked nicely."

She stood up. She looked down at her carrots then looked up.

She saw Melvin waving briskly, a bright smile on his face.

"Hi. It's me."

She smiled, flushed with warmth and joy, and waved back.

Rene

An excerpt from
When We Were Young

I was surprised when René knocked on my door. She asked if she could come in. To say I was surprised would be an understatement. Without my answer, she entered the room and I closed the door behind her.

She wore a faded, yellow dress. It was frayed at the edges. She was thinner. But her smile was as iridescent as ever. She could tell I was happy to see her.

She walked over to the chair by the window and sat down.

"How have you been?" she asked.

"I was about to ask you the same thing. I've been busy. Little acts of resistance. Occasional *as*sistance. But mostly *subsistence*."

She smiled. "Yes, I've heard."

"You?"

"I have been away. I was about to be apprehended when last we met. I was sent to Grenoble for safekeeping. Since I am fluent in

German, I worked translating radio messages for the local FFI radio station." She paused, "It was rather dull."

"The Allies are not far. They have taken Paris. De Gaulle marched down the Champs-Élysées. Triumphant, I suspect, as if he had taken it single-handedly."

"Yes, no doubt."

"The crowds adored him," I said.

"Yes, no doubt. At least for now."

"I am surprised to see you."

"They came to me a few days ago and told me there was a bridge in need of blowing up. And that some assistance would be required."

"And you volunteered?" I asked, somewhat surprised.

"I was asked forcefully. No, better to say I was encouraged. With the approach of the Allies my services were rapidly unnecessary. So, I said yes. I had no idea you were the one needing assistance."

"I was surprised they would even ask me in the first place. Knowing, of course, my, shall we say, limitations."

"Yes, I share your surprise." She smiled again. "They want the bridge blown up today."

"We need *plastique* and the *accoutrements*."

"I have brought them. Plus, two pistols with silencers"

"I still wonder why me. They should take out the bridge with bombs. Instead, they want me to do it."

"No one to spare." She looked dejected as the words left her mouth.

"No one?"

"Besides, you are familiar with the bridge, no? Do you have a plan?"

A plan. I thought whoever was bringing the fireworks would have the plan. I did not want to reveal my stupidity or surprise, so I acted like I was being reflective.

"There is a small wood at the south side of both tends of the bridge. When I helped blow it last time, we were able to get very close without exposing ourselves. I know the way. The woods on the right were very badly burned. I will take the bike and carry the explosives, wire and detonator up a path that runs just parallel to the canal then slip up to the railroad embankment. You will go with me and leave your bike there. Double back and cross the canal to the west bank and walk up to the woods on the other side. It is not far, maybe a quarter mile or so from the crossing. Give me a wave when you are ready. You can make some sort of demonstration with the guard on the west side. I will cover the guard on the east side. When you give me the signal, I will shoot the east guard while you do the same to your guard." I wondered if she could tell I was making it up as I went along.

She nodded. I could see her thinking of the role and task I had just given her. She stared into middle distance. I could almost hear her mind working the risks and probabilities.

"When do you want to do it?" she asked.

"Now."

"Broad daylight? Don't you think that is too risky?"

"Perhaps, but by the late afternoon the sentries are hot and tired, and I have found easily distracted. Besides, I am still new at this and I need to see what I am doing."

My logic must have been well received because she nodded and said, "Let's get going."

"No, let's give it another hour or so then we can head out. Repeat the plan back to me."

She did. And as she repeated the details again, it sounded simple but not fool-proof. What else could I come up with? Especially on such short notice.

"We must move quickly once we kill the guards. The sound of gun fire will bring them running."

"Yes. But hopefully we will be the only ones shooting and no one will hear the little chirps of the silencers. The blast, of course, is another matter." She winked at me and we proceeded to chat idly for an hour.

We set out at four o'clock.

We reached the woods in no time.

...

I moved slowly through the burned trees to the embankment. I was a dozen yards from the east end of the bridge. Each sentry stood at the opposite end of the span and moved back and forth at a slow almost ambling pace. They looked hot and bored. They appeared to be German but from the distance they could be foreign conscripts. Either way, whatever René had in mind would get their attention. I took position close enough to cover her but not so close that a casual look in my direction would reveal me. I could not move quickly to her aid if it was required as I did not have the agility to pick quietly through burned timber, but I had a clear shot at the nearest guard. I could easily shoot him with the pistol at this range. The far guy was beyond my ability to see part of the time and I could not hit him with certainty even when he was in view.

Rene's plan was to come up to the guard at the west end of the bridge, make a show of some sort, and deal with him. I was to take care of the one closest to me. Seemed simple enough. I had the satchel full of plastic explosives, the detonator and spool of wire at my side.

I waited.

...

"Bonjour, monsieur," I heard her say sidling up to the German. "Five francs, I make you very happy."

The soldier looked surprised and delighted at his sudden good fortune.

She reached down between them and rubbed his crotch causing him to look both ways and glance at his smiling companion at the other end of the bridge. She snuggled into his neck as she rubbed more forcefully. He laid down his rifle and separated himself to reach for his fly. She put the barrel of the pistol against his chest below the breastbone and fired. The sound was muffled. He fell against her. It must have taken a second for the brain of his companion to process what he had just witnessed. Suddenly he raised his rifle to his shoulder. I was about to pull the trigger and kill him when she lifted her right hand and fired hitting him square in the face. The report of the pistol was unmistakable this time. A soft, twerping sound.

I ran up the sloping hill as best I could with an artificial leg. With two quick strides, I was standing above the second German. I lifted him up with an ease and strength that, for an instant, surprised me. I pushed his body down the opposite slope and it rolled into the bushes. I grabbed the rifle and headed for the center of the bridge. I was moving quickly, only vaguely aware of René hefting the first German's body into the canal. I marveled at the ease with which she seemed to do it. I was already pulling the explosives out of the satchel when I heard the splash.

René, the front of her yellow dress covered with blood, took two steps to me and reached into the satchel removing another brick of *plastique* and started tearing at the wrapper. She kneaded the compound onto the exposed girder beside and below the rails. I glanced at her, admiring both her concentration and efficiency. I molded my two bricks onto the girder on my side.

In the matter of a minute, she had the explosives set then put the detonator wire into it while I did the same. She passed the wire under the rail to keep it from being noticed or cut by the wheels of a train. I had already done the same.

Almost in unison we moved quickly down the embankment, avoiding the tangle of burned trees and brush. The very same embankment I had guarded several weeks ago. I pulled the spool behind me as we ran down the narrow path. Based on my recent experience with Lizard, I made her follow me well down the path to the place where I had left the detonator.

I connected the wires, charged the detonator and told her to duck.

The resulting simultaneous explosions shook the ground, threw up a massive amount of smoke, wood and rail. It was not the stupendous eruption of recent history but when the smoke cleared the bridge was sagging badly onto its one intact girder. We watched it for a second, both of us laughing involuntarily. The steel gave way and buckled sending the two halves of the span into the water with a loud, satisfying splash.

We turned to look at each other, prone on the ground. We were still laughing when our eyes met. I reached into my pocket and pulled out a five-franc noted and said, "I hope this is enough."

She snatched it from my hand and put it into her bra.

She threw her arms around me and kissed me on the lips. She paused a second and looked into my eyes. She let go, we got to our feet and ran to the place where we had hidden the bikes. She pulled off the bloody dress without missing a stride and tossed it into the canal. Surprisingly, there was little blood stain on her slip.

She grabbed up her bike and darted across the field east in the direction of the safe house while I, according to plan, headed south down the path parallel to the canal.

I heard two rifle shots in the distance. Then a third. I pedaled as fast as I could afraid my metal and plastic leg would sail off. I reached the outskirts of town sweating and out of breath. I hurled the bike into some brush and went swiftly to a narrow alley where I sat down and tried to catch my breath. I hid behind some trash and made myself as small as possible. I could hear vehicles and shouting in German from the street. The noise was disturbed by the sudden appearance of RAF Typhoons overhead, great flocks of them, and the volley of rifles and distant AA fire.

When I thought it was safe, I slowly crept on all fours into a field to the west of the village. After I had crawled about half a mile from the town, I rolled onto my back and started to think. I wondered what had happened to René. No, she was a very clever girl and was probably fine. Of this I was certain.

I waited until dusk and finally lifted my head up enough to see the back of the town. Something to the south was ablaze. I figured it was not safe. I waited until dark. A thunderstorm moved from the west to the east and poured all night. The sky was lit up by marvelous bolts of lightning and booming thunder. I was still hot, and the rain was cooling.

By dawn the rain had cleared out and the sun was starting to peek over the woods to the east. I reversed my crawl and got close to Jordan's building. I went into the back entrance which I had the foresight to leave unlocked. I went up the stairs to the flat and stripped off the damp clothes. I shoved the German stump under the bed and scanned the street below. There was a lot of activity. German soldiers were up and down the street. A line of tanks nestled against the stores on the far side of the street. They were up onto the sidewalk in hopes of not being seen by a passing fighter-bomber. Some were scorched and scarred. All looked worse for the wear. The panzer crews were milling about smoking, working on the tanks or pissing on the storefronts.

By ten o'clock I grabbed the crutches and made myself look as pathetic as possible. I slipped on a black beret and went down to the street. Not a soul seemed to pay attention to me. I walked up toward the park for a smoke.

When I reached the entrance, I saw René hanging from the same limb Jordan had once graced. There was a noose around her neck and her face had been pulverized her genitals mutilated. I knew it was her by the slightly blood-tinged slip. She had been shot in the back twice. These were the sounds from yesterday. They had likely been fatal. The ruined face, mutilation and the lynching were for show.

I looked around and saw six crumpled bodies lying at the base of the wall of the florist across the street. I recognized Madame Delacroix as one of them.

God and Ford Motor Company

It was a rainy Thursday night. The physics of the action were easy to explain. Inertia, velocity, mass. But the principal culprit was lack of adhesion between tire and pavement. The irresistible force meets the immovable object. The tree never stood a chance.

My wife, son and his girlfriend had just completed a meal at a favorite Japanese steakhouse. I waited for them as they ran into a local market for a few items when I spied a rainbow that appeared after a passing heavy shower. I should have taken it as an omen. But at the time it seemed like just an ordinary rainbow.

They say your life passes before your eyes as death is imminent. To a person in the car there was none of that. Instead a calm lasting a few nanoseconds was experienced by all. The airbags deployed at the sound of impact. I could see the buckled hood through cracked glass. Everyone was moving. We were banged around but there was no blood. That was only the last miracle.

The first was the person at Ford Motor Company who designed the car to withstand such an impact. And the individual who first thought up the idea of an airbag. Or the person who made seatbelts mandatory. And the person on the assembly line who put it all together just so.

Most of all I thank God. His hand can be found in all of this. Why that particular tree? It snapped like a twig. Why that particular tree and not an oncoming car?

The rainbow He showed me was a message that He would look after me and my family that night even though at the time it was just an ordinary rainbow.

If there is any other explanation, I'd like to hear it. Be forewarned, however, nothing you say can shake my faith in His power or through Him, Ford Motor Company.

Amen.

Smegma

Smegma was lazy. He hated to put out effort of any magnitude. His nightly walk was an imposition and he let me know it. For years it had been a test of wills. What I interpreted as sloth was merely his idea of energy conservation. Cats would tempt him with unbridled aggression, and he would stop and stare at them as if viewing for the hundredth time a rerun of the Brady Bunch until finally they gave up the effort and let him pass with indifference. Same old houses on the same old tree-lined street. Same bushes to pee on. A favorite dumping ground. The only time he came alive was the ritual treat of a Milk Bone upon our return to the kitchen.

Tonight was different. His ears were cocked, anticipation in his eyes. Or perhaps a wariness. Maybe tonight was the night he would address his feline issues.

We arrived at the far end of the street at our usual turn-around point. It is dark and the road curls off into the woods. There are only a few houses here.

I was startled by a flash of light, a muffled pop, glass shattering, and a woman's scream. There was another flash then silence.

Instinct sent me behind a large oak. My mind reeled. The dog and I had witnessed a murder like something straight out of a movie. And the dog knew it was coming. We exchanged glances. I was terrified. Proven right that this night would be different, he was smiling with a sense of accomplishment. Sick, demented animal.

In the dead silence that followed, I gathered my wits and retrieved my cell phone. I dialed 9-1-1 and whispered, "I just witnessed a murder."

I was surprised how long it took the two police cars to arrive, lights off, no sirens. Stealthy in the night, they parked some distance from the murder house. Smegma could not contain himself, anxiously shifting back and forth on his haunches while glancing between the two cops, the house and me.

He watched intently as the two cops hid behind a tree, guns drawn, formulating a plan. I guess Smegma thought they were taking an inordinate amount of time as he started a soft, but persistent whine.

The cops suddenly charged the house and kicked down the door. The lights went on. A woman screamed. I waited for the sharp report of gunfire. There was only more yelling and shifting shadows.

Several minutes later, the two cops walked out and approached me. There had been no murder. The pop was from the explosive release of a champagne cork which shattered a mirror across the room. The flashes were from a cell phone as the husband took salacious pictures of his naked wife on their first anniversary.

I must confess I was mildly disappointed and perhaps even embarrassed as they drove away. They told me they would have the township pay to fix the door.

The dog stood up on all fours and wagged his tail as we watched the poor guy, wrapped in a towel, try to replace his door. I thought of offering to help but would probably get punched in the process.

We turned and walked home. Smegma seemed disappointed the walk had ended. Not only was he lazy, he revealed himself a pervert.

Fun

Please stop, she begged. But I liked it. Eventually, so did she.

Somebody's Red-headed Stepchild

AN EXCERPT FROM
The Business of Killing

The next day, the 58th Wing launched daylight precision strikes against two separate targets. The first task force, composed of the 40th and 444th, was to hit the Sumitomo Metal Works near Osaka and the other, 462nd and 468th,were to hit the Kawanishi Aircraft Factory at Takarazuka, north of Osaka. Takeoff for both strikes was scheduled for 0400. Hollis had **B-san,** his search and rescue B-29, in the air by 0300. They flew north and arrived on station on a bearing of 180 degrees, one hundred miles south of Shiono Cape, Sugarloaf.

The two strike forces passed by Iwo Jima and picked up an escort of several dozen Mustangs. Hollis could see them pass by on their way to the targets. The P-51s had big, teardrop- shaped tanks slung beneath their wings.

An hour after they disappeared northward, Hathaway received the strike report. Half an hour later the two task forces reappeared on the horizon and flew past headed south. The Mustangs were not with them. After bombs away and clearing the target, they were released to go down on the deck and shoot up anything even remotely resembling military significance.

Hathaway picked up a distress call from Actor Four Six, a 40th Group bomber. They were down to two engines and the pilot wanted to make sure everyone was alerted to his predicament.

Actor Two Niner had buddied up with him. After a time, they must have been OK for Hathaway never heard anything else.

Well past the last bomber and with all channels free of distress calls they turned for Home. Mitchell gave Hollis the bearing for home and he set the autopilot. He figured they were not at the optimum search altitude, but everyone had certainly cleared the target.

He had just leaned back to snooze when Johnlee tore around in his seat as if his chest had been struck by an artillery shell. Hollis glanced over at Hialama and then at the Cajun.

"I see green. Somebody's red-headed step chile is in da wata. Goodyear. He got Emily on his lap."

Hollis yanked himself erect in his seat. Translated it meant somebody's red headed stepchild was in a rubber raft surrounded by green marker dye in the water. A radar reflector on his lap.

"Where?"

"We jus' past right ova him. He's eita' dead or asleep." "This'll wake him up," Hollis muttered.

Inexplicably, having never experienced it in flight before, Hollis found himself covered with goose bumps.

"Hey son, wake up. You 'bout to get saved," Johnlee said.

Hollis shoved the throttles forward, the acceleration pushing him into the seat. It nearly hurled Pettitmore back out of his perch in the nose onto the flight deck. Hollis put the bomber into a diving turn on the reciprocal course leveling off at no more than a hundred feet as if *he* was on a strafing run in a Mustang. They passed right over the boy in the one-man raft giving little heed to the possibility of blowing him into the water by the prop wash.

"He awake now, Boss. You take us down any lower and dey be rescuin' us."

Hollis had radio ring up the closest sub. Mindful this close to the coast the only thing out of the water would be its antenna.

"Nellie's Nipple, this is Songbird Six One. I got one redheaded step chile in a Goodyear ten miles off Sugarloaf. Bearing one seven zero. Evergreen. Can't miss him. He's waving like a whirling dervish."

After a long pause. "Roger, Songbird. We will attempt to lasso." "Roger will stand by."

Hollis flew low over the boy again, the foam from the waves cascading over him. Hollis could see him smiling. He chucked his Emily radar deflector into the sea. After about fifteen minutes of circling Pettitmore spotted a periscope in the water. Its direction foretold by the thin feathered white wake it left.

"Nellie, target is dead ahead about five miles, bearing 275 true. I will pass over him." "Roger."

Hollis did it again. The kid in the raft never stopped waving as if he was still unsure, he had yet been seen.

"You are within a mile."

Hollis started a tight circle, the epicenter the bobbing yellow raft.

Soon the periscope sidled up to the raft. The kid in the raft paddled furiously to the periscope which had become stationary in the water. When he got close enough to touch it he looped the painter around the periscope and waved his hand in front of the lens.

"You got him."

The sub slowly turned and dragged the raft out to sea at the pace of a brisk walk. Hollis laughed as the boy held on for dear life, determined to not to let go until they reached the wharf at San Francisco.

"See any bandits?" "Negative. Do you copy?" "Negative bandits."

Still within sight of the Japanese Empire but further out to sea the periscope sank suddenly into the water. A few minutes later the conning tower broke the water some distance away from the raft and the sub's gray-black hull rose out of the ocean. Men scrambled onto the dripping deck and one hurled a line to the airman. Suddenly the boy was lost from view as the hull came between Hollis and the raft. He could see some rapid movement on the deck. The sub seemed to absorb the men through various holes and it quickly disappeared beneath the waves, its former presence marked only by the foam spewing from its vents and the sudden churning of the screws.

Hollis settled back. Just another day at the office.

In the headphones, he listened to Tommy Dorsey and "The Sunny Side of the Street." It made him smile before he fell asleep again.

Two weeks later, the war with Japan was over.

Hollis sat on his cot picking white sock lint from between his toes. He would head for the shower, dress and head to the flight line to go home.

"You Major Hollis?" "Yes, I am Hollis."

Hollis was looking up at a lanky second lieutenant. Probably not more than eighteen. "You are?"

The kid took off his hat and Hollis immediately knew who he was. There were tears streaming down his freckled cheeks.

"I'm somebody's red headed stepchild. The boys on that sub got a big kick out of that." The boy shook Hollis's hand and handed him a bottle of Old Grand Dad.

"I won this in a poker game with some Gyrenes. My squadron CO told me I was too young to drink. So instead of having it confiscated I wanted to give it to you. Until I saw you guys, I thought I was a goner. I was out there for two days. The sharks were circling me."

"Sharks, really? You are the first guy who ever told me he actually saw sharks." The boy still showed evidence of his sunburn.

Passage

An Excerpt from
BOMBING

Thursday, January 27, 1983

He awoke from a fitful sleep. For weeks his bloated, ascitic belly had compromised his breathing and he could sleep only when sitting in a chair. But tonight was different, he felt well enough to try sleeping in bed next to his wife. Propped on three pillows, he chatted with her in the dark until she fell asleep. Soon he dozed, too.

An hour or so later, he awakened and struggled to his feet, trying hard not to disturb his sleeping wife. He slipped into his bathrobe. It hung loose on his cancer-ridden body. He could not resist an ironic reflection that the long, painful course of radiation treatments and chemotherapy had prolonged his life sufficiently to allow him to slowly suffocate. He looked down at his beloved and long-suffering wife, studied the gentle rise and fall of her chest. Holding the headboard for balance, he leaned over and, saying goodbye, kissed her cheek.

He went to the kitchen for a can of beer. He took great delight in the knowledge that this would have given his oncologist apoplexy. He thought the doctor was, deep down, a reasonable man and would understand. Sipping the drink, he went to the front door and stepped outside. It was bitterly cold, and the night was as still, dark and clear as any he had ever seen, yet his state of mind made him impervious to the cold. His breath made large clouds of steam which evaporated slowly into nothingness. A fresh snow had fallen that afternoon making the scene peaceful and idyllic. He recalled the neighbor kids digging out his sidewalk that afternoon and smiled. He looked up at the stars, spotting Orion, the Hunter. It was his favorite constellation. How many times in his life had he gazed intently at those particular stars? He thanked God for this night. It was how he wished to remember earth in his last moments.

He returned to the house and went to his study. In a room crammed with pictures, mementos, medals and books on shelves from floor to ceiling he sought out a single, small, faded snapshot resting in a plain black frame. The photograph was of a group of ten men kneeling and standing beneath the nose of an old army bomber. Each man had long ago scribbled his name beneath his face. All ten men grinned widely. It was the grin of camaraderie, youth and innocence. They were the finest; the very best America had to offer. Ten stories, ten paths converging on one instant in time caught forever in a faded black and white photograph. If America and democracy needed defending, it was fitting that these ten should be among the ones chosen to defend them.

He held it in his hand while he looked at the other pictures on the wall. They were of his four daughters, their husbands and his grandchildren. He sat on a leather couch and carefully placed the photograph on the coffee table. He got up and went to a cupboard and pulled out an old wooden ammo box filled with brittle, ancient 78 rpm phonograph records. The box was heavy, and it took nearly all of his remaining energy to move it. He carefully placed the box beside the photograph and returned to the couch. He picked up the picture, studying every face in the soft light. He knew every name without reading the signature. He had pictures of their children and grandchildren on his wall, too.

He struggled back to his feet and returned to the wall and took down a recent picture of the same pose in front of a shiny, restored Flying Fortress in a museum. It had been their last reunion before he had gotten sick. Some spaces in the pose were missing, left empty by passage. They grinned broadly as before, now silver-haired, heavier and bespectacled. One was in a wheelchair. His smile was a little feeble, but no less genuine.

He sipped his beer and looked at the pictures for a long time. His mind brimmed with thoughts and emotion. He studied the outline of the old B-17, sleek and dark, beautiful and sinister; the new one pristine, and cleansed innocent by restoration and fading remembrance.

Revisionists with selective memories, he knew, would have him wear the mantle of an unrepentant destroyer, the murderer of innocent women and children, totally devoid of morality, particular in the abject brutality of his method. He rejected this. He did the job he had been asked to do in good faith, choosing instead to leave the morality questions to the collective wisdom of a higher authority. Maybe it hadn't been a "good war", but it had been a righteous one. If he had been required to do penance, he had done none. If he should feel guilt or remorse, he was unmoved. He smiled to himself. It was too late anyway. Judgment was a few breaths away.

Finally, he laid back and rested the older photograph on his chest. Contented with a life well-lived, he closed his eyes and fell asleep, sure in the knowledge that the grass in Europe grows especially green over the bodies of the missing and dead airmen who were his friends. No one was there to mark the last beats of his proud, tired heart as he left this earth to join them.

Advert

"Womb for Sale
Cozy. Like New"
Maybe, he thought,
She meant 'For Rent'
Or, perhaps, 'Sub-let.'
He wasn't sure.

The Strait

An excerpt from a forthcoming novel
Boats

The only sound was the lapping of the Strait against the chines. No one dared cough. The birds squealing and the animal noises in the jungle behind the boat was something they had become used to but it still annoying. The only light was the canopy of stars. It was just enough to illuminate the dark hulk of the nearby islands. The boat rolled gently with the swell.

Chip lifted his faded, salt-stained ball cap from his head and ran is hand over his blonde, tightly cropped hair. His head itched. The rash in his groin was starting to burn. He desperately needed a cigarette. The ember of a burning cigarette could be seen for miles and he dared not go below for one. He was in tactical command of the ambush. He needed to be topside in case something happened. The wait was tense and tedious.

The two transport destroyers had been expected hours ago and they had sat still against the backdrop of dark Savo Island for practically the entire night waiting for them. The resupply runs had been predicted with uncanny accuracy every night for the past week. Where they got such information was a mystery. They said it was because they were spotted heading south by reconnaissance flights, but Chip figured they were reading someone else's mail. Tonight, was different. They did not come. The intelligence people had simply gotten it wrong.

He glanced at the luminous dial on his watch, an expensive gift from his father so long ago. The sweat, tension and the elements had faded the leather band, bleaching it. He never took it off. He was afraid of losing it.

The Jap cans had been expected a little after midnight. They would never be this far down the Strait this late for fear of getting caught by the rising sun. Their usual course of action was to scoot down the Slot or through the Strait between Cape Esperance and Savo Island, which they now guarded this evening, drop their cache of resupply and high-tail-it out back from whence they came before the sun came up. Were that to happen the flyboys from Henderson would feast on them like flies on a fresh turd.

He would give it another half hour. If the bastards didn't show by then he would radio Kelsey in the other boat and tell them call it a night. They did not want to get caught in the open either lest the Japs were to feed on them. For the moment, though, they were well concealed by the dark backdrop of the jungle behind them.

Two and a half hours ago Christmas Eve had become Christmas. Half a world away, many hours from now as the earth rotated, his parents, sisters and their husbands and his fiancé would be celebrating the birth of Christ with the exchange of gifts, consumption of a roasted turkey and innumerable stiff martinis.

A Manhattan would go down good right about now. So would a cigarette. And more balm for his chafed testicles.

Chip nearly jumped with the presence of a soft touch on his arm. It was almost a caress. His musings had caught him off guard. The nearness of the man beside him had been forgotten hours ago.

"They're here."

Chip raised the binoculars to his eyes. There was a small gap between the western extent of the Island and the northern cape of Guadalcanal. It provided the western entrance to the Strait. It was unmistakable. The darkness of the forecastle and the mast momentarily blotted out the stars on the horizon as the destroyer passed. Like the blinking of distant lights. They were late. He looked to see how many were behind him. It was impossible to tell but his instinct told him there had to be two other cans close behind. The plan had been for him to go after the lead Jap and Kelsey would go after the one behind. Whoever was in third position would be dealt with in detail. Hopefully they would have enough torpedoes to deal with however many ships arrived. Had they had more boats it might be different. As it was, they were operating on a shoestring. No radar, only eight sometimes unreliable torpedoes between them and occasionally cranky engines. Their intelligence estimates were suspect sometimes, too. As now. Once they left the sanctuary of the base on Tulagi, they were on their own. They didn't even have accurate nautical maps. But such concerns were supplanted by the arrival of the enemy convoy.

He put the mike close to his lips, "Kelsey, they're here. Execute as planned. See you on the other side."

Kelsey acknowledged by keying his mike twice.

Chip called the engine room. "Open the mufflers."

The throaty muffled rumble of the idling engines exploded into the pitch-black night from both boats simultaneously. The instant the anchor was on the deck, only a matter of a few seconds, Chip pushed the throttles forward. Impossible to imagine the roar not carrying across the open water as the two boats came alive, the likelihood of an alert lookout missing the approaching phosphorescent wakes was nil within the confines of the Strait.

Chip aimed the boat for the place where he expected the first can to be, accounting for drift, the slow pace set by the shallow water and the approach to the beach that had recently become their favorite disembarkation spot. Dead slow, feeling for the soft sand to rest their bow, they were sitting ducks. It was a perfect set up. All they had to do was race across the open water, let fly the torpedoes and scram. It couldn't get much easier. No need for maneuver. Until they fired up the engines, they had the element of surprise. And speed.

Chip looked over at Kelsey. He could see the boat on a parallel course riding the waves two hundred yards to his right. They would be within range to fire the torpedoes in a matter of minutes. The width of the Strait was about ten thousand yards. Very narrow in nautical terms. At thirty-five knots they would cover the distance to effective torpedo range quickly.

Yet the targets remained silent. And dark. He and Kelsey expected them to open fire and turn on their search lights making target acquisition easy. What was wrong with the stupid Japs? How could they not know we were coming for them? Chip and Kelsey would be firing into the dark. It suddenly dawned on him that the hunter had become the prey.

The night was instantly illuminated by a ball of fire. A Jap destroyer had sliced into Kelsey's boat. The flames lit up the night blinded eyes that had seen only darkness for many hours. Straight ahead Chip saw the old *Fubuki*-class destroyer that had passed before the stars. To his right he saw a larger destroyer passing through the flames that had once been Kelsey's torpedo boat. Chip made the swift calculation that it would pass behind them. They were too close to engage with anything other than machine guns. Chip spun the wheel around to pass the marauding destroyer broadsides. The machine guns and twenty-caliber cannon lit up without spoken order spraying the starboard side of the Jap can as they passed each other, raking its decks with tracers and hot lead. The entire Strait was suddenly illuminated with search lights, gunfire and the crisscrossing ribbons of tracers. But they were too close and moving too fast for any of the deck guns of the Jap to hit them and in short order they were past pounding over the foaming wake of the Jap can which was already turning to port. The *Fubuki* held fire for fear of hitting its mate.

Chip gave the order for smoke but was too far past the destroyer to let go a depth charge that would have any meaning. They had been caught flat-footed in their own trap. He glimpsed the burning wreck of Kelsey's boat as he increased the distance, the burning bow pointed upward. Beyond that he could make out the Number Two Jap can turn to pursue. The lights turned in their direction but all they illuminated was smoke. Best he could tell there were only the two destroyers for he could not spy the third destroyer.

He made another quick calculation. Going back for survivors, if there were any, would be suicidal. Engaging the Jap can might prove suicidal as well. It was churning the water in an effort to sprint after them. Suddenly the water erupted with ear-crushing explosions as the first volley landed behind them. They were firing into the smoke.

When Chip felt he had gone far enough, the rounds hitting the water well to their stern he slowed down and turned hard to starboard. He did the only thing he could think of. They had made good their escape.

"Chief, make ready the tubes! We're going after that fucker."

The Jap made it more convenient by playing his searchlights back and forth on the water. That was his first mistake. His second was slowing down either in an effort to pick up survivors or, more likely, to avoid running hard onto an uncharted shoal this close to the beach. Either way he had inadvertently limited his range of maneuver.

The idiot in the *Fubuki* suddenly backlit the Jap can before he realized his stupid mistake, but it was enough. Chip gunned the engines like a bull charging the matador and aimed the boat dead amidships. Their previously laid smoke drifted into their path concealing them. Once through it they were about two thousand yards from the Jap. Sprinting over the water, the boat pounded against the waves. When he figured he was close enough, about eight hundred yards, he salvoed all four torpedoes and passed to the stern as the first torpedo exploded against it.

The water around them churned with the impact of exploding shells, but they had made their escape for they all fell short. Chip looked back. The Jap can was dead in the water. The *Fubuki* no doubt throwing overboard everything they had arrived to deliver. The lone PT boat sprinted away planing over the ink-black water.

The whole encounter had lasted no more than five minutes.

Smiles

It was warm, pleasantly so. Not the raw furnace heat he expected. He tried to maintain His good graces after all I have done. He wanted to be an upright man. He had not always been so.

He had killed men. He betrayed his vows. He had lied. But he raised good citizens and loved my wife. Perhaps she deserves to be here more than he. He had grown old poorly.

When he emerged from the mist into the light, he smiled not by what he saw, but by the surprise. He was amazed at all the people. Numbers beyond counting. Men and women in all shapes, sizes and colors. Boys and Girls. Infants. Babies not yet born.

He looked for friends but did not see any. He wanted to see his mom and dad. They had a hard life and deserved to be here. Though his father was not an easy man.

He stepped to the edge of the grass: the greenest, sweetest lawn he had ever seen. It glistened with fresh dew.

Around him were people who held their detached heads in their hands. Others were charred beyond recognition the only thing visible were their sad eyes. Some were still bleeding. No one spoke. There was nothing to say. They had crossed over.

He saw his boss. He did not understand why he was here. He saw his drill instructor who smiled at him as if all had been forgiven.

There were contorted children in wheelchairs. Soldiers with missing limbs. Old people who held their heads high for the first time in years, maybe decades.

When we got to the end of the grass, we came face to face with Him. Everyone was whole. No one limped. No one missed a limb or a head. No char. No pain. Only smiles. He saw his Dad. He waved. He saw my Mom. She blew him a kiss. He found a place to sit. He would wait there until his wife joined him. The kids could catch up with them later.

Rocky' Eyes

I went to the animal shelter to try a dog. Girls were not working out as I'd hoped. Or perhaps I was just lonely for someone, anyone. I should not have taken the acquisition of another living being quite so casually. But I did.

So, one bright, fall Saturday morning I trucked off to the shelter in search for my new best friend. Were it not for Google Maps, I'd have never found the place tucked away in the woods several dozen yards off the road. The engine, the crunch of tires on cinders and the slamming of the car door triggered the voices of a hundred dogs echoing into the woods. It was the sound of hopeful redemption. Amnesty.

The place was warm, brightly lit and, not surprisingly, smelled like dog. I spoke to the fellow behind the desk. He smiled broadly. "You here for a dog?"

No, a kilo of fissionable plutonium. "Yes. Sounds like I'm in the right place."

"We have forty-one dogs. Lotsa different breeds. All of 'em need good homes. Go have a look." He was much too cheerful for such a grim place. "The ones closest to the door are the ones that are next to go."

"Go where?"

"Doggie heaven."

There were forty cages. Each one occupied. One had two nearly identical cocker spaniels.

The warden followed me.

"Run out of cages?"

"No, these two are brother and sister. We decided not to separate 'em." They were two cages down from the desk. All were very excited to see me. Some twirled and danced around. Others wedged their noses against the vertical bars of the cages. Hoping, no doubt, for the long-awaited return of a familiar scent. One had to admire their unbridled enthusiasm. A few were less active but equally attentive.

I grew annoyed at the warden following closely behind me like an over-persuasive salesman anxious to get rid of any car on the lot. I thanked him curtly telling him I could take it from here.

Half-way down the long aisle of cages, I came upon a little black and white dog cowering tightly in the corner. He was unmoved by my presence or the commotion I had started. He sat in the corner, his head down as if ashamed, his eyes fixed on the junction between the back wall and floor. He knew I was there because he turned his head slightly but did not look at me. The three-by-five card taped to the cage read "Rocky. Shit zu (Mostly). Five years old male."

As I walked on, he lifted his head almost imperceptibly, and we locked eyes. They were dark, the white rim slightly exposed.

"Oh, that's Rocky. He's been here a while. His owner passed away. And no one wanted to take him."

Rocky's owner died, but it was Rocky who had been condemned to Hell.

I knew enough about dogs to know that you're not supposed to look directly into their eyes. It pisses them off. But even as I walked on, Rocky's eyes remained fixed on mine. They reflected abandonment, uncertainty, and grief. I know because I kept glancing back. When he knew I was moving on, he lowered his head and resumed staring at the floor. During the entire encounter, Rocky's little head moved no more than an inch or two. They say animals don't have a conception of their own death. Looking at Rocky, I disagree.

The warden told me he hadn't left the corner since he arrived five weeks ago. He wouldn't even move to eat so they would set the food and water bowl right at his front paws. I walked on. That was just too sad, even for me. Poor little guy.

There were a few dogs that seemed good candidates to be my best friend. An Irish setter stood out. Beautiful animal. Probably too big for the apartment.

When I walked past him, Rocky was sitting at the gate of the cage, head still bowed, his eyes averted.

"I'll take this one."

When I lifted him up, he was trembling. He was so light.

Instead of joy at salvation, he sat on the passenger's seat shivering, head still down. I worried I was too late. We drove away breaking forty hearts.

The warden gave me recommendations about feeding and general care. I wasn't sure, so I Googled it.

When I went to bed that first night he sat on the floor and whimpered. Finally, I lifted him onto the bed. He shoved his little butt firmly against my thigh. I reached down and stroked him from his chest to his rump until I fell asleep. Sometime later, I woke up. Rocky's course little tongue was licking my hand.

A few days passed and Rocky slowly came out of his funk. His animation increased about one percent per day. By spring, I figured I might have a normal dog.

I took him to the park. We went for long walks. Girls made a fuss over him which we thoroughly enjoyed. I tried to teach him to fetch a Frisbee. He sat on his haunches staring at me with that WTF look while I retrieved it.

We even went to the beach once. He didn't care for it.

We fell into a routine. He hated when I left for work each morning. There would be a single small turd in the hallway waiting for me when I came home.

We'd sit for hours watching football or Netflix his body against my leg. He had a soft little snore.

As the years passed, Rocky got set in his ways. One could open the dictionary to 'curmudgeon' there would be Rocky's picture. We finally reached an understanding about the turd.

He gradually developed back problems the result of jumping down from heights like the bed or the couch. His little spine started to lose its recoil and he would shiver with pain. The vet helped a lot. I got a ramp which he refused to use even when bribed with a slice of lunch meat. I made other accommodations but as the years passed, he grew less flexible and had trouble getting around. He developed a gimp. I carried him out to attend to his necessaries and carried him back in. But no matter how hard it was for him to walk around he would always be waiting for me when I opened the front door or slam his butt up against me when I turned out the light.

Eventually, I realized I had kept him alive too long. He had trouble walking even to eat. It was torture to watch him squat on the grass. I am sure it was for him, too.

The vet worked pharmacologic wonders with him. She would try a new medicine or therapy and put off the inevitable for another year. But now it was clear her treatments only postponing the inevitable. I would hold him in my arms and rub his head and arthritic body while he trembled in pain. If a dog was able to but a good face on this situation it was Rocky. He wagged his tail with the same vigor when I got home or gave him his treat. He smiled with his eyes.

Finally, she said we could go on like this for a while longer but was that fair to Rocky? Think about it. Bring him back tomorrow.

I said okay.

I knew I kept him alive longer than I should have. I could see in his eyes his pain. I knew that he knew tomorrow would be different.

I took Rocky home and fixed a nice dinner for him. He tried to eat it but could not. He seemed to appreciate the effort. We went for a walk. He peed on his favorite trees and street signs. He knew. I could see it in his eyes. We cover ourselves with a blanket as we watched the Monday night game. We ate some popcorn — one of his favorite treats. I think it was the salt.

I lifted him into bed and laid down beside his warm, little body. He woke me up as he licked my hand. It was only the second time in all the years he did that. I knew I had kept him alive longer than I should have. I could see in his eyes his pain. I knew that he knew tomorrow would be different.

The next morning, I carried him to the car and placed him on the seat beside me. I remembered the first ride we took together and had to pull over until I regained control.

The vet took him gently and placed him on the table. He did not take his eyes off me. They say in their final moments a dog will look desperately for his master before he passes. This is true. She placed Rocky in my lap. He breathed gently, looking comfortable for the first time in a long while. He lifted his head, and our eyes met for the last time. He closed them forever, rested his head on my arm and, lapsing into an endless sleep, crossed The Rainbow Bridge.

They say animals cannot conceive of their own death. I disagree.

Football over Cabernet

She walked into the restaurant as if she were the absolute monarch of all she surveyed. Intimidating in a mid-thigh black dress and Louboutin heels, she carried herself with grace and elegance. Pulling the chair away, this goddess sat down before me folding her lithe, sculpted legs under the table. She was stunning. I sat back down more than a little surprised to see her.

Her eyes sparkled in the flicker of the candlelight. She smiled revealing perfect teeth. Her brunette hair framed her flawless face and fell easily onto her shoulders. The décolletage was mesmerizing; a tit for tat with gravity.

"So nice to see you," she said. "What are you drinking?" she asked. It was more a purr than a question.

"A delightful cabernet. Would you like some?"

"I would love some," again with the purring.

I took the decanter and poured. She lifted the glass to her nose and savored the aroma as if trying to identify its heritage. She swirled the glass and sipped the wine. Her smile deepened.

"Quite right. Excellent choice. You are a man who knows his wines."

"Yes but, I must confess I have visited the vineyard in Napa. It is true loyalty."

"A connoisseur of wine. I like that. Very becoming."

"You flatter me."

"It's not flattery if the talent is a perfect fit."

She leaned forward, and my eyes instantly went to the warm, dark valley formed by the curves of her endowment. She crossed her arms and leaned slightly forward which only served to deepen the canyon. And my expectations.

"So, tell me again what it is you do for a living?" she asked just before she placed her glistening red lips on the rim of the wine glass.

"Bureau chief for the Times."

"New York?"

"London."

"Funny, you don't sound English?"

I smiled. So did my loins. I wondered if the drapes matched the rug; if there was a rug. We laughed again.

The G-rated, non-threatening conversation grew dull as she slipped into a discussion of Upper East Side real estate inflation. I lived in Soho so I couldn't have cared less except for the fact she was becoming more relaxed by the wine with a concomitant increase in animation. I continued nodding my fascination appropriately with this woman growing with each syllable.

Launching a Hail Mary, I made a slightly off-color joke. Her laugh was genuine and reassuring. There was some ambiguity and subtlety I'm sure she could not have missed. When it was apparent I had not stepped out of bounds I felt a little more emboldened.

She took another sip of the wine. I could tell she was savoring it by holding it in her mouth momentarily letting it coat her tongue before swallowing. She tilted her head slightly and nodded, appreciative of and rewarded by the piquant flavor. My eyes were repeatedly drawn to the pearls encircling her delightful neck.

I stretched my leg slightly until I could feel her knees. She did not withdraw. This was like making a first and ten in the Red Zone down by three.

I was tempted to introduce a lurid compliment, an acknowledgment of the persuasive sexuality she so richly deserved and likely anticipated just as one might give praise to a thoroughbred or an excellent meatloaf. But there were risks. Where was the defining edge? Would I recognize the out of bounds markers before I wandered over it? Exactly where were the out of bounds markers? And what was my path to the end zone? End it with one quick play, a pass perhaps? A quarterback sneak up the middle? Or take a more measured approach, gain ground gradually, in an orderly, thoughtful, even respectful, effort with its inherent risk of a fumble, the lousy ball handling or misreading a last-minute defensive maneuver. Or incur a penalty that would push me out of any reasonable opportunity to score? Or, most egregious, do something stupid and/or rash and be disqualified before I had the ball in play?

Perhaps I should be more alert to her defense. Was she feinting one way while intending the opposite? One does not like to be played. I could either score and win the contest, face another embarrassing loss or end it in a tie. Either way, I needed to be cautious but not reserved. Bold but not extreme. It was now or never.

"Would you ah–like to—"

She leaned forward expressing her décolletage and took my hands in hers.

"I really must go," she said. "The wine was terrific. As was the company."

She released my hands and stood up.

"Thanks for stopping by. It was fun. I enjoyed your company."

"Me Too."

I watched her walk away, the seams in her stockings straight as yard markers.

The funny thing was, I had never laid eyes on this woman before in my life.

In retrospect, I should have expected a price quote.

Thirteen Days

A novella

Chapter One
Day One: The Operation

"Get in here if you want to rearrange the living room. This goddamned furniture isn't going to move itself." It was his second beer and still only ten a.m.

Mary was putting breakfast dishes away. "I'll be there in a minute. What's your hurry?" Chet returned to his easy chair and felt a sudden, fleeting pain in his chest.

Chet shrugged it off as he always did when confronted by an unpleasantry in his life. *Muscles,* he thought. *It will pass.* He tried to convince himself it was from all the leaf-raking the day before. So, he sipped his beer and lit another cigarette. At the end of the second drag, the pain became unendurable pushing through to his back, taking his breath away. It felt like something was ripping inside of him.

He tried to stand, but his feet would not hold him. He fell to the carpet.

Mary, in the kitchen defiantly putting a K-cup in the machine, heard the thump but disregarded it as just Chet impulsively rearranging the furniture himself.

After waiting patiently for her coffee to brew, she decided it might be prudent to see if Chet needed a hand with the bigger pieces.

Chet was on the carpet, lying on his side, curled into the fetal position, his face contorted as if he was trying to speak.

"Chet! Dear God!" She knelt beside him and touched his head as if to check for a fever. She rolled him onto his back and lifted his head. As she rolled him, his eyes moved to keep her in sight. He winced. *Perhaps*, she thought, *he was more comfortable on his side* and she rolled him back over. It didn't seem to make a difference.

"Chet! Chet!"

He looked up at her blankly. He was trembling, growing increasingly pale. She reached into her pocket, retrieved her cell phone and dialed 911.

She tried to comfort her husband but there was little she could do. She knew how to console an injured child. A brush-burn on the knee, a boo-boo on the forehead. But nothing like this.

Anybody who looked this tortured by pain, she knew, was surely dying.

...

The paramedics worked quickly to stabilize the man on the floor. They checked his vital signs. They placed him on high flow oxygen. In hushed tones and in a code only they understood, they discussed intubating his airway, but his breathing was not labored, and he seemed aware. They knew that whatever was wrong with their patient was going to kill him soon.

She read their concern. The tall one stood and ran to the front door to retrieve the gurney. When he returned, they placed him gently onto it and strapped him in, careful not to dislodge the green oxygen mask from his face or cause too much discomfort.

Mary noticed the little plastic bag at the end of the mask made shallow, cyclic inflations and deflations. Then it appeared to stop.

"C'mon, Chet, hang in there buddy," the tall one said.

"Braintree Memorial, this is Medic Twelve. Picking up sixty-nine-year-old white male with chest pain. Blood pressure one hundred over eighty-eight on the right, less on the left. Pulse one hundred-ten and thready. Oxygen sat ninety on four liters rebreather."

"Okay. Twelve. Move quickly. No TPA."

"Roger."

Mary understood virtually none of it.

The short one turned to her. "Mrs. Pettigrew, we have to move quickly. Do you want to ride with us?"

She thought quickly. "No, I must bring my son." She turned toward the entrance to the hall. She saw Benny standing there with the same blank countenance he had for twenty years. "I'll be along directly."

She followed them out. She took Chet's hand and squeezed it tightly. They exchanged glances. As the paramedics closed the back door of the ambulance, she thought this would be the last time she would see her husband alive.

Mary hastened back to the house to put on more presentable clothes and took Benny to his room and dressed him as well. She figured she was only about five minutes behind the ambulance.

When she arrived, there was a helicopter spooling up on the pad behind the emergency entrance. The high whine of the machine drew Benny's attention. The electric doors opened with a hiss and she led Benny into the ER. She bypassed the receptionist and went right to the first nurse she could find.

"My name is Mary Pettigrew; they just brought my husband in. Chet."

"Oh, yes, Mrs. Pettigrew, the doctors are evaluating him now. They have determined he needs to be transferred to University Hospital for further evaluation."

"What's wrong with him?"

"I'll let you speak with the doctor, but he is quite ill, and the University Hospital is more equipped to handle this kind of emergency."

"What *kind* of emergency?"

"Mrs. Pettigrew, I'll let you speak with the doctor." She glanced at Benny. "Perhaps you should have a seat in the waiting room and Dr. Quintana will be right out." She turned and left.

With a combination of fear, isolation and anger, she took Benny to the waiting room and sat down. She found the talking heads on CNN irritating as they sat behind their desk laughing about something trivial. She could not hear as the volume was turned down, but she didn't care if she could. Her only thought was of Chet. She squeezed Benny's limp hand and waited. She was convinced Chet was gone while they were probably lounging in the breakroom discussing a clever way to tell her that.

A few moments later, a mother and her kid sat down in the waiting room. The kid had the sniffles and kept snorting up tallow-green, liquid snot. The mother looked fine. On the other side of the ER her husband lay dying and this little kid had a cold. She wanted to tell her to take the little bastard home and deal; there were more serious things going on here.

"Mrs. Pettigrew, I'm Doctor Quintana. I've been looking after your husband." He glanced over at the snotty kid and extended his hand to Mary. "Perhaps we can discuss this someplace else." "Please tell me. Is Chet still alive?"

"Yes."

She followed him, her hand still clutching Benny's, to a small conference room.

"Mrs. Pettigrew, your husband has a very serious condition. We believe he has what's called a dissecting aneurysm of his aorta. It's the big artery coming out of the heart. It is a very critical condition and beyond our capacity to treat here at Braintree. He has been stabilized sufficiently to be transferred to University Hospital in Boston where they have experts who can handle this condition."

"Is he going to make it?"

"I can't answer that. But time is critical, and we are taking him to the helicopter for transfer." "Can I see him?"

Quintana was slightly surprised she did not say 'we.'

"I'm sorry, he's been loaded onto the helicopter now and they are leaving." "He's dying. I should have had the chance to see him before you took him away."

"Yes, I'm sorry. But, as I said, time is of the essence. The ward clerk will give you a detailed map and instructions on how to get to University Hospital." He stood. "I wish you all the best."

He glanced at Benny again and left.

...

She studied the instructions. Understanding most people had some sort of driving software on their phone, she threw the anachronistic instructions onto the floor after buckling Benny into the passenger's seat. It was Saturday morning. She figured it would take forty-five minutes to reach the hospital.

She knew in her heart he was already dead and all they would need from her were the funeral arrangements.

...

The team was pulled together quickly. Atticus Reynolds, the Director of the University Hospital's cardiac surgery program, was just dressing after his second case when he got the stat page from the Cath Lab. His first inclination registered at some more primitive level of his brain told him to ignore it. He had completed a busy Saturday morning doing cases left over from Friday's Cath schedule. He wanted to go to the office, finish some departmental paperwork, go home and leave whatever problem the catheter jockeys had gotten themselves into for the guy on call. "Reynolds," he said

"Atticus, this is Dawson. I have a sixty-nine-year-old male with a Type A dissection on the table here."

Son of a bitch!

"I'll alert the OR and be right down."

"Good. I'll get him ready. This guy's got one shot."

Reynolds changed into a fresh pair of baby-blue scrubs, pulled on his white coat and headed for the cardiothoracic recovery room. He paused at the end of his most recent post-op, looked at the monitor, felt the pulse in the man's foot and walked on.

Arnie Sedgewick, one of the cardiac anesthesiologists sitting at the Nurse's Station, said he heard there was a dissection in the wings, and he would get ready. Atticus merely nodded.

Reynolds went to the catheterization suite and found Hancock in the dark room viewing the digital images he had just taken of Chet's heart and chest vessels.

"Oh good, you're here," Dawson Hancock, the interventional cardiologist, said. "This guy's in trouble. His coronaries are fine, but he dissected from just above the root all the way to the renals."

Atticus stared at the images as Hancock played the video back and forth showing the flailing interior part of the vessel.

"There's perfusion into the carotids but he's sheared off his spinal artery."

"I'm not so sure about the carotids."

"You'll soon find out."

"I guess we will won't we. Thanks, Daws."

With the images set in his mind, Atticus formulated his approach. They had to move quickly if they there was any chance to save the man. Chet had been taken to the pre-op holding area, intubated and sedated by Sedgewick. Lines were being placed by the anesthesia resident and the cardiac surgery fellow sat at the computer entering data. He had very little to go on from the transferring hospital, as there were no relatives present from which to obtain a history. He was told the wife and son were on the way but there could be no delay. They could not wait for formal introductions and explanations. There simply was no time.

...

Ordinarily, the Cardiothorcic Fellow would make the long incision, open the chest, splitting the breastbone with a compressed-air-driven saw and have the patient on bypass before Atticus arrived. Not this time. One false move and the aorta would explode as if it contained a stick of dynamite. Atticus opened the chest himself while the fellow dug out the artery in the groin for heart-lung bypass.

In a well-practiced ballet where few words were required, the nurse placed the scalpel onto Atticus' outstretched hand.

"Let's see what he brought to the party," Atticus said as he made the cut.

With the breast-bone split, he opened the sac around the heart. Dark blood sloshed around inside the heart sac, a sign of impending doom had they not arrived in the nick of time. The tense, distended, reddish-purple aorta emerged dominantly from the heart, like a large tube of meat hanging in a butcher's window. The outer layer was thin and fragile as wet tissue paper. Sometimes, the wizards of the Cath Lab could repair these with catheters, balloons and stents but this one was beyond their technical reach. The blood in the sac was a clear indication the aneurysm would blow open into the sac and instantly kill him.

Atticus took a suture and placed it into the floppy right auricle, snipped quickly and directed the large tube into the heart. Moments later, the Fellow said he had the artery exposed and was inserting the cannula for blood return from the heart-lung machine. "We're ready," was all he said.

"On bypass." A moment later, "Coldest water."

The machine, resting on the floor behind Atticus, started to twirl its little pumps and Chet's heart became irrelevant. His life was suspended on a machine, dutifully powered by a reactor somewhere in the hinterlands of rural Massachusetts.

As Chet's heart slowed in response to the cold blood flowing through it, Atticus placed a large clamp on the aorta after the body was sufficiently cooled, then slit open the tense aorta and looked inside. He put paralyzing fluid into the heart and packed ice around it, rendering it cold and dormant and still. He looked at the tear in the aorta's inside lining and followed it as far as he could see.

Using quick, practiced motions, he stitched a cloth tube into the aorta, repairing the tear. It was fragile tissue and he was very careful. It took him an hour.

When he was done, he closed the aorta over the Dacron tube and purged the air. He slowly rewarmed Chet from his cold, suspended animation.

In response to the fresh, warm blood, Chet's heart started to contort as if stretching out the kinks after a long nap. Eventually it resumed its faithful rhythm, undamaged by the cataclysmic event and the instantaneous catastrophe it narrowly avoided.

He swapped places with the Fellow and closed the groin incision after it was safe to go off bypass. The Fellow mopped up the bleeding in the chest, wired shut the breastbone and closed the incision. By then Atticus was long gone to seek out the family. He needed to explain to them the nature of the problem, what he had done to fix it and what her husband's chances were of remaining alive.

...

Mary drove as fast as she dared to the University Hospital. Waze directed her with GPS precision to the emergency room where she parked the car and led Benny by the hand to the receptionist.

"My name is Mary Pettigrew and they brought my husband Chet Pettigrew by helicopter. Can you tell me where he is and how he's doing?"

"Uh, yes ma'am. Your husband was evaluated and admitted. I don't have any other information to give you, but I can get Doctor Reynolds' PA to come see you and let you know what's going on." She glanced at Benny. "Please have a seat over there and she'll be right with you."

Mary took Benny and found two seats in the crowded waiting room much too small for so much urban suffering.

A short time later, a fine-looking young woman wearing a white coat, approached Mary and bent down slightly. "Are you Mrs. Pettigrew?"

"I am."

"My name is Sandy Williams"—she extended her hand— "I am Doctor Reynold's Physician's Assistant. Doctor Reynolds is your husband's surgeon."

"Surgeon?"

"Yes. Your husband has sustained a tear in the big artery in the chest, called the aorta." Williams glanced around the waiting room. Her discussion would be better served elsewhere, she knew. Explaining the intricacies and ramifications of her husband's condition should be carried out into a private space away from the low intensity turmoil of a big-city hospital waiting room. Mary helped Benny to his feet. It was the first notice Sandy made of the young man sitting beside her. Sandy noted the blank stare on the young man's face.

In a small consultation room off the expansive ER, Sandy proceeded to describe in layman's terms what had happened to Chet and what was being done to correct it. She walked a fine line, a line she had come to nurture between the technical aspects of her husband's conditions and the gravity of his catastrophe. She repeatedly glanced at the mute young man with the blank stare who was clearly orbiting in his own universe. She wanted to offer sympathy and concern without being maudlin.

Mary asked the inevitable question: "Will he survive?"

"Too early to tell. Dissecting your aorta is a very serious condition. I will let Dr. Reynolds lay that out for you. All I can say is that he is still in the operating room and we will get word to you as soon as we can.

In the meantime, let me take you to the CTS ICU waiting room. I'll let Dr. Reynolds know you are there."

Mary and Benny took seats in the large waiting room across the hall from the double doors that led into the Cardiothoracic Surgery Intensive Care Unit. The only thing she knew was that

'Cardio' meant heart.

She looked at the clock every few seconds, her mind racing with the possibilities, her heart filled with dread. She wasn't sure how much time had passed when the electric doors opened and out stepped a thin black man with a slight afro. Sandy was by his side.

"Dr. Reynolds, this is Mrs. Pettigrew," Sandy said softly.

Mary came to her feet and extended her hand which the doctor warmly shook. She noticed they were soft, gentle hands, his grip firm.

"Hello, Mrs. Pettigrew. I am Dr. Atticus Reynolds. I am the Chief of Cardiac Surgery here. I just finished operating on your husband. He is not yet in the recovery room from the OR but he should be in the ICU in another few minutes."

At least he was alive, Mary thought. Relieved, she expected him to tell her Chet would get to go home in a few days.

"I need to tell you that your husband has a very critical problem." He proceeded to describe the details of the dissection of the aorta in patient, practiced layman's terms. Mary appreciated the caring tone in his voice.

Reynolds held back his greatest concern. Blood flow to the brain may have been severely compromised during the tearing. Brain damage. He couldn't be sure until Chet woke up from surgery. If he woke up. He thought it best to keep that to himself for now. In addition, he knew he had sheared off the artery to his spinal cord likely leaving him a paraplegic even if he did survive. If he woke up, fine, and he hadn't put his wife through the uncertainty. If he didn't, then he would come clean.

When he finished, he asked Sandy to check if Mary and her son could go into the ICU to see her husband. He excused himself and told Mary he would be in touch if there was any change. Mary thanked him and waited for Sandy to lead them in to see her husband. As she sat and held Benny's hand, she wondered how Chet would feel knowing his life was saved by a black man.

Mary grew impatient sitting in the waiting room. She knew it was time to tell the children. She took out her cell phone and called their daughter. It was Saturday, she expected her daughter to be home. Rhiannon was a pediatric oncologist at Children's Hospital. A brilliant doctor, perhaps she could help her through the complexity of the crisis that had befallen her father.

"Hi, Mom."

"Hello, dear. I'm calling from University Hospital. Your Dad has done something to his aorta," spoken as if he'd done something drastic to his hair or repainted the car pink.

"He's what?"

"They told me he has dissected his aorta whatever that means. The surgeon explained it to me."

"Jesus, Mom!" Mary hated when her children swore. "Is he still alive?"

"Oh, yes, dear. They took him to the Catheterization Lab. They must think he has some problem peeing. They took him to surgery right away. Benny and I are here waiting to be let in to see him. I don't know what all this means. Can you tell me?"

Rhiannon's mind raced at light speed. What could she say? She didn't know much about adult cardiovascular disease but knew enough to know this was as serious as it gets. She knew that marvelous and clever remedies and procedures had been developed in the field, but she couldn't tell a stent graft from a ventricular pump even though she could write a book on Ewing's Sarcoma. So, she excused herself from Saturday afternoon rounds and ran the three blocks to the University Hospital.

When she arrived, breathless, she found the CT waiting room empty.

...

It was only when Mary finally had a chance to see Chet that the magnitude of his calamity seized her. He had a large tube taped into his mouth. A machine was breathing for him. Tubes projected from his body like transparent plastic appendages. His blood bubbled back and forth in each until the droplets made their way to the canisters hanging on each side of the bed. His eyes were covered. His hands were cold and pale. She was confused and frightened by what she saw.

She could not imagine what was going through Benny's mind as they stood holding hands, a few feet from the bed. For all she knew, it had the impact of staring at a tree trunk.

There were many similar patients arrayed around the large room in various states of electrical dependence. She counted a dozen.

When Rhiannon stepped up to the bedside, the doctor part of her was pushed aside and the daughter part took over. "Jesus Christ, Mom."

"Rhee, please…"

"Look at him. What's going on? I need to talk to somebody."

Chet's nurse arrived at the bedside and introduced herself to Rhiannon.

"Yes, this is my daughter," Mary said, smiling with irrepressible smile of a proud mother.

"She's a cancer doctor at Children's." The doctor part took over now.

"Tell me what's going on?"

The nurse clad in pink scrubs with a name tag that read 'Amy' didn't look old enough to be out of high school let alone managing a critically ill patient who just had his torn aorta fixed. With the natural smile of compassion and expertise, she explained in terms only Rhiannon could understand what had happened and what had been done to beat back her father's brush with death. Rhiannon found the explanation chilling.

She stood with her mother and brother at the bedside, transfixed at the sight of her father in so unnatural a state.

"We need to get word to Chet."

"I think he's out boating."

"We better hurry," Rhiannon said quietly to her mother. Rhee moved over and took her brother's hand.

She looked down at her father her heart gripped by uncertainties and fear.

Chapter Two
Notification

"Mother's weather, few at two thousand, ceiling ten thousand broken. Visibility five, altimeter three zero point zero two."

Chet Junior replied in his usual calm voice, "Four-zero-one, angels ten. State seven." He took note of lightning on the horizon.

"Four-zero-one, roger angels ten. State seven."

Chet entered the pattern. Marshal was busy checking on the remainder of the planes aloft.

Marshal: "Four-zero-one, radar contact twenty-one miles. Final bearing three-zero-five. Check-in button fifteen." A few moments later, "Four-zero-one, dirty-up."

In the few minutes required to enter the pattern, the visibility had deteriorated significantly. Rain streaked the windshield. He was suddenly furious but had to keep his emotions in check.

Approach control took over. "Four-zero-one, lock on. Final radar contact eight miles. Fly bullseye until lock on. Final bearing three-zero-five."

"Four-zero-one," Chet replied, the pace of his breathing slightly increased.

"Four-zero-one, lock on six miles, say needles."

Chet went through his final checks. He was ready. It had grown suddenly dark. He didn't have time to be pissed at the unexpected squall line Mother was sailing toward.

"Right and up," Chet replied.

"Four-zero-one, I show you left and up. You are well right of course. Fly left and up." Chet adjusted.

"Four-zero-one, you are slightly above glide path, coming down. Left of course correcting slowly."

Silence.

"Four-zero-one, well right of course. One mile," Approach said calmly.

The landing signal officer took over. "Four-zero-one, you're Paddles contact. Lined up right. Come left."

Chet adjusted. The LSO said, "Approaching center line. Little right for line-up." A few seconds passed. "You're on center line. Three quarters of a mile. Call the ball."

"Four-zero-one. Hornet, ball. Six-point-five," Chet replied. The carrier grew larger by the second.

"Roger ball." A moment later, "Little power. Power... Easy with it."

He had made dozens of landings in conditions far worse than this. Why should this one be any easier?

A few seconds later, the ramp flashed out of sight below him and the fighter slammed down on the centerline of the wet deck catching the three wire. Chet fell forward in the jarring, familiar, happy deceleration against the harness of another successful trap.

After a moment the tailhook disengaged from the wire and the plane director, using lighted batons, guided him off the landing area to the starboard Row where he parked the FA-18 and shut down the engines and systems. When he opened the canopy, he could feel the rain strike his face. #

With the stress of landing over, Chet became infuriated at the botched preflight weather forecast by the Meteorology Section. All they could ever tell you for sure was when the isobars are close it gets windy. He still had two rookies, Nuggets, up there waiting to get down. As their commanding officer, his stress level approached that of the rain-soaked landing made only a few moments before. Compounding the problem was the fact that they would soon be approaching critical fuel levels.

Chet went to Flight Ops and had them spot a second tanker on the deck for ready launch to refuel the two if things got critical. There was still one aloft, but he needed to get back on board soon too. The bingo field, the landing location of last resort, was Oceana, Virginia. They were a hundred miles off the coast doing run-ups for imminent deployment to the Mediterranean. The two Hornet pilots were capable men, or they wouldn't have been sent to the squadron. They should be able to handle a little unexpected bad weather. They were due on board in the next ten minutes. Still in his flight gear, he went down to the flight deck. Then he thought better of it and went back to Ops. He didn't want to be perceived as a mother-hen waiting for her wayward chicks to show up.

In the fading wet daylight, he watched the monitors as an E2C trapped, then a FA-18 from another squadron. Then another. His boys were next. He listened to the exchange between the Nuggets, Approach Control and Paddles, the Landing Signal Officers standing in the rain, ears to the telephones, eyes staring into the dark rain for the approach of landing lights and flashing strobes.

He went out to the island catwalk and stared into the same dreadful night. His eyes strained to see the first of his two planes. He willed the pilots not to fuck up.

Then he saw it. The pilot was "Checkers" Hazlett. Chet figured he was the better of the two. The landing lights lit a cone of moisture. He looked like he was in the slot. Checkers cleared the ramp and slammed down onto the deck leaving a trail of sparks behind as it dragged the hook across the deck. He caught the Two Wire. An acceptable landing if not ideal. The jet came to a pleasing stop and was directed off to the Row.

Good. Now for "Zipper" Slocum. The weakest of all his pilots. Somebody in Meteorology would feel Chet's wrath. Had he known of the approaching storm, he'd have cut short the qualifying. He didn't want to baby his young pilots, but he didn't want them dead either.

Zipper wagged his wings slightly. His approach looked a tad high but from this vantage in the rapidly fading light, it was sometimes difficult to tell. Zipper crossed the ramp and dropped onto the deck, leaving a slash of sparks but did not stop as twin flames of the afterburners pushed his jet back into the wet night. Bolter.

Shit. Fucking shit.

One more missed trap and Zipper would be in trouble with marginal fuel load to allow getting juiced by the tanker. He ran down to the flight deck and saw that the ready tanker, being flown by the executive officer of the other squadron was hooked up on the number one catapult, his engines on idle. Breaking all rules, he ran to the side of the line of deck crew, their backs to the wind-driven rain, and gave him a thumbs-up. The exec gave him the middle finger. Chet could not see the exec's face behind the oxygen mask, but he knew he was probably sticking his tongue out too.

If Zipper boltered again, they would fire off the tanker. It would be dicey fuel-wise for Zipper. He would have to climb above the murk, rendezvous with the tanker, all the while sucking up precious fuel and complete the transfer of enough fuel for more attempts to land on Mother or head for the bingo field.

Chet looked down the length of the dimly lit flight deck awaiting Zipper's return.

"Come on you little fuck, get it on."

The fighter appeared out of the dark. From this vantage it looked high again. Even worse than before. He was going to miss the wires again. He knew Zipper was being given the precise adjustments by the LSO in short but firm coaxing bits of advice.

As if in slow motion the fighter cleared the ramp, slammed the deck and caught the three wire. He was down. Chet left quickly. He did not want to see the mixture of dread and relief that was no doubt etched on his face. He would catch up with Zipper and the others in the squadron ready room to join in on the razzing Zipper would receive for his nerve-wracking performance.

Chet dumped his flight gear in the equipment room then headed for the Ready Room. The pilots and RIOs cheered his arrival like the winning quarterback. They had already started giving Zipper the business. The atmosphere was more like Animal House than a military staff room. Tension was being released after the dark, rainy evolution. Everyone was safe. Chet overheard Zipper protesting, "I meant to do that."

Everyone in the room knew it was a lie. He was probably close to shitting his pants. Clark, the Squadron Executive Officer, pulled Chet aside. "CAG wants to see you." "Shit." *What does he want?*

Chet left the Ready Room and walked up to the CAG's office. He was still wet with rain and sweat. He knocked twice on the door with the sign "Commanding Officer. Carrier Air Wing 7."

"Enter."

Captain Jensen, the Commander of the Air Wing, informally and universally known as

CAG, was a good friend of Chet's. Jensen was captain of the Naval Academy football team when Chet was a plebe halfback. Their career paths paralleled, Chet's just three years behind. Jensen was a rising star. He would be easily selected to rear admiral someday soon.

"Hi, Chet. Come on in."

"Thank you, Sir."

When the door was closed, all formality ended.

"What's up?"

Jensen walked around his desk and handed a small slip of paper to Chet. "We got word your dad is very sick. The family requested you should come to Boston ASAP."

Chet looked at the note. It provided no more information than that which Jensen had given.

"Geez. We're right in the middle of workups." Carrier Quals would not be complete for another week. Longer if the weather did not improve. "I can't go. Besides, how will I get home?" "There's an E2C with an equipment breakdown the techs on board can't fix. It's returning to Oceana at first light. You can catch it."

"You sure?"

"Fuck man, it's your dad for Christ sakes. Besides, that twit of an exec of yours can use a little leadership experience. We'll be in Norfolk by the end of next week. Hopefully, you'll have things worked out by then and your dad will be eating Jell-O bitching at someone to get him a beer." He paused. "Besides, your old man is too mean to die."

"Thanks."

"No sweat. You'd do it for me." He smiled at Chet. "At least I think you would." "No chance."

He shook the CAG's hand, saluted and left. "Hope the old bastard gets well soon," Jensen said as Chet closed the door behind him.

Chet returned to the Squadron Ready Room. With the stress of the day's flying dissipated, it was again boisterous like the locker room of a winning high school football team. Chet took his exec aside and explained the situation. "Tell them I was called away," he said. "Don't tell them why. And while I'm gone, you're in charge. Don't fuck up."

Chet went to his stateroom and packed. He sent Rhiannon an email and waited but there was no reply. He turned in but did not sleep. There were questions he wanted to ask his father but never found the right occasion. There were also things he needed to tell the man but never got around to it. Important things. Milestones good and bad.

Chapter Three
Day Two: The Lake, Pee Wee and the Prom

Chet climbed into a flight suit, put on his floatation vest and pulled the white cranial onto his head. Carrying his bags, he stepped out onto the flight deck. The deck crews were already busy preparing for the morning's launch. He saw the E2C, the pilot and copilot walking around for final inspection.

The copilot walked over to him and shook his hand. "Good morning, Commander. You're hitching a ride with us."

"Good."

"Here, Sir. Let me get that," the plane captain said. He took the bags and carried them to the plane.

"Morning, Commander," the pilot said as he walked over to greet him. "Looks like it's going to be a beautiful day for flying."

"The boys will be up early."

"We should have you back in Oceana in no time."

The three men entered the plane and the engines were soon humming.

"Strap in, Sir," the copilot said. Chet strapped into the radar operator's seat directly behind the cockpit. The other two seats to the rear were empty.

After several minutes, pre-flight checks completed, they taxied the plane up to the end of the number one catapult, unfolded the wings and placed the plane precisely at the end of the catapult. From his vantage point Chet could see very little of what was going on outside, but he knew the choreography of launching so he watched the pilots. He saw the pilot give a quick salute and braced himself. The roar of full military power made the plane tremble. He rested back on the headrest and waited.

He hated flying off a carrier with somebody else at the controls. It was a relinquishment, the surrender of destiny to a complete stranger even if he had a familiar, confident face. It was unnatural: a matter of blind trust that didn't sit well.

...

It was the one place on the lake that had a decent little beach. It was nicely shaded. There were rocks around, some of them big ones which jutted out of the cool clear water, others hidden just below the surface. The rocks were the reason few others picnicked there but if you knew the rocks well and were careful, they did not present a problem. It was a familiar place and they picnicked on the spot many times. Even camped there once or twice, although his father seemed to have an aversion to the process of camping. It was pleasantly isolated too, as if they were the only ones who knew about it. Across the lake, maybe a hundred yards or so, was the big camping ground with rising smoke from barbecues, loud voices, beer-induced laughing and brisk conversations that sometimes seemed to carry across the water despite the constant roar of the rapids downstream.

Their father taught Junior and Rhiannon to be good swimmers, but they never went into the water above their knees unless Senior or their mother was in attendance, either with them or sitting on an aluminum folding chair near the water's edge.

Occasionally Junior and his sister would take Benny by the hand and lead him to the beach, wading out until the water's depth rose to their waists. They always assumed Benny liked it, but they had no real way of knowing.

It was on such an idyllic, hot July afternoon when Junior and his sister took Benny into the water. Abruptly their father leaped past them like an Olympic swimmer off the block. The splash startled Benny.

For a moment Junior thought his father had lost leave of his senses or else was suddenly very hot. Their puzzlement at the seemingly abrupt display of athletic prowess was quickly explained. They heard the distant, high-pitched voice of distress but its origin was not immediately apparent. All they saw was the receding splashes of their father swimming as fast as he could. Junior and his sister pulled Benny from the water and stood beside their mother, her gaze fixed on their father. That was when they saw some little kid in a bright orange floatation vest being swept toward the rapids where the river exits the lake. Their father was swimming toward him. It was a race: their father trying to rescue the kid before he was sucked by the current into the rapids.

There was screaming from the campground and splashing.

Senior stopped swimming and they lost sight of the orange vest. After what seemed like an interminable few seconds, they could plainly see their father slowly swimming back. He was halfway back to the beach when they saw the orange vest in tow.

Mary and the three children stepped away from the beach as their father bent down and picked up the little boy in the orange vest. He was crying. Chet picked him up and carried him to their campsite. He took the vest off the terrified child and wrapped him in a towel. He was shaking severely. It was only then they saw the rivulets of blood running down Senior's abdomen, soaking the front of his tan trunks. Everyone saw the scraped skin that ran vertically from just below his nipple to his navel.

"Hey Dad, you're bleeding."

"Oh dear," Mary said and reached for a towel. Senior looked down and saw the blood.

"Must have scraped it on a rock when I dove." But his attention was more focused on the little boy in the orange vest. Mary threw another towel around the whimpering, trembling little boy. He looked about eight.

Junior walked over to the cooler and pulled out a Popsicle and handed it to the boy.

A short time later, the quiet was shattered by the roar of a pick-up arriving at the camp, raising a cloud of dust and a shower of cinders. The driver and a woman jumped out and ran toward the boy. The man was obviously drunk. Convinced their boy would live, he turned to the bleeding Chet and offered his hand.

Chet slapped it away and lit into the man.

"You stupid fuck. You should keep an eye on your damned kid. It would have served you right if he'd've drowned, you stupid bastard."

The man was so taken aback he couldn't seem to decide whether to thank Chet again or just leave.

Junior thought the man might take a swing at his father. This would have been a monumental mistake. So, the man did the best thing and took the woman and his traumatized son to the pick-up and left.

Junior also knew that his father was so wound-up that it would take a while for him to calm down. His mother stayed silent and dabbed at the blood until it stopped bleeding. Benny, his interminable blank expression unchanged, handed his father a popsicle. A short time later, they drove home. It was a long time before they returned to the lake.

A moment later the catapult fired, pressing Chet into his seat, the plane instantly accelerated down the deck and, with a satisfying jolt, separated from the shuttle and banked out over the Atlantic.

Chet sat back and smiled as he thought about the lake.

About ten minutes into the flight the pilot turned around smiling and said over the engine noise, "The CAG must really like you."

"Why?"

"There's nothing wrong with this airplane."

...

Chet arrived at Oceana Naval Air Station, thanked the pilot and copilot for their time and, still in his flight suit, took a shuttle to Norfolk International Airport. The next flight to Boston would be after noon. He found a comfortable place at the airport bar to sit and read. Mostly, he thought about his dad.

He phoned Rhiannon.

"Hello, Chet. Thank God you called. Where are you?"

"Sitting in the bar of the Norfolk airport. What's going on?"

"How did you get off the boat so quickly?"

"Catapult."

"Listen, let me go somewhere I can talk." There was a protracted silence.

"Chet?"

"Yeah, Rhee. Tell me what's happened to Dad."

"He did something bad to his aorta. Tore it. It's called a dissection. A bad one."

His first thought was to wonder what his father had been up to to tear something inside his

body. "How did he do that? And what does all this mean?"

She proceeded to describe, in terms he would understand, what a dissection of his aorta meant. It sounded very complicated. And ominous.

"How is he now? The surgery was successful, right?"

"I think so. He's still alive, anyway. He's on a ventilator to help him breathe."

"Is he awake?"

"Not yet."

"How's Mom taking all of this?"

"You know Mom. The eternal optimist. She expects him to yank out his tubes and reach for a beer."

"In other words, she doesn't get it?"

"None of it."

"Shit. Did you talk to the doctors?"

"I've spoken to the surgeon and the Fellow. I also spoke with the cardiac anesthesiologist who's running the ventilator. They are cautiously optimistic. The anesthesia guy said with his history of smoking it may take a while to get him off the vent. No rush, he said."

"Cautiously optimistic. That's like telling me 'I think it'll fly.' Does Mom know I'm on dry land?"

"No, she thinks you're still out flying around the middle of the ocean."

"She sent me the message."

"No, I did."

Protracted silence.

"Listen," she said. "I have to get back. I'll tell Mom you're on the way. Let me know when you takeoff and I'll pick you up at the airport. When do you get in?"

"Around four."

"Good. I'll come get you. You can stay at my place.

"'Kay. I'll be in touch." "Okay, see you soon."

"Bye." Chet hung up.

...

With an hour to go, he headed for the gate. He was still in his flight suit which was against protocol but the last thing on his mind was protocol, except that it prevented him from drinking alcohol. He drew glances from the flight crew as they walked to the gangway. He nodded to them. Recognition of brethren.

The gate manager called him over to the counter and told him if he wanted to be first on, he could board ahead of the others. He thanked her and took the first window seat. One of the pilots saw him take his seat and leaned over from the aisle. "Where you headed?"

"Boston. My father is ill."

"Sorry to hear that. I was with the COD squadron out of North Island and the *Carl Vinson.*"

"You don't say. I'm with the Jolly Rogers off the Ike." He tugged at his sleeves. "It was a hasty departure." "Looks like it."

It must have appeared that Chet did not want to reminisce or exchange war stories for the pilot said, "Well, good luck to you and your dad."

"Thanks."

A few moments later the attendant reached over and placed a drink in his hand.

"Sorry, I didn't order this," Chet said.

"Compliments of the First Officer."

"Oh, thank him for me."

Chet finished the drink just as the first passengers started boarding. The drink did not allay his anxiety about strangers in the cockpit. Having a tail-hooker in the dummy seat helped.

Chet spent a semester at the Air Force Academy as part of an exchange program. One night drinking beer with his blue-suited colleagues, he remarked that anybody could land on ten thousand feet of stationary concrete but it took a real man to land a plane on a moving, pitching piece of steel 120 feet wide and 800 feet long, at night, in the rain with marginal fuel reserve or even on a perfect Case 1 day.

He tried to doze once the airliner left the ground, but he could not: his mind was flooded with 'Dad' stories.

...

It was a cold, rainy October day. That didn't stop the spectators. They all had skin in the game.

Chet Junior was the starting running back for the Pee Wee football team. They were called the Crusaders, so named by their sponsor, the local dealer of Catholic artifacts and Bibles.

The field was a quagmire and the Crusaders were down by a touchdown in the fourth quarter. The quarterback for the Crusaders handed the ball to Chet in an end-around and there was no one between him and the goal line as the other players collapsed into a scrum. Chet ran as hard as he could, spurred on, no doubt by the near-hysterical encouragement of his parents and sister.

From the opposite side of the field an opposing player hit Chet at full tilt. It knocked the ball from Chet's arms and sent him sprawling into the mud. The impact was so severe that everyone stood to see if Chet had survived.

In the meantime, the other player, so triumphant with his hit, picked up the fumbled ball and started jumping up and down, seemingly unaware of his next tactical move.

His hysterical coach practically ran down the field beseeching him to take off for his opponent's goal line. Everyone started laughing. Except Chet Senior.

Chet leapt from the bleachers and ran toward his son lying prostrate in the mud. Chet knelt beside him. Junior's eyes were closed. Senior carefully removed the oversized helmet from his son's head. Senior then gently slapped his son on the cheek.

"Chet, you okay buddy? Come on, Son, snap to."

For an interminable moment, Junior did not move. He was barely breathing.

There was sudden cheering as, against all odds, the opposing player ran across the Crusader's goal line and spiked the ball. He was mobbed by his team.

Junior opened his eyes, recognized his father and said, "Sorry, Dad. I lost the ball."

Senior helped Junior to his feet and once underway to the sideline, Senior took off after the opposing player

"Hey, you little son of a bitch, that was a bad hit. You could'a hurt somebody, you little prick."

The boy's father grabbed Senior by the arm and spun him around.

"Hey, asshole, you can't talk to my son like that!"

"I'll talk to the little fucker any way I want. Did you see the hit your little bastard made on my son? He could'a killed him."

"Lighten up, asshole. They're just kids."

"Yeah," Chet could not contain his fury and grabbed the opposing player by the jersey.

"They're just kids."

"Take your hands off my son, you dick."

Chet pushed the kid to the muddy ground. The boy's father

reacted instantly grabbing Chet by the front of his windbreaker. Those who knew Chet instantly recognized this as a tactical mistake.

Chet decked him before anybody could intervene.

Those present wisely restrained the other father who yelled, "Your son sucks. If he can't play the game, have him take up checkers."

Chet turned and said, "Mind your own business, asshole. I don't see a Heisman in your son's future."

Junior grabbed his father by the arm, and they walked off the field, Mary and Rhiannon trotting along behind them.

Chet Junior was excommunicated from the Crusaders and never played Pee Wee football again even though he loved the game.

Chet, Senior was banned from attending any of the games.

The next season, the owner of the Catholic supply store withdrew his support of the team. "It was way too violent," he said. "They're just kids."

...

Rhiannon ran up to Chet as he exited the security zone and hugged him. She noted he was in his flight suit. "Gee did they let you fly their little plane?" "No." He kissed her cheek.

"I'm so glad you're here. Thank you for getting here so quickly. I don't think Mom is going to handle this well."

"That's okay, I called in a favor I didn't even know I was owed. How's Dad?" "No different that when we spoke."

"What do you mean, Mom is not going to handle this well? What aren't you telling me,

Sis?"

"Let's get your luggage and then we'll talk," she said as they got onto the escalator. It was her way of telling him he was not going to like what she had to say.

They'd bonded closely since way before Benny was born. It intensified after Benny was born and his disabilities became apparent. From that point on, they had a certain level of communication that few siblings were blessed with. She fawned over her older brother and he was like her knight in shining armor, as clichéd as that was when she said it. Rhee could come to him with things she dared not share with their parents, especially their father. They even had their own language, a code they shared from the time they were little. The fact she seemed to want to withhold things from him now was quite unsettling. Her silence persisted at the baggage carousel.

In the car, he turned in the passenger seat and said, "Okay, Rhee. Stop fucking with me. What's the story?"

The question caused her eyes to well.

"I don't think Dad is going to make it. I know doctors. Christ, I am one. Especially surgeons. They can tell you a lie and make it sound like the truth from God's own mouth. I do not think he's going to pull through. They as much as said so. They think his brain was deprived of blood flow during the dissection and he's probably braindead." She wiped a tear from her cheek. "And of course, Mom thinks he's going to be sipping beer and eating pizza any second now." "Rhee, you need to tell her."

"I can't. It will kill her."

"She might be stronger than you think."

"Ya think?" It came out of her mouth too quickly as if it were a hope rather than a confirmation.

"Well, I guess she'll find out soon enough," Chet said finally.

When they arrived at her townhouse, Chet carried his luggage into her spare bedroom, showered quickly and changed into a pair of khakis, running shoes and his USNA sweatshirt. She had a cup of coffee waiting for him when he entered the kitchen.

"Have you told Helen?" she asked.

"No. Since the divorce we communicate rarely. I want to check things out before I call her."

There was a long pause. Chet and his sister, close since youth had grown apart over the years as each pursued life's diverging pathways. It seemed inevitable. They had spoken only periodically over the years while he flew planes and she became a pediatrician.

"Ever sorry you two never had kids?" She asked the question already knowing the answer.

"The way things turned out between us? I'm glad there were no offspring to suffer that calamity."

"Wise."

"You?"

"I am too involved in my career to start anything serious. I've had a few near misses. The last one was a keeper, but I found out just in time he had straying eyes. He thought he was being clever. A woman knows."

"Ah, yes. Helen revealed her intentions with sparkling clarity."

"I've never asked you and, if you don't want to you don't have to tell me, but what happened between you two?"

Chet grew pensive and sipped his coffee. The silence was prolonged as if he was cataloging each episode. "We fell in love. She was the most beautiful woman I had ever seen. Still is. A bunch of us rented a place on Virginia Beach and had our frat party activities. She was there with her folks down from Richmond. We met on the beach and it was lust at first sight. God she was gorgeous. One look at her in that bikini and I was hooked. She was good too. She could suck the chrome off a trailer hitch. From that point on we saw each other as much as we could. After six months of 'dating'"—he made quotation marks with his fingers—"we decided to get married. She thought it was all glamor being a naval aviator's wife and cocktail parties at the Officer's Club. I call it the '*Top Gun* Effect.' We wanted to get married at the Chapel at the Academy, but her folks didn't want her wedding militarized so we had that lavish ceremony as you well remember"—she nodded—"and, for several years everything was smooth sailing until I finally got deployed to the Med. She flew over for shore leave in Naples, but she wasn't the same. Those six months killed it. Several glorious years then the arrival of the bitter end."

"She cheat?"

"Of that, I have little doubt. When I got home, she wasn't there to meet me at the fly-in.

When I made it home from the base, she greeted me with divorce papers. The rest is history."

"Funny, I never liked her."

"You made that plain just as she made her disdain for our father quite obvious."

"I think he saw her for what she was. Say what you will about his tact, or lack thereof, he called that one right."

"True. Perhaps she figured I was going to turn out like Dad and wanted no part of it."

"Perhaps. But then again, she never really got to know the old man. Or wanted to."

He paused as he sipped his coffee growing increasingly pensive. Finally, he continued, "Our mother is such a mixture of beauty, grace and tolerance. Long-suffering. I sometimes wondered over the years what she ever saw in our Dad. I guess in Helen I was looking for Mom.

Uniquely warm and quietly dignified. It didn't take long for the blush to leave that rose. I was looking for Mom and she wasn't it."

Coffee finished, they headed to the hospital.

...

Mary saw her son walk into the glass cubical but didn't say anything, letting him take in the sight of his father.

Chet was shocked and pissed at his sister for not warning him on the way over. His father was lying in bed, plastic goggles shielding his eyes; a breathing tube in his mouth held in place by a plastic apparatus; the gentle rise and fall of his father's chest punctuated by the soft, episodic hiss of the breathing machine. The soft beeping noise of the monitor kept a metronomic rhythm. A tube taped to his nose emerged from his nostril. Tubes on either side of his chest filled with dilute blood. A sheet and blanket covered his chest. He lay perfectly still, inert. The only way he knew his father was alive was by watching the bouncing light on the heart monitor.

Benny stood, walked over and put his arms around his older brother. Automatically, as if by subliminal muscular reaction, Chet placed his arm around his brother. When his mother stood to hug him, Chet snapped out of his trance, only then did he see his brother and his mother. His first reaction was that she was smiling up at him.

"Hi, Mom," he said in a croaking voice, holding her close. He could not remove his eyes from his father. "Jesus, Mom, what the hell happened?"

"He was rearranging the furniture in the living room and he collapsed. I thought he had a heart attack or stroke or something. I called 911. He ended up here. As you see."

His arm still around his brother, Chet turned to his sister, "Tell me what's going on here."

"He's sedated on a ventilator. I gathered from what was said this morning on rounds that they believe he is stable hemodynamically, but they are concerned about him waking up and getting him off the ventilator."

"Sounds serious," he said in a patronizing voice. "As we discussed, it is," patronizing back.

Chet tried to clear his head. "I need to talk to the doctor."

"He was here earlier, he said he'd be by later this evening. He will talk to you then." "Get him now."

"He's a surgeon. He's a very busy man and you are not on the deck of your carrier."

He ignored her. "You okay, Mom? Have you slept at all?"

"I'm okay. Benny and I have been looked after nicely by the staff."

"You look terrible. Have you slept?"

"Benny and I have been napping in the waiting room across the hall. But we don't mind sitting here. We don't want to miss anything. Besides, the nurses have been very kind to us."

Growing increasingly agitated, the Navy Commander, always in control, wanted answers.

"Please settle down, Chet," Rhiannon said in a more sympathetic tone. She might be an important doctor, but she was still his sister.

"Listen, to your sister, Chet, they are doing everything they can. He's in the best hospital in the country."

It was enough. He took control of his anxiety and approached the bed. Taking his father's hand in his, he squeezed. He looked for something familiar to assure himself that this man, lying still on the bed was his father. He watched the monotonous rise and fall of his chest. He reached for the sheet that covered him and pulled it down, revealing the long white dressing on his chest and the long, hard, pink scar from the rescue at the lake. Tears welled up in his eyes. He squeezed his father's hand as if this might arouse him from his medically induced coma or infuse in him some miraculous healing powers.

"Are you staying with Rhee?"

"What?"

"Will you be sleeping with Rhee?"

His smile was inadvertent. "Yes, Mother, I will be sleeping with Rhee."

"Oh, Good."

It was a marvel of neurobiology that his mother had been a copywriter for a publishing house for over twenty years.

Even Rhee smiled at that. He looked at her and winked. He hugged Benny who had not let go of his older brother since his arrival.

"First of all," Mary said. "I wasn't sure you'd get off your boat—"

"Ship, Mother. It's a ship. A boat is a submarine."

"—in time. I'm so glad you made it. Can you stick around until we get your father home?"

"We'll see." He thought the likelihood of Senior leaving the hospital was not good and actually returning to his home even less likely. He looked at his sister as the thought formed in his head. "I'll stay as long as the Navy will let me."

A short time later, after the small talk had subsided, a nurse came into the room to check something. She noticed Chet standing by the bedside.

Mary, ever the courteous one, introduced the new arrival. "This is Nurse Amy. She's taking care of your father. This is my son, Chet Junior. He's a Navy pilot. He just flew in off his bo— ship."

Amy turned to Chet and shook his hand. "Nice to meet you."

"She's not married."

"Thank you, Mother. I think that's enough."

"Chet is a Commander."

"How nice," Amy said, trying in vain to diminish her embarrassment.

When she was finished, she turned to Chet saying, "Your father is stable. We are going to try a sedation vacation later today to see if he can breathe on his own. That way we can see if he is strong enough to have the ventilator turned off and the tube removed from his throat. Doctor

Cummings, the intensivist will be by later to see how he made out." "Is he strong enough to have the machine removed?" Chet asked.

"We'll see." She said it with a warm but reserved smile.

Chet nodded and looked at Rhee whose expression did not change. Amy saw this, finished what she was doing and left. Chet thought Amy looked too young and fresh to be a nurse in such a critical, tension-charged atmosphere. He wondered how long she had been out of nursing school or if she'd started her menstrual cycles yet.

A short time later, Amy returned. "We're going to move Mr. Pettigrew." Mary stood up alarmed. "Why are you moving him?" Chet asked sternly.

"We are going to move him to a bigger cubicle. One with more space so you can all sit in comfort."

"Oh," Chet said. "Thank you. Does this mean his vacation will be postponed?" "Not at all. Just so long as there is no other disturbance in The Force." She winked at him. When she left, Rhee turned to him and said quietly, "Junior, this is going to be a long haul.

You need to relax. Not everything that happens around here has life and death implication." "Okay. I get it," he said even though, as a military officer, he disagreed.

"Relax, boy," she said, patting him on the arm as if he were a mischievous dog.

A short time later, a small contingent of nurses and aides arrived to unplug the machines and transfer Chet Senior to a more expansive cubicle. They moved the bed carefully into the central part of the ICU and directed him to the larger glass-enclosed cubicle in the corner of the unit. When he was all plugged in, they let the family back in. There were now two large reclining chairs and a small sofa for the family to continue their vigil. For a while they remained silent.

"When was the last time you guys had something to eat?" Chet finally asked.

Mary said, "I don't remember. Benny and I had a snack from the machine in the waiting room last night and the nurses have been fetching me coffee and a soda for Benny but that's about all, now that you mention it."

"Mom," Rhee said, "why don't I take you guys down to the cafeteria and we'll grab a real meal." "Sounds good."

"I'll stay here," Chet said. "Maybe you could pick me up a sandwich and a Diet Coke.

Tuna if they have it. Or maybe egg salad. I want to stick around to see how Dad enjoys his vacation." "As you wish," Rhee said, admiring and yet annoyed at her brother's obsession with command and control.

...

Chet Junior, like his father, had always been protective of his sister. Even solicitous at times. From the very beginning, the Old Man had a softspot in his heart reserved exclusively for his daughter. Whenever possible she took advantage of it. In his eyes she could do no wrong. If he was hard on his older son, he was more thoughtful toward his only daughter. However, the young daughter rejected it, preferring to carve out, with annoying persistence and optimism, her own path in life. Yet, when Benny came along and his difficulties were apparent, she looked after him the same way she did for her father and older brother.

Chet pulled the chair close to the side of the bed, rested his hand on his father's and smiled at the balance of nature.

...

Rhiannon was in a tizzy, as her mother put it, for two weeks. The invitation to the Junior Prom had come from one of the star players on the high school football team. She was overwhelmed and distracted by the possibilities and requirements. Everything had to be perfect. "Settle down and don't screw up," was all Chet Senior said from behind his newspaper. "You'll be fine." Unusual for his succinctness.

That was not enough for his daughter. She had to have the perfect dress, the perfect hairdo, the finest shoes... This took place in an orbit far above Chet Senior's notice.

Finally, the big night arrived. Her father, again reading the paper and sipping his beer, took little notice of the young lady, hair in plastic curlers running around the house in barely contained hysteria. He only took notice when he went to the fridge for another beer. "Yeah, you look great," was all he said as they passed each other. He again marveled at the process of biology that allowed her to develop into such a fine young lady. Just like and probably because of, her mother.

The football player was scheduled to pick her up at five and they would get something to eat then go to the prom, which started at seven-thirty. Rhiannon waited patiently for her date's arrival. By five-forty-five it was apparent he wasn't going to show. As Rhee grew increasingly distraught, Chet suggested they call the kid's home and see if was on the way. "Maybe he's got car trouble," he said from behind his paper. "Maybe the tux didn't fit."

Yielding to the uncertainty, Mary finally called the boy's home. "I'm sorry, Robbie's decided not to go," the boy's mother said.

"He what?"

"He didn't think it would be as much fun as he thought so he decided to hang out with some of his friends instead."

"Chet, he's not coming. He's hanging out with his friends instead," Mary said with disbelief.

Chet leapt from his chair, barreled past his bawling daughter, grabbed the phone and yelled,

"You tell that little son of a bitch, he's going to take my daughter to prom if I have to dress him in his tux myself. Tell him get ready, I'm on my way! God-damnit."

This burst sent Rhee running up the stairs to her room in hysterics.

"Chet, now stop this," Mary said as her husband continued to harangue the kid's mother to the point where she hung up on him. Chet turned, his face red and disappeared.

Fifteen minutes later her daughter descended the steps holding her father's hand. Chet was in his dress Marine sergeant's uniform. Rhee was smiling broadly.

They stopped in front of her dumbfounded mother. He bowed as Rhiannon curtsied.

"Maybe you shouldn't do that, Chet. You don't want to blow out the seat of your pants."

"Fear not, woman. It still fits. Except don't look directly at the buttons. One might fly off and poke your eye out."

Chet put out his arm and Rhee placed hers around his. Chet bowed again, his sabre rattling slightly in its scabbard. They turned and left.

When they arrived at the elaborately decorated gym, all eyes turned their way. She did not have a corsage as there had been no time for one, but she was on her father's arm and nothing else mattered. Chet stood to one side while Rhee fetched them some punch. One of the chaperones walked over to him and introduced himself. Chet made him for a Spanish teacher. Or maybe Home Ec.

"You are here with Rhiannon?"

"Yes. Her date bailed at the last minute, the little fucker."

The man stiffened slightly. "We don't like to use that sort of language on school property."

"Not even the gyum? Well, Sir," Chet said, "you can call him whatever you want. I should've run the little bastard through with my sword. *Comprende, Amigo*?"

"Um. Yes, I do."

"Was there anything else?"

"Yes. Please leave your sword in the car."

At that moment Rhiannon handed her father a cup of punch. He toasted the chaperone,

"Here's to you, Sir, and the fine job you are doing with all these young people."

Rhee beamed as they clinked their plastic cups then simultaneously tossed down the punch as if it were a shot of fine scotch. They laughed.

The chaperone bowed slightly and said, "Enjoy your evening. You make a fine-looking couple."

Finishing their punch, Rhee and her father mingled with her friends. Soon several young men gravitated to the couple and asked questions. What significance was the red stripe on his pant leg? Did he ever guard the President? Was he in Vietnam and how many people did you kill? One said his father was in the Marines. When Chet asked him what outfit, the boy responded, "I don't know. He never talks about it."

Rhee was proud of her father as he showed remarkable forbearance, patiently answering every question, addressing every comment. All the more compelling a demonstration because it was so out of character.

At the end of the evening, slightly past one a.m., the prom concluded. Chet took his daughter to the I-HOP for, as he put it, some grub. Not long after taking their seats, the waitress approached and took their order.

"She's a little young for you, eh soldier?"

"I'm not a soldier. I'm a Marine. Now, get our food and be quick about it." Chet talked with his daughter for nearly an hour. She never looked at her father the same way again. When the waitress returned with the check, he thanked her for looking out for his daughter and left a big tip.

Chet Junior was in his second year at the Academy. He heard the story directly from Rhee by phone. She was so proud. He could tell by her effusive language and the pitch of her voice.

...

While the rest of the family was still down in the cafeteria, Amy entered the cubicle and

made some adjustments to the ventilator and told Chet they were starting his father's breathing trial.

Chet jumped from his seat and stepped to one side.

"So, you're one of those *Top Gun* kind of guys?" she said as she worked.

"Yes. Same thing. Different aircraft. Different ship."

"Wow. That must be exciting," she said as she disconnected his breathing tube from the machine and connected another.

"It is. It's the best job in the world. In fact, I was an instructor at the Top Gun school for about six months."

"Wow. That must have been something."

"It was."

They exchanged glances.

"We'll let your dad breathe on his own for a while. I'll check his blood gases in about half an hour. We should know how he'll do by then."

"And if he fails?"

"We'll try again later. He needs to be strong enough to breathe on his own. He's been through a lot." She smiled and left.

Chet watched his father's chest rise and fall. Puffs of humidified air came out of the breathing tube like warm breath on a winter's day. He wondered, with the sedation turned off, why his father did not stir. He squeezed his hand, but it remained lifeless.

"Hey, Pop," he whispered softly. "Time to wake up." A short time later, his family returned to the cubicle.

"Nothing to report," Chet told them. "They've started his breathing test off the ventilator."

He looked at his mother. "He hasn't stirred."

"He's probably still sleepy," Mary said.

Rhiannon looked concerned, but it was clear to Chet she was trying to conceal it.

"How long has been off the machine?" Rhee asked.

"Twenty minutes or so."

"He's barely breathing," she said softly.

As if on cue, Amy returned and put him back on the ventilator. Chet studied her. He could tell she was disappointed by the outcome of the trial.

"We'll let him rest a while longer," she said quietly. "We'll try again later." "He failed," Rhee said softly. She made no effort to conceal her disappointment.

"Yes," Amy said. "But his surgery was only yesterday, and he needs to be a little stronger is all. He'll come around. You'll see."

Chet was sure his sister spotted the lie.

They sat quietly while Chet ate his egg salad sandwich and sipped on his Diet Dr. Pepper. He studied his sister for a moment, looked at his mother and walked over to Benny and put his arm around him and kissed the side of his head. Benny reached around and hugged his brother. *Poor Benny,* he thought. *What must be going on inside his feeble head? If anything.*

A short time later, Dr. Cummings entered the cubicle. He was a short, bald little man with a ketchup stain on the lapel of his white coat.

"Good evening, everyone. My name is Dr. Cummings. I am the critical care physician overseeing Mr. Pettigrew's care. I came by to fill you in on his progress."

There followed introductions including Benny whose absent affect made Cummings pause.

The doctor spoke softly. "Do you want me to discuss this in front of him?"

"Oh, yes, Doctor. He may not show it, but he hears and understands everything you say."

After a fleeting puzzled expression, Cummings continued. "Mr. Pettigrew, as you know has suffered a catastrophic tearing of his aorta. Doctor Reynolds was able to repair it quite expertly. My concern—our concern—is that he is going to have trouble getting off the ventilator. This may be because of brain injury from the tear in his aorta and the subsequent efforts to repair it." He paused and looked at Rhiannon. "My understanding is that you are a physician."

"Yes, pediatric oncology at Children's. I understand perfectly." She turned and looked at her mother. "We all understand."

"Good. It may be too early to tell if this is the case, but we will give him a few days to rest and try each day to wean him from the ventilator." "Then he can go home?" Mary said.

The doctor smiled sympathetically. "He has a long road ahead of him. He has had a lot happen to him and managed to get this far. We'll take our time and do our best to get him home."

He turned to Rhee. "We'll have to work with what he has left."

Rhee nodded. Chet understood, as well. Sweet, befuddled Mary stared intently at the doctor. Benny focused on his father.

"I will keep you abreast of Mr. Pettigrew's progress and any changes."

When he left, Rhee took her older brother out of earshot of their mother and said quietly,

"Dad's finished."

"Rhee, you need to tell Mom."

"No. Not yet. Let it play out. There's a chance I'm wrong."

"You need to tell Mom."

"No. Let's just keep it between you and me for now."

"What are you two whispering about?"

"Sleeping arrangements," Chet said.

They sat at the bedside for the rest of the evening. Locked in private thoughts, little was

said.

Finally, Mary suggested Chet and Rhee go for the night. She would call them if there was a change. Amy, as she was ready to leave at the end of her shift, brought in some blankets and pillows for them. She showed them how the chairs shifted into recliners, so they could sleep at the bedside. She introduced DeVonte, the nurse on duty for the night. She mentioned they would do another breathing trial around two a.m., but Chet Senior was stable, and they would keep a close eye on them.

Rhee and Chet kissed their father, mother and Benny good night and left. They offered to take Benny with them. It would be, Chet said, one less thing for their mother to worry about. She declined the offer. "Oh," she said, "we will be fine. Not to worry."

...

Chet and Rhiannon said little on the way to her home. They could sense what the other was thinking. Settling into the two-bedroom townhouse just a few minutes away from the hospital, Rhee opened a bottle of cabernet and some Ritz crackers. Chet sat on the couch with his third glass of cabernet in his hand while she curled up beside her. He could practically sense the distress transmitted through the weight of her body against his. He was afraid I might not get in and would wallow in disappointment and self-pity for the rest of my life as a failure. He even went so far as to talk me into another profession. Teacher or something. Or was it guidance counselor? Funny,

Dad never subjected me to the lectures he gave you. Chauvinist pig." Chet gave her an elbow.

She continued, "Dad was always concerned about my desire to be a doctor. He probably thought I was over-reaching just trying to get into Boston College. I don't think he could endure my disappointment.

"You were his Golden Boy. His only disappointment with you was not becoming a Marine officer. I'll never forget the look in his eyes when you walked up, accepted your diploma in your gleaming white uniform and shook the hand of the Vice-President.

"Then when I got into BC he was blown away. Then when I got accepted to Tuft's Medical School and yelled, 'Dad, I got in!' he hugged me so hard I thought he might dislocate one of my ribs. He went into the bathroom and cried. He could not conceal his joy even though he tried. He acted like my acceptance was a forgone conclusion. But he had the same look on his face you had when you shook Biden's hand.

"Not just a doctor, but a pediatrician. I think he secretly thought of it as a way to figure out Benny's autism.

Chet was exhausted. He had started his day being flung off a carrier in the Atlantic. Rhee had been summoned away from rounds the day before and never finished. They toasted their father and went to bed.

...

During the night, Chet Senior failed his breathing trial.

Chapter Four
Day Three: Tet

Chet and Rhiannon were up by six. Neither had slept well. She made coffee. She offered to make eggs, but Chet said he was not hungry and aa headache from the red wine. It was Monday morning and she had to make rounds before returning to the bedside. She offered to drop him off at the hospital, but he said he would walk. Besides, he needed to do his morning run. He tucked the spare key into his pocket, put in his earbuds and they left.

His mind was filled with competing fret over his squadron and his father. Instead of finding the run invigorating, he climbed in the shower filled with sadness and dread.

Chet nuked some coffee and left for the hospital where he found nothing had changed. Dr. Reynolds had been by early to check on his handiwork. He had made the statement that, "surgically, he is recovering without complication."

Mary asked him, "What about his brain, Doctor?"

He hemmed and hawed, telling her that there was reason for cautious optimism then left.

"Has Cummings been around yet?" Chet asked his mother.

"No, Dr. Reynolds said he would be by sometime later today.

Mary resumed her position on the chair beside the bed. As always, she took her husband's hand in hers.

Chet decided to take Benny for a walk. He held his hand as they went to the CT ICU waiting room to get sodas, then took him to the bathroom. While they were gone, Rhiannon joined her mother.

When Chet and his brother returned, they sat down on the couch.

Their mother still held her husband's hand then said, to no one in particular, "He used to hate cutting off ears."

Rhee bolted forward in her seat. "What did you just say?"

"Your father said he didn't like cutting off gook ears as much as he thought he would. Some of the Marines did it. Like taking scalps. They'd string them on a necklace. Cutting off an ear while the gook was still alive was like counting coup. He told me he did it once or twice but found the practice unappealing. He discouraged the others from it. He said he saw no purpose served by mutilating the enemy dead or alive." Rhee and Chet exchanged glances.

...

Chet sat on the floor beside his father. He studied the framed picture on the wall behind his father's chair. It had always held a dark mystery. For some reason, his father never explained it. It was a *Life* magazine cover of a young Marine, running down a street, his head down as if into the slash of a blizzard, M16 in one hand clutching a naked Vietnamese baby in the other. Chet asked his father about it once but never got a response.

"Why the Marines?" he asked his father.

"Because," his father answered, an answer even more succinct than he was used to. Chet Junior expected yet another long lecture about the importance of a college education.

Instead, his father lit another cigarette, took a sip of his beer and rested his head back, memory obscuring the present.

...

Bucky said it was theirs for the taking: a brand new 1966 Dodge Challenger just sitting by the curb, unlocked. Just a quick joyride to see what it could do, then they would put it right back where they found it. Nobody would be the wiser. It was a recurring theme with Bucky who, as Chet repeatedly pointed out, was only a cunt hair away from being arrested for something.

Bucky had this knack. He could talk a zebra into relinquishing his stripes. Chet frequently surrendered wisdom and caution to Bucky's dark charisma. As if under a spell.

"Sure, why not." *I mean,* Chet thought, *what could happen? Reform school? A real jail with bars and child rapists and stoner-cold killers? Dead with their crumpled bodies in a smoking wreck against some tree?*

Bucky hot-wired the car after midnight, and they were away. Once they got beyond earshot of whoever the car belonged to, Bucky floored it. Chet watched the tach needle brush up against the red. Tonight was the night he was surely going to die. At the hands of his best friend no less.

The town was dark. Bucky pulled the Challenger to a gentle stop at a red light in the center of town. He looked both ways. Nothing. The place was shut down for the night. *Good,* Chet thought.

When the light turned green, Bucky floored it again. Trying to overcome the inertia of a stationary position in time and space, the tires spun until there was enough grab to propel the car forward. Chet looked through the rearview and saw the cloud of rubber smoke. A moment later the flashing red lights emerged from through the smoke.

"Man," Chet said, "you're fucked."

Before the smoke had properly dissipated, he and Bucky were hunched over the hood with handcuffs around their wrists. The hood was warm, Chet remembered. Another cop car arrived, and they were hauled off to jail where they were photographed, finger-printed and tossed into a cell where they spent the night. Chet's dad was so pissed he refused to come down to the jail. Ultimately, it would lead to another beating.

...

High on the bench, the judge looked down over his glasses at Chet.

"Ya un'erstan o'course, Young Pettigrew, that this is a serious offense. Theft of an automobile not belonging to you? And I make no distinction who ak-chally stole it, ya un'erstan. You were in it at the commission of the theft. That makes you an accomplice. I make no distinction who was at the wheel of said automobile. You being eighteen and nearly outa high school, I could charge you as an adult. Un'erstan where I'm coming from?"

"Yes Sir," Chet said as contrite as his genetic code would allow.

"So, I'm going to offer you a way out. Your record is clean. You have not previously run afoul of the authorities. I will grant you some susceptibility to the guiles of one Mr. Bucky Wallace, a name familiar to us by prior acts. He has his own fish to fry. I'm going to give you a choice. It should be easy for a bright guy like you. Here's the deal: you finish high school, graduate with no more infractions of the law or social order and enlist in the Marines and I'll wipe your slate clean.

No record of your indiscretions. We got a deal?" He looked over at his father, stone-faced as ever. He nodded almost imperceptibly.

"Helluva choice, Judge. I'll take the Marines."

"You better hope they'll take you."

With the whack of the gavel, the deal was done.

July 1, 1966 Chet arrived at Parris Island. It was the longest thirteen weeks of his life. #

Horace told Chet they were moving up. It was Tet and there was a cease-fire to observe the Vietnamese New Year. Lance Corporal Chester Pettigrew dutifully gathered his gear and they boarded waiting trucks. The sun wasn't even above the horizon, and his fatigues were already wet with sweat. Somebody at Topside thought that during the lull they could move up an artillery battery of 105s into a better position to protect the northern entrance to Hue. Made sense. As a mere Lance Corporal in the Marines, anything Topside wanted either made perfect sense or was incomprehensibly stupid. On occasion, they were not mutually exclusive.

After a long, dusty ride up from the coast, the battery unlimbered at the northern edge of a suburb of Hue and set up four howitzers at the edge of a flat, featureless rice paddy the size of four football fields guarded by a line of dense trees in the distance forming the limits of the jungle. The sergeant placed Chet's platoon in a covering position but first they had to help the arty fuck-offs sandbag the place. It was dark before they had a reasonable position. Even though Chet was in the best shape of his life, he was exhausted and dehydrated. His squad, of which he was the second in command, spread out on the floor of an abandoned storefront. Must have been some sort of grocery as there were desiccated chicken carcasses hanging from a string suspended from the ceiling. The place, like just about every other place he had been in South Vietnam, reeked. Rotting vegetation, strange cooking aromas abetted by random piles of cow shit. Chet thought he would be used to it for as long as he had been in-country, but he wasn't.

It was early on January 29th. Chet was assigned to place the squad in position to guard the left flank howitzers and watch as one of the artillery privates lowered the tube into a horizontal position. Probably going to clean out the barrel. Chet distracted himself with the slow, plodding water buffalo pulling an ancient plow through the rice field guided from behind by a thin old man in a gray loin cloth.

Curiously, the gunner seemed to bore-sight the howitzer. He watched as the gunner loaded an armor-piercing shell and closed the breech. *Odd,* Chet thought. There was no reason for him to do so. The guns hadn't fired since they were emplaced. The gunner pulled the lanyard, and with the booming discharge of the cannon, the cow disappeared in a red splash and flying sinews. The poor Vietnamese farmer was bowled over by the flying hindquarters. The shell passed right through the cow without exploding.

For a moment, Chet was paralyzed with disbelief at what he had just witnessed. He saw the gunner was laughing. The bloody farmer was standing over the carcass screaming and gesticulating wildly. Within seconds Marines came running up to the gun, but Chet was there first. He grabbed the young gunner by his shirt and started pummeling him with his fist. By the time he was pulled off, the gunner's face was a bright red pulp with missing teeth.

The Marines hauled both men away: the gunner to the aid station and Chet into custody.

The company gunnery sergeant started howling at Chet until the company commander appeared. Outside, the acrid smoke was starting to clear from the line of the four howitzers and a crowd that had gathered. A Navy corpsman attended the Vietnamese farmer. It turned out he was unhurt except for a few bruises inflicted by the impact of the cow's hindquarters. He was howling and crying hysterically as Chet was escorted away.

Chet sat silently as he was harangued for beating the shit out of a fellow Marine. When the rage was exhausted, the company commander said, his face so close to Chet's he could feel the impact of spittle on his cheek, "What do you have to say for yourself, Lance Corporal?"

Eyes fixed on a nail in the wall, Chet finally spoke, "That cow was that poor bastard's most valuable possession. A member of his family. And that little cocksucker blew it to pieces just for fun. All due respect, Sir, how would you react? We came here to liberate these people not ruin their lives."

Tirade spent, the Captain asked, "What do you think we should do about this, Marine?" "Buy that poor bastard a new cow."

After a brief silence, the Captain turned to the Gunny and said, "Get this mother-fucker out of my sight," and charged out of the room.

Chet bolted to attention ready to withstand the burgeoning, prolonged fury of his Gunnery Sergeant. Instead, he spoke softly.

"Get the fuck out of here. Have one of the swabbies look at your hand." It was only then Chet noticed his knuckles were bleeding.

Returning to the position, the cuts on his hand bandaged, Chet got the cold shoulder from the arty guys. Horace walked over and put his arm around Chet. "That was some shit, man. Way to go."

...

Two mornings later the artillery position was overrun by North Vietnamese regulars. Trying to fight a delaying effort, the artillery battery only managed to save two of their guns. It was a bloody, chaotic affair.

Two days of fierce fighting drove the Marines back into the city. They took heavy casualties, relinquishing territory inch by terrifying inch. The street fighting was fierce and chaotic. Chet's company was severely depleted and ordered to stop the advancing enemy against all hazards in an effort to halt the People's Army of Vietnam. They threw up a roadblock at an intersection and placed make-shift barricades while the supersonic crack of the bullets passed their heads.

Chet knew he would be dead within the hour. He raised his head high enough to see approaching NVA soldiers about fifty yards down the road. He mused this was how Custer's troopers must've felt. Chet then sprayed rounds down the street and ducked when an RPG streaked into the building across the street. Chet could feel the blast of heat and shower of dust and wood planks. The ensuing silence was profound. From the recently destroyed rubble of the building, Chet heard a baby crying.

Powered by something other than reason, Chet ran across the street into the smoking rubble. Bullets whizzing after him. A moment later he emerged with a baby under his arm and dashed toward the rear.

Horace lifted his head to take in the astonishing sight then immediately resumed firing.

An hour later, Chet returned. They had held their position and were about to pull back to a more defensible line closer to the center of the city.

"What did you do with the kid?"

"I took him back; we shoved a bayonet up his ass and roasted him on a spit. Those young ones are mighty tasty. Juicy, too. I got the drumstick."

"Jesus Christ." When Horace rose to fire again, he was greeted by a dull thud and fell over dead.

...

Finally, one day when he was on leave, Chet Junior asked, "Seriously, Dad. What's with that picture?"

"The baby's mother was killed by a mortar round," he explained. "The baby was still alive, and I took the baby back to the aid station where later we cooked him up," Chet said. "Mighty tasty." Seeing the horror on his son's face he added, "Only kidding. Just because I liked killing doesn't mean I lost *all* my humanity." He paused, resting his graying head back, "Some go back to where they were. Others not. Some never returned at all. But no one left unchanged."

It proved to be one of the most profound things his father ever said to him. It was all he would ever say about Vietnam or any other subject.

He eventually reached the point where they asked Chet to become a drill instructor where, they explained, he could use his meanness to noble purpose. But he declined and left the Marines as a sergeant.

Were it not for the bouncing point of light signaling the electrical activity of his heart, the slight rise and fall of his chest and the rhythmic hiss of the ventilator, Chet Junior might be looking at a dead man.

When Cummings came around, Chet followed him into the hall and asked him when they were going to try withholding sedation again. His expression turned grim and he responded, "He's not had any sedation for the past twenty-four hours."

"What does this mean? He's braindead?"

Cummings looked Chet in the eye. "I assume so. We won't know for sure until we do an

EEG and brain scan."

"What will that tell you?"

"If he has electrical activity in his brain and whether his brain is being perfused with blood." "When will you do these tests?"

"I'll give him another day or so. Then we'll decide. I'm not in any rush. I'd like to get a neurology consult first. His brain may just be stunned. These things happen sometimes when a major cardiovascular event occurs. The most important thing right now is letting him rest and stabilize. His kidneys are not working so well either. We may get by without hemodialysis, but we'll see. That decision will probably need to be made within the next twenty-four hours. That will be our next decision point."

"Decision about what?"

"Whether there's any hope of recovery."

"Have you had this discussion with my mother or my sister?"

"I have not broached any of this with your mother, but I did have a chat with your sister. She's up to speed on this."

Why didn't she talk to me about it? Chet wondered. *Where was the communication between brother and sister?* He resisted the reflex to be instantly pissed at her. As if explaining things to him in medical terms would involve words he was incapable of understanding.

"Thank you, Doctor."

"Sure. I'm around. The decision to withdraw life support for your father is still a way off."

The words struck him hard, like a hammer to his brain. The thought had been there but never formally as had just occurred. Cummings nodded, turned and walked away. Chet looked back into the cubicle where his mother sat beside the bed twirling his wedding ring and Benny stared blankly at his dad.

He desperately wanted to talk to his sister, but she had left to go to the Children's Hospital to start clinic hours not long after the cutting off ears comment.

Chet sat down and looked at his dad. His mind wandered through memories of his father coming home from work, grabbing a beer and putting on music as he lit a cigarette.

Chet Senior loved all kinds of music. From Mantovani and Johnny Mathis to James Taylor and The Beatles, although he shied away from the classics and opera. After several beers he would rest his head back and fall asleep, losing himself in rhythms only he could hear and dreams only he could see. At least he looked like he was asleep, even dreaming perhaps. Occasionally, Chet would see his father's foot tapping to the beat between snores.

Sometimes he would make Junior sit on the floor in front of him as he lectured his son on the value of a college education. "Study hard, go to college and make a lot of money so you don't turn out like me," he would say. Chet Senior was a child of a child of the Depression who didn't give a rat's ass about his son or his future. Chet Senior refused to make that mistake.

So, when Chet Junior came home Thanksgiving of his plebe year in his United States Naval Academy uniform, he thought his father would melt with pride. Junior recalled the expression on his father's face when he stepped through the door. It was the proudest moment in his father's life rivaled only by his daughter's subsequent graduation from medical school.

Yet when Chet graduated from the Naval Academy, he handed his father his greatest disappointment. His son chose not to be commissioned a second lieutenant of Marines and instead graduated an ensign and went off to flight school. Chet Senior never quite forgave his son even as he rose steadily in stature as a Naval officer and pilot.

Through his two successful children, he figured he more than made up for any transgressions he might have been a party to in his life.

Chapter Five
Day Four: Benny

Reynolds and his Fellow came into the cubicle. They greeted Mary and her children politely and he checked the pulses in Chet's feet and gently peeled off the dressings that ran down the center of his chest and the one covering his right groin. The nurse applied new dressings as Reynolds guided them into the hall.

"Mrs. Pettigrew, I believe your husband"—he turned to Junior and Rhiannon— "and father is doing quite well surgically. His heart is stable, and his kidneys are working better. I think the status of his brain, however, is in question. He should be awake by now and breathing on his own. He has failed every trial off the ventilator we have conducted. I have spoken to the intensivist and I know he shares these concerns." Reynolds looked back into the glassed cubicle at Benny who had found his way to the discussion, drawn to the stimulation of nearby voices.

"He could go on like this for an indeterminate period of time. I'm not saying he is in a permanent vegetative state, but it is something we will have to confront at some point. We'll talk again tomorrow. Any questions?"

Chet could see his sister's head shake almost imperceptibly. His mother held a tissue to her mouth. When Reynolds and his fellow walked away, Mary turned to Rhiannon and asked, "What does this all mean?

"His brain is fried," Chet said pre-empting his sister who turned to him with a look of fury.

Benny was a surprise. Chet Junior was thirteen and Rhiannon was two years behind him when Mary found out she was pregnant.

"Are you sure?" Chet Senior asked. "It's been so long, how would you know?" He thought she must be joking. She wasn't. "Maybe you just skipped a period. It's happened before."

"No," she said softly, "my breasts hurt."

"Maybe you bumped your tits doing the wash."

"Chet, I'm pretty sure I'm pregnant."

A flash of incredulity passed over Chet's face. "How could this happen?"

"Remember, Chet: your little swimmers find their way in the dark narrow tunnel looking for the target they know is up there somewhere. They can smell it right out of the starting gate.

They have this race to see who can get their first." She made a doggy-paddle gesture. Chet stared at his wife. Her sarcasm did not add to the discussion.

Rhiannon, of course, was thrilled. Chet Junior not so much. For the first several months of the pregnancy, Chet Senior waited for her tits to stop hurting signifying yet another miscarriage. She had been plagued with them in the past, losing more than she knew how to explain. Each one was a heartbreak. Chet would console his wife and the issue gradually went away. Each one was heralded by the sudden and inexplicable resolution of breast tenderness. She would cry, Chet would try to console her, and life went on. Chet secretly hoped that would be the case here. Their lives had arrived at a status quo that a new child surely would disrupt.

This time, though, Benny was a keeper. When she went into labor, Chet left work and raced home happy his driving skills prevented him from wrecking on the icy roads.

"Come on," Chet said cheerfully as he helped her to the car. He made sure she was buckled in and they left. Junior and Rhee were at school and they had planned for the kids to be picked up at the end of the school day by a neighbor. So, when school discharged and they saw Mrs. Johnson waiting for them, they knew their baby brother or sister was about to arrive. Rhee was thrilled. Junior not so much.

Chet drove with requisite caution. When they arrived at the entrance to the emergency room, Chet helped his wife, now clearly in pain, out of the car. She slipped on a patch of ice the size of a dollar bill and broke her fall with her right hand. She noted the pinky finger was slightly askew. Then, as she was righted and placed in a wheelchair by her husband and the nurse, she was attacked by another hard contraction and her water broke, flooding her seat and spilling out onto the macadam.

"Well, that settles that," she muttered as she was whisked away, and Chet left to park the car. In the few brief moments it took him to do so it started snowing. Mary lost all awareness of her bent finger.

As Chet tried to catch up to them all he heard was, "Jesus H. Christ, that one really hurt!" Chet smiled. Mary was in rare form.

In the labor room, Chet held her left hand, taking no notice of the angulation of her right.

It took less than two hours for her to deliver a howling baby boy. They had agreed to call him Benjamin after Mary's father. As she held the fresh baby boy in her arms, she failed to realize her finger had thankfully straightened itself. She was glad later. She didn't want to incur any more expense than that associated with her delivery. Unfortunately, it never flexed quite right again. But at least it was straight.

The next morning, the pediatrician delivered the news that Benjamin was a healthy, perfect, little man. Ten toes, ten fingers and of strong voice. "We even sharpened his pencil. Congratulations."

When they arrived home, they took Benny to the nursery. They purchased a new crib and chest of drawers, a rocking chair and a bassinette. Not figuring they were going to have any more children; they had donated their nursery furniture to the Goodwill a few years after Rhee was born. They settled into their role as parents of a newborn.

Mary detected the first hint of a problem when Benny turned three months. He didn't seem to recognize her when she entered his room. He did not emotionally engage. He did not smile when a smile was called for.

Each morning she was greeted by a blank stare. His eyes would not fix on hers, instead they seemed focused at middle distance. He would not look at her when she brought him up close to her face. Babies early on recognize their mothers; their eyes fix onto those of their mother. It is their first form of communication after crying. Her first thought was that perhaps his vision was bad. She made a little test to see if he would follow a light or blink if she held something abruptly to his face. She could make him startle. Maybe he needed glasses. She prayed he wasn't retarded.

Mary was conflicted about whose attention she should bring her concerns to first: Chet or the pediatrician.

"Here," she said. "Put down your beer and hold your son."

She dropped him suddenly onto Chet's lap and watched closely to see if Benny's reaction was different with his father. It was not.

Chet shook the boy gently saying, "How's my big little man?" Nothing.

"Look at his eyes, directly I mean." Chet did as requested.

"They look fine to me. You think he has pink eye of something?" Mary started crying.

Chet looked up at her. "What's wrong with *you*?"

Between sobs she said, "I think he needs glasses." As she spoke the words, she knew his problem could not be corrected with optical lenses.

"Calm down, woman. There's nothing wrong with our son."

"Okay. Okay." She lifted Benny from her husband's lap and walked away. She went to the kitchen and made an appointment with the pediatrician. She hoped her concerns were premature and the visit would settle the matter.

The next afternoon, Mary, with Benny in her arms, was led into the examination room.

"Good morning, Mary. What seems to be the problem?"

"I want you to check Benny out."

"What's the matter?"

"See if you can tell?"

It was an interesting challenge, but the doctor accepted it. He walked over to the baby and silently proceeded with his examination. He laid Benny on his back and felt his skull, rubbing his fingers easily over the soft spot and looked into his eyes. He opened his mouth and felt the neck.

Then kneaded the baby's abdomen.

He was a patient, caring doctor who had been with the family, attending Chet Junior and his sister since birth. He knew Mary to be a thoughtful and reliable mother. If there was something wrong here, he was not seeing it. Then he brought Benny's face close to his and looked into his eyes. The doctor's expression changed. He knew, and she knew he knew.

"I see your concerns. If there is a developmental issue with Benny it is still too early to tell."

She knew he was lying.

"I'll check him again at his six-month checkup and we'll see where he is."

At six months, it was obvious, even to Chet. Something was not right. Benny didn't coo, he never smiled. He displayed no satisfaction on sucking the milk from his bottle.

"Something is wrong with your son," he said.

"*Our son*!" she screamed with a fury he had never seen. "He won't talk, he won't even babble, for Christ's sake."

"You mean he's a God-damned retard?"

Mary took her son from his father and went to their bedroom, crying inconsolably.

After a while, he went to the bedroom to find his wife asleep beside their son. He picked up the boy, careful not to disturb his mother and took him to the living room where he sat the boy on his lap and started talking to him. In all respects, he seemed perfectly normal. *Maybe,* he thought, *the boy is slow, and he will catch up over time.*

It never happened. Chet could never grasp the biological coding error that had randomly and inexplicitly afflicted their son. Even when it was carefully explained to him, he refused to accept it. What little solace he took resided in the fact that 'tards don't reproduce and the genetic or developmental error would extinguish itself with him. That, whatever mistake had occurred in his seed, would not be passed on to another child. It did not assuage his guilt.

Acceptance was slow in coming. Oh sure, he would cry appropriately when he was hungry or had poop in his diaper, but he would never respond to his mother's voice to calm him down; he remained in his primitive state with each passing birthday. Benny never spoke. Ever.

Mary, both Chets, but especially Rhiannon, worked diligently in a vain, frustrating attempt to remedy whatever deficit that might have occurred inside Benny's mind. Autism was considered a new diagnosis and did not have the horrific ring to it that would become apparent to the world as time went on. Benny was just a little slow, behind on his developmental milestones. In fact, he met none of them. The density of his autism was almost paralyzing. It was an unspeakable tragedy when they finally came to grips with the eternal vacancy that existed inside Benny's skull. He would remain a perpetual infant even as he grew to be a man. It was *The Long Hello* of raising a densely autistic child.

...

The respiratory therapist adjusted the settings on the ventilator. Rhiannon remained snuggled into the chair, snoring softly. Benny sat on the couch, resting his head on his brother's shoulder, both sleeping soundly. All three of her children still and asleep.

...

It was a perfect summer day. Mary stood at the sink peeling potatoes when she saw out the kitchen window Chet guide Benny onto the little hill out back. He brought with him a beach ball, a soccer ball and a soft ball. Chet was going to teach his five-year-old son to catch.

Chet knelt down a few feet in front of Benny and she could see him explain the physical and mental process of catching something tossed at him. First, he demonstrated the principle of gravity by dropping the three balls in succession, repeating each demonstration several times as Benny watched. She admired Chet's patience. Finally, he handed the beach ball to his son who held it momentarily and let it drop. Chet looked pleased.

Chet moved away from his son and tossed the beach ball at him. The ball fell off his chest with no effort to catch it. Chet took the ball and threw it again with the same result. Benny didn't even react to the impact. He repeated the maneuver over and over, each time hoping his son would grasp the concept. Mary could see Chet's frustration mount with each toss until finally he threw the ball violently against Benny's chest, rebounding it into the yard.

Benny stood perfectly still, arms at his side and cried. Chet sat back on his haunches, grabbed his son and hugged him tightly against his chest. Chet started crying. Mary wanted to run out and comfort them both but resisted. Chet and his son were close from that day forward. Mary could not decide if she had witnessed defeat or acceptance.

...

It was a perfect storm: the contact of living flesh and kinetic energy.

"Christ!" Chet yelled the contact with the doe was instantaneously violent. The hood buckled with the sound of or metal impacting living flesh. He pulled the car over instantly to make sure it was a deer and not something else. He looked at the front of the car. The hood was slightly buckled, the grill was caved in and the left headlight was out. But there was no hiss of steam, so the radiator was intact. He could drive it home. He noticed a smear of red blood and patches of fur on the metalwork.

He went back to check on the animal. It was a doe that lay on the road. Her legs were twitching as if she was still running. Frothy blood bubbled from her nose and mouth. She was wide-eyed trying to process in her primitive brain what had just happened to her. He was sure by the angle she was laying that her back was broken.

"I'm so sorry," he whispered. He stood and pulled the deer to the gravel shoulder. She struggled at first but relented. He stroked its head. The doe swallowed twice, seemed to look around and died.

Mary was already asleep in bed when he got home. Before he climbed into bed beside, he visited his son, stroked Benny's head, kissed it and went to bed.

Chapter Six
Day Five: Fire and Rain

Mary stared at her husband. She twirled his wedding band around his finger. It was loose and twisted easily in one rotation after the other. It hadn't left his hand since the day she slipped it on his finger. He had once told her about men getting their wedding bands caught on machinery at the mill, resulting in the flesh being ripped off the bone. When he told her this, she insisted he not wear it to work but he refused her request. He lost weight as he aged, and she once suggested he have it tightened up. He refused.

"You losing weight, she asked.

"Not really," he said. "Why do you ask?"

"Your face looks thinner."

"I weigh the same, woman. It's just been redistributed. He tugged at his belt, which she noticed, had been let out a notch or two. Belts, she knew, acquired memory.

...

She woke up, facing her husband. "What are you staring at?" she asked him.

"I wake up every morning thanking God it is you. And every night before I go to sleep, I say a prayer that I will wake up beside you and not roasting in Hell."

"You don't believe in God." It was a statement not a comment. She clearly knew the answer.

"He gave me you, didn't He? That's proof enough. When I die, I want you to know my last conscious thought will be of you."

She propped herself on her elbow. "Now what brought that up?"

Inconsiderate of the evolving moment, Baby Chet started crying and she tossed off the covers and pulled on her housecoat.

"You're really something, you know that?" she said as she padded out of the bedroom. #

"Mom," Rhee asked, "why are you smiling? Something funny?"

"Something your father did."

"Care to share?"

"He loved that car. Broke his heart to get rid of it."

...

"Here to buy a car, Marine?"

"Yes, Sir." *Christ, you idiot. Why else would I be wandering around a used car lot on a dark, cold January morning?*

"We got some mighty nice used cars here. Low mileage. Great shape. Most of 'em single owners who traded 'em in for something new."

The salesman's New England brogue made his word almost unintelligible.

"Sergeant, I see. Got lots o' ribbons there. Been to Vietnam?"

"Just left. For the third time."

"Gee. I see you got a slight gimp. Wounded?"

"How much for the Mustang?"

"That one over there?"

"Yeah"—*you twit*— "the one right there."

Chet pointed to a Mustang fastback, a metallic aquamarine color. It was pushed back against the cyclone fence that ran the perimeter of the lot.

"Oh, that one." He took steps toward the car. "Yes Sir. That's a nice car. Two-eighty-nine V-8. Four speed stick. Only two barrels but that could be remedied easy enough. She's a honey. Not sure why the guy who owned it got rid of her. Nineteen sixty-four and a half. One of the first fastbacks off the production line. Not quite a '64, not yet a '65. I ran the VIN. Sure enough, she's a classic."

"How much you want for her?"

"If it's power you want, I got a nice GTO over there."

Chet turned to look. "Naw. Like the man said, 'That's jack-off. This one is pure pussy.'"

"Well, then. I'll sell her to you for two thousand dollars."

"She needs a little work. Fifteen hundred cash."

The salesman extended his hand. "In that case, the pussy is all yours." Chet shook the hand. "Let's go write it up."

The salesman was mildly surprised when Chet peeled of fifteen one-hundred-dollar bills from a large wad he pulled from his pocket.

"Where you stationed?"

"Lejeune."

"Where's that?"

"South Carolina."

"What brings you up here to Massachusetts?"

"I'm getting out and a friend told me about a job in the mill near here."

"I didn't know they were hiring."

Chet finished the paperwork, got into the car and drove off the lot ruing the fact that he only had a quarter of a tank. The bastard should have at least had the tank filled before selling it, but he was so excited about his purchase he chose not to argue the point.

As he drove the car off the lot, he thought of Bucky. Poor Bucky. Probably still in jail for something. Amazing, he thought, how sometimes things in life come full circle. Chet had come to realize that poor people, white or black, faced a different system of justice in rural communities. Would a rich white kid be offered an opportunity to make amends for some delinquency by forced conscription into the Marines with Vietnam his certain, final destination? He thought not. #

The next day, Chet finished furnishing his small apartment in the town of West Concord.

Everything he purchased he bought new. The only hand-me-down, he liked to say, was that car. He hung a shadow box filed with his medals which included two Purple Hearts, a Bronze Star and the Navy/Marine Distinguished Service Medal among others. Medals for exceptional marksmanship. And the Navy Cross. His wretched, old father would be proud.

Chet's father routinely beat the shit out of him until he became a teenager and was in a position to strike back. Induction into the Marines was a Godsend. He had very little communication with the man when he went off to boot camp. In his entire first tour in country he only received two pieces of mail from home. One wishing him a Merry Christmas, the other a request for cash.

He had no idea about the status of his mother. She walked out on the marriage not long

after Chet was born. She couldn't take the abuse anymore. He had no clue where she was or even if she was still alive. He had no desire to find out.

One morning, several months after settling into his new life and a burgeoning relationship, the phone rang. It was only the fourth or fifth time it had rung since moving in.

"This is Greenfield's Nursing Home. Are you Chester Pettigrew?"

"Yes. What is this about?"

"I'm sorry to inform you that your father passed away two days ago. It took us two days to find you and provide notification."

"Are you sure he's dead?"

After a moment's silence, the voice said, "I beg your pardon?"

"Okay, what do you want me to do?"

"He gave us directions to have him laid out at Klassen's Funereal Home then buried at Eternal Solace Cemetery."

"Okay."

"We need you to sign some papers. You were named Power of Attorney. You have to

dispose of his estate."

"He had an estate?"

"A little bit of money but, not much else. A few personal artifacts."

"Get what you can for what he has left and give the rest of it away. Why don't you just go ahead and cremate him and scatter the ashes in some field?"

"Those were not his wishes."

"I see. Okay, I'll leave tonight. I can be there by tomorrow afternoon. Do whatever you need to do in the meantime."

"Very well. We will see you then."

Chet hung up the phone. Transiently saddened but also greatly annoyed.

...

"I never told you this," Mary did not take her eyes of her husband as she continued to twirl the wedding ring. "He hated his father."

"I didn't know we had a grandfather," Chet said.

"You kick a dog enough times and he either dies or becomes mean. Your father vowed he would never lay a hand on his children. If he ever lost control and struck one of you kids, I had his permission to instantly kill him and make it look like an accident. If you needed a spanking, I was the one who had to do it."

"That explains a lot," Chet responded with a whiff of sarcasm.

She stared silently at the plastic goggles over her husband's eyes, protecting his corneas from being scratched. She smiled. She often thought their courtship and love affair could be made into a movie that would rival *Love Story* without the tragedy.

...

Mary sat in a booth at Cole's Diner finishing breakfast. It was a ritual every Sunday after Mass. She looked above the rim of the paperback she was reading as a man came in and took a seat at the counter. He was dressed in a tee shirt, khakis and work boots. She noted his muscular arms and flat belly. She had never seen him before. She figured he worked at the mill. He turned to look out the front window as a noisy motorcycle passed on the road outside. Their eyes met. He smiled, and she smiled back then quickly returned her eyes to the book. From that point on she looked at the words without reading any of them.

When he finished his coffee, he turned to look at her again. When their eyes met a second time, she felt herself blush. She wondered if he noticed. She picked out one word on the page and locked her eyes on it. When she looked up after a few moments, he was standing above her. "Hello," the man said. "What's your name?"

"Mary. Mary Kellogg."

"Huh. Like the cornflakes."

"Yeah. Like the cornflakes."

Chet reached across the table saying, "My name is Chet. Chester Pettigrew."

She shook his hand as demurely as her excitement would allow. She thought he was the finest looking man she had ever seen strong, rugged and handsome like the hero in a romance novel.

"I couldn't help notice that we noticed each other. You come here often?" he asked.

"Every Sunday after church."

"I work at the mill."

"Lumber?"

"Toilet paper."

"Oh, that mill."

"Yes. You work around here?"

"I do copyediting for a Boston publisher."

"Oh, yeah? That's cool. What's a copyeditor?"

She smiled. "I check for spelling errors, punctuation mistakes. That sort of thing." "Huh. Sounds interesting."

"Is that your Mustang out front?"

"Yep."

"Short haircut. Did you just get out of service?"

"Yes. Marines."

"Vietnam?"

"Yeah. Spent some time there. May I join you?"

"As you wish." She closed Goldman's *The Princess Bride* as Chet motioned to the waitress to bring him another coffee. He asked if he could get Mary something. She declined his offer.

Chet studied her. She was beautiful, her features perfectly proportioned almost delicate. Her hair was long and blond, framing her face. Staring at her across the table, she repeatedly pulled her hair back off her shoulders only to have it fall back as she spoke.

They continued chatting about unimportant stuff when Chet asked, "Listen, would you like to go to a movie sometime or get dinner?"

"I've known you for all of what? Twenty minutes? How do I know you're not some serial rapist or mugger?"

"Oh no. That comes later."

She smiled. "Well, I guess we can try a movie sometime."

After half an hour of dry, pointless conversation, they parted. Before doing so, she handed him the slip of paper with her number on it.

Through the window she watched him climb into his Mustang. He waved at her through the windshield as he backed up and peeled away. She wondered if he would call. She hoped so. He seemed like a decent guy. Recent experience suggested such men were few and becoming increasingly hard to find.

After the first week with no phone call, she gave up hoping. Two Sundays passed and no Mustang. Next Sunday she would try some other diner. Maybe someone equally charming who filled a white tee shirt just so might drop by. It was a sarcastic thought. She pushed him out of her short-term memory.

So, the phone call was a surprise. More like a shock to the system. He apologized for his failure to call citing shift work, a bad cold and some other excuse she took to be bullshit.

"Would you still like to go to the movies?"

"I guess but if this is your way of being aloof or hard to get, it's not working."

"*Jaws*. You seen it yet?" "No, but I read the book."

"I didn't know there was a book."

"Read it."

"So, you know how it ends?"

"Yes."

"And who eats who?"

"I do." She wanted to say 'who eats whom' but decided against it.

"That's too bad. I'm out of surprises."

"Well, maybe the movie doesn't completely follow the book," she said. "I'd still like to see it."

"Okay, I'll pick you up Saturday at seven. We can grab a bite afterward."

"Sounds good. See you then." She detected a hint of excitement in his voice. Maybe anticipation. Maybe both.

The phone clicked in her ear.

Ten silent minutes later the phone rang again.

"Say, where do you live?"

...

The date was a huge success. Chet was charming. He even presented her with a long-stemmed rose. The ride in the Mustang was thrilling, made more so by the wet roads.

When the shark launched itself at Brody's chum, she flinched and grabbed Chet's hand. He held it in his rough, workman's hand until the credits finished.

She was fascinated by the aggressive approach Chet took with his burger. Two bites and half of it was gone. He'd already drained two beers by the time it arrived on the table. He dumped enough ketchup on his fries to make her think they were just a convenient vehicle to deliver the condiment into his mouth. He wasn't sloppy just enthusiastic. She found him mysterious and strangely irresistible. *Perhaps,* she thought, *his lack of refinement added to his appeal.* He was a work in progress.

"Can I ask you what you did in the Marines?"

"Sure." "And?"

"I was a rifleman. Every Marine is a rifleman. It was either jail or go into the Marines."

"What?"

"My buddy had me go joyriding in a stolen car. He went to jail. I was given the choice of jail for six months or the Marines. Jail would have been easier."

"How so?"

"Ever hear of Parris Island?"

"No. Must say I have not."

"It's where men are men and boys are scared. Some of the mosquitos in South Carolina are big as dragon flies."

He took a swig of beer and continued, talking as he chewed.

"You need to swallow. All that beef and bread makes you unintelligible."

'Huh?" He wiped the ketchup from the corner of his mouth and made an exaggerated swallow. "Oh, yeah. I don't know why I eat like that. Bad habit I picked up in-country."

"Which country?" "South East Asia."

He needs a lot of work, she thought.

"Can you talk about Vietnam?"

"Sure. I'll answer anything you want to know. Why do you ask?" "Well, it seems like some of you guys don't want to talk about it."

"I know some guys were—what's the word—traumatized by the experience but I was just over there doing what my country asked me to do. Ask away. Then you have to tell me about copyeditin'"

"Deal." "I went over as soon as I got out of Infantry School. I was a private. By the time I was done with my first tour I was a lance corporal. I was wounded during Tet in '68. By the end of the second tour I was a sergeant. They wanted me to become a D.I. but I said no. I had enough."

"What's a D.I.?"

"Drill instructor for Marine recruits at MCRD. Nasty business." "For the D.I.s?"

"The recruits."

"How badly were you hurt?"

"Which time?"

"There was more than one?"

"Yeah, I got clipped three times."

She reached across the table and wiped a dollop of ketchup from his finger, putting it onto her tongue. The gesture instantly stopped the conversation, making him look into her eyes.

"You must have been lucky."

He continued his fixation on her eyes without saying a word. With the ketchup gone, she took his hand and held it firmly.

His next thought was how he was going to finish his burger.

In a subdued voice he said, barely above a whisper, "I figure God was not done with me."

She also whispered, "Did you kill anybody?"

"That's a question you should never ask a man." He could see the regret of the question on her face. "It was nasty business."

After a protracted silence, she bowed her head. "Copyediting can be fun." He saw the tear run down her cheek.

Good, Chet thought. *She gets it.*

She knew he was proud to be a Marine. She knew he had done all that was asked of him.

She never spoke of it again.

They went out a couple more times, then silence.

It annoyed her greatly when days or then almost a week went by without getting together or a call or even a postcard. She figured he was not as enamored with her as she was of him. She hoped it was because he was busy at work or otherwise distracted. She called him on two occasions and there was no answer. She tried not to be disappointed, but it was unavoidable.

...

Her heart started pounding in her chest when she heard his voice at the other end of the phone Saturday afternoon.

"Hi."

She wanted to launch onto a tirade about his absence from her life but played coy. "Oh," she said diffidently. "Hello." Whatever excuse he was about to offer, if he offered one at all, would be summarily rejected. Just who did he think he was?

"Sorry. I had to go out of town to bury my father. It was short notice."

"Oh, I'm so sorry, Chet. Was it sudden? You never spoke of him before."

"Well, I haven't talked to the bastard in years. Don't know what killed him. Probably meanness. I had to make arrangements to bury him. He had just enough life insurance to put him in a cheap coffin and drop in a hole. Sorry I didn't get a chance to call you. I had to drive to Virginia in the middle of the night."

"So, I take it you were not close."

"Hardly. I didn't even know he was still alive."

"Gee, Chet. I'm sorry."

"Don't be. The planet is a better place without him." She didn't know what to say.

"Can I see you again?" he asked

"As you wish."

"You busy tonight?"

"No. You?"

"Can I treat you to dinner?"

Her heart swelled. "Let me check my calendar. Why, yes. I believe I am free."

"Pick you up at six?"

"That will do nicely."

"'Kay." He hung up.

He took her to a place dark and cozy. They sat near the lit fireplace which, for May, was a bit uncalled for. It was a warm and humid night even by Central Massachusetts' standards.

All Mary wanted to talk about was the dark relationship Chet had with his father. She wanted her sympathies known. He would not have any of it and cut her short.

Her heart went out to Chet, but he rejected politely any discussion of his father. He alluded to the abusive relationship he had with the man and barely mentioned his mother's middle-of-the- night escape.

Before dessert, he cut off any further discussion. After a prolonged silence he reached across the candle-lit table and took her hand.

"Marry me."

Had a comet crashed through the ceiling, she could not have been more taken aback.

She stared at him, seeking his expression in the candlelight to ascertain if he was either drunk or kidding. Maybe both.

"Can I sleep on it?"

"Sure."

After the proposal any meaningful conversation ended.

"Go for a ride?"

"Sure."

He paid for dinner, climbed into the Mustang and they drove into the humid, starless night. She did not know where he was going and didn't care to ask.

Chet was surprised at how much he was in love with her, and how quickly it had overtaken him. Or, perhaps, how desperate his father's demise had made him. He had no one left. He did not know he possessed such an emotion. Lust was one thing. It arrived easily and without investment. Love, adoration and tenderness were quite another. He was on uncharted waters. He was still a relative stranger to this woman. He wondered if she felt the same way, drifting into the same uncharted waters with an uncertain outcome.

Chet drove off the main road up a long hill and parked the Mustang in a small clearing. He shut off the engine, keeping the radio on. He leaned over, took her face in his hands and kissed her. It was a gentle, almost beseeching kiss. She kissed him back, suddenly compelled to inject released passion into the force of her lips on his.

He abruptly pulled away and opened his door. He pulled the seat forward and dropped the back deck over the seat forming a flat place where they could lie down. It was a tight space and when she laid on her back, she could see a few scattered stars through the hatchback glass. He held her in his arms as he climbed clumsily in beside her. He banged his head against the glass roof. To stretch out completely they had to put their legs on the folded front seats.

He removed his shirt. In the dim light of the dashboard she could see the deep scar on his right shoulder. She touched the cratered of skin. She reached around and touched the corresponding scar on his back. She understood trajectory. She ran her fingertips lightly over the blanched skin as if touching it might sear her fingers.

"What happened here?"

"Bug bite."

"That must have been some bug."

"The bugs are big in Southeast Asia."

She leaned up and placed her lips lightly onto the scar placing her tongue into the depression.

In the confined space of the backseat of the Mustang they finished undressing. Were it not so desperate and awkward it might have been amusing. But it was fueled by accumulated, pent-up passion. Their groping and effort were punctuated by a flash of lightning. He could feel her arms tighten around his neck and he found his reward. Then another flash.

"Let It Be" came onto the radio. She held him tight as he found his stroke.

After the climax, it started pouring. He spoke softly, "You don't need to tell, and I don't need to ask. You came." "No. I was liberated."

Still breathing heavily, he whispered, "I never had a best friend until you came along. I'm not counting Bucky. He turned out to be a dick. All he did was cause me trouble."

"Without him, you wouldn't be here. *We* wouldn't be here. I will never cause you trouble," she whispered. She folded her arms around his neck. He shifted his weight off her as another bolt of lightning lit the interior of the car. She looked past him at the steamed back window and giggled. The downpour beat on the roof in a steady rumble.

"Yes," she said.

"Yes, what?"

"I will marry you."

After staring into her eyes for a moment, he kissed her again.

She marveled at how much love and passion could fit into the turned down backseat of a '65 Mustang Fastback lit only by the glow of the dashboard radio and the intermittent bolt of lightning. She held him tightly as James Taylor sang "Fire and Rain."

...

"Gosh, he loved that car. Broke his heart to get rid of it."

"Why did he?" Chet asked.

"You."

Rhiannon, curled into a ball in the lounge chair in the corner, lifted her head and asked,

"What car?"

Chet covered her with a blanket then sat beside Benny on the small couch and fell asleep as well. Benny rested his head on Chet's shoulder and dozed off. Chet put his arm around his brother and drew him closer.

Mary looked at her daughter and remembered something Chet said when Rhee was eighteen. "I saw our daughter completely naked this morning. It was an accident and she didn't see me. I lingered for a few moments admiring her. She is a beautiful woman. You did well with your uterus." "*We* did well. She's a fine, bright young lady. You should be proud."

Mary got up, walked over to her daughter and kissed the crown of her head. Rhiannon barely stirred.

"Can he hear us?" Rhiannon whispered.

"I'll bet he's heard every word."

Mary curled up in the chair and looked over at Benny then at her husband. Random thoughts entered her head. Chet Senior always thought Halloween was a trumped-up holiday foisted by confectioners and costume makers. His own father never let him out to sample the tradition. So, when Mary and the kids went out trick or treating, he thought it was a waste of time and money. Some sort of commercialized pagan ritual. While Mary had Junior and Rhee out to trick or treat, he would stay home with his son, sit on the porch and dole out candy with a contemptuous sneer. Benny sat beside him oblivious to what was transpiring nonetheless watching each child as they accepted some candy then watch them as they walked away. If he understood what was transpiring, he never let on.

Then one Halloween, Junior and his sister felt they had grown out of Halloween. Whether it was concern about caloric intake, a silly excuse to beg for something was never clear. That didn't stop neighborhood kids from coming around, ringing the doorbell and receiving, by way of veiled threat of arson or hurled eggs, their bounty. Yet Benny, with his seemingly narrow scope of things, always seemed excited, or what passed for excitement, when the fake pumpkins came out and the Snickers and Baby Ruths were poured into the plastic pumpkins on the front porch.

Inexplicably as the day arrived, Chet ran around the house clearly distracted and determined. She initially thought this might be the year Chet would booby-trap the candy, set up a Claymore mine or simply darken the house and refuse to answer the doorbell. He did not let on what he was doing, and Mary did not want to ask. When he requested a wire coat hanger and aluminum foil, the mystery deepened. The request for a pillowcase only deepened the mystery. When he asked for an early supper, she was convinced he was up to something. Some sort of counterinsurgency.

She became distracted cleaning up after dinner. Chet, she assumed, grabbed a beer and went into the living room. When she finished she went to join him. She was only mildly surprised he was not there.

Perhaps, she thought, he was in the basement doing whatever he did down there.

A short time later, Chet walked into the living room dressed like a farmer in bib overalls and plaid shirt. His face darkened with burnt cork to make him look like an old bum. He was holding Benny's hand.

Benny was ensheathed in a white pillowcase with the end cut open for his head and the sides slit for his arms. Perched on Benny's head was a coat hanger bent into the configuration of an angel's halo. It was wrapped by shiny aluminum foil.

"Mind the door, woman. We're going out."

Before she could release herself from the grip of astonishment, they disappeared into the evening.

Mary sat on the porch rocking chair. She had witnessed something quite surreal. She handed out excessive amounts of candy but kept her eye out for the boys. They were gone for a long time.

After the Trick-or-Treaters tapered off, she stayed on the porch. She saw them approach. Chet and his son emerged from the darkness. Benny carried a bag filled with a significant bounty in one hand and his father's hand with the other.

They greeted Mary on the porch, and she leaned over and looked into the bag of loot.

"Nice haul," Chet said.

Mary hugged Benny with all her might. Tears fell onto the pillowcase.

Chapter Seven
Day Six: Mugs

When Mary woke up, Benny was still lying close to his sister sleeping soundly. She snuggled next to him, covered with the same blanket. Chet was gone. He must have slipped out sometime before the nurses made their six-thirty rounds. They were in and out so quietly she hadn't noticed. Were it not for the fact there was a new bag connected to a thin tube depositing white fluid into Chet's stomach, she wouldn't have had any awareness of their visit.

Mary was glad to see Nurse Amy had returned from a day off. She and Chet Junior had spent a lot of time chatting with each other. Small talk mostly. Decorum prevented them from deeper conversation, she suspected, but it was clear Amy had taken a shine to her son. When Junior wasn't around, Amy would ask after him.

Doctor Cummings had been by last evening to tell Mary they were going to do an electroencephalogram, whatever that was, to see if there was any electrical activity in her husband's brain. After that they were going to do a perfusion test to see how much blood was getting into Chet's brain. He and a neurologist, whose short Russian-sounding name she could never remember, had gently broached the subject of Senior's failure to wake up. She was convinced they were being subtle by using big words and couching them in sympathetic tones. All she remembered was the not so subtle implication her husband was never going to recover.

When she first heard that, she was shocked. But they knew vastly more about hearts and brains and kidneys than she ever would and when they broke it down in words, she understood their conclusions seemed obvious. She was tormented by how she was going to break the news to her children. She would wait until the test results came in then have a serious conversation with her three children about their father's future.

Yet, looking at Rhee and Benny she knew it would be a hard conversation. Braindead. Even the words were difficult to say.

Mary often thought the reason Rhee chose pediatrics was because of her younger brother. She was particularly attentive toward him and tried to teach him things although she was never sure how much of what she told him was retained or even registered in his brain.

Rhee spent hours trying to teach Benny how to tie his sneakers. Every session she was closer and closer to pulling it off. Feat of the Feet, she called it. Finally, after patient, indulgent hours he did it. He managed to tie his shoes.

When her father came home that evening, she told him that she and her brother had something special they wanted to show him. He had acquired a new skill. They made Chet sit down in his chair while Benny tied his shoes. When Benny stood up to walk, he tripped and fell ending up with an egg on his forehead. It was only then they realized he had tied the shoelaces of both shoes together.

Chet stood up and headed for a beer. "Maybe you ought to get him a pair of loafers," was all he had said.

Rhee stirred, looked at her watch and said she needed to go to her apartment, shower, dress and go to Grand Rounds at Children's. She would be back later that afternoon and hopefully by then they would have Chet Senior's results.

...

"Where's he off to?" was all he said.

Mary turned quickly; she already knew who it was.

"He's off getting a brain scan."

"You think they'll be surprised when they find he doesn't have one?"

"Oh, Charlie!"

Mary left her chair and ran to the large African American standing, hat in hand, at the door of the cubicle. She threw her arms around his bulk and held him tightly. His arms encircled her as he said, "Oh Mary, I am so sorry to hear about Chet. I only heard about it last night when I had dinner with Skorskie."

Charlie was tall and hefty like the linebacker he once was. But those days were long gone. While he retained his bulk, some of it had drifted down to his waistline. His dark, bald head was shiny in the light, the gray hair circling his head like a crown of Roman leaves.

Whatever it was, I suspected he'd be home sipping beer by now," Charlie said. "I wish." She left his embrace and they stepped into the cubicle.

"Hiya, Benny."

Benny, of course, turned his head to the source of his name but did not emote.

Mary directed Charlie to the couch. "So, what happened to the Old Man? Skorskie said he had an emergency operation."

"He had a torn aorta and he had to have open heart surgery. How that happened I don't know. I'm still not sure what all this means. Rhee understands but it's lost on me."

"He tore his aorta? How did he do that?"

"They said it is caused by hardening of the arteries and high blood pressure. But it was under control. He was moving furniture and he still smokes. When I found him, he was on the floor, I thought he was already dead. But the EMTs took good care of him and he ended up here. They operated on him right away. He seems to be stable from the operation, but the bad news is he may have brain damage. That's why he's not here. He's off having a brain scan. They seem to think he might have brain damage form the tear. He hasn't woken up yet."

Charlie took it all in. "I'm so sorry, Mary. Is there anything I can do?" He paused. "Where's

Chet? He still on his carrier?"

"No, he flew back right away. He's off doing something, and Rhee had to go to the Children's Hospital."

"Can I get you a coffee or something?"

"No, thanks. I'm good."

"Something for Benny?"

"No, Charlie. Thank you but we had breakfast a little while ago."

After a prolonged, pregnant pause, they wheeled Chet back into the cubicle. It took a few minutes while they reconnected him to the machines. Mary stood and asked the nurse what the scan showed.

She said the doctor would be by in a little while to go over the results.

Mary knew the nurse was very likely aware of the results but could not reveal them mainly because she was in no position to explain the implications. She returned to her seat beside Benny and looked at her husband, his chest rising up and down to the monotonous rhythm of the ventilator.

She looked at Charlie. He looked perplexed. Perhaps he was contemplating his own mortality.

"Let me tell you a Chet Story," she said and glanced briefly at her husband. "Many years ago, Chet came home all excited that he had been selected to help start up a new product line at the mill. I don't even remember what it was. Some plastic wrap or something." "Yes, I remember."

"You were named as the director of the second shift and he of the first."

Charlie nodded. "Yeah. They wanted to get the kinks out of it before hiring a third shift." He smiled at the reminiscence.

"Surely, you must know Chet, growing up in rural Virginia, was not particularly enamored with black people. And spending all that time with you, a black man, was, well, intimidating." Charlie gave a nod.

"His father was as bigoted as you get. And back in those days apples tended not to fall far from the tree."

"Coconuts, either."

"Yes. So, he was, shall we say, anxious at the up-coming interaction. Call it trepidation." "Yeah, good word."

"He didn't want his racism to get the better of him, so he bought a pair of green ceramic coffee mugs you two could use at the office. Since he hated to drink out of Styrofoam or paper cups. He thought it would somehow be awkward."

By now she had his full attention. "I remember those mugs. They suddenly appeared one day not long after we started."

"Anyway, he took some masking tape and wrote 'Chet' on one and 'Charlie' on the other. I was livid. So, I told him, 'Chet dear, black people know you don't like them, why advertise it? Hot and parched out in the boonies and a Negro hands you his canteen are you really gonna be concerned with whose lips last touched it or the cold water inside it?'

"'Not the same,' Chet said.

'It's *exactly* the same.' I washed the mugs, tape still on them mind you, and we went to bed.

"The next morning when I went to make his coffee, the tapes had been removed from the mugs."

"Huh."

"He grew quite fond of you."

"And I him."

"Any word?" Junior asked. "Hey, hi Mr. Simpson." Chet extended his hand, but Simpson slapped it away.

"Gimme a hug, you peckerwood." Chet embraced Simpson tightly.

"Wow, Charlie. I haven't seen you in years. How've you been?"

"Boy let me look at you. Last time I spoke to your father he told me you were the executive officer of a fighter squadron."

"I own it now. I got promoted."

"Damn, boy. The old fart must be proud."

"Yep. Although he still thinks I'd've been better off as a Marine."

"No, Son. You done well for you'se'f. You don't need to explain you'se'f to anyone." Their conversation was interrupted by the neurologist with the Russian name.

"Good afternoon, Mrs. Pettigrew." He nodded to Junior, "Mr. Pettigrew." He looked at Simpson and smiled then returned his gaze to Mary. "I'd like to give you the report on your husband's brain perfusion scan and the most recent EEG." Charlie excused himself and left the cubicle.

"Yes, Doctor. What do you have to tell us?" she asked.

"I'm afraid it is as I suspected based on repeated neurological assessments that your husband and your father has almost no electrical activity in his brain."

"Almost. That means some," Chet asked. "Even if it's not much. So technically he's not truly braindead."

"You are a very bright man, Mr. Pettigrew so I don't want to parse words with you. His scan shows minimal flow to the brain stem and cerebellum. Not enough to give him any cognitive

function or even allow his breathing center to let him get off the ventilator. I'm sorry."

"No hope?" Mary asked softly, perhaps not wanting Benny to hear.

"No hope."

Chet stiffened, "No hope?"

"'Fraid not."

"Can we get a second opinion?"

"Of course. I can make several recommendations. But I expect the opinions will be the same." He paused. "Are there any questions?"

Chet's brain was flooded with them. A virtual tsunami inside his skull. He needed to talk to Rhee. Where the hell was she?

"How long can he go on like this?" Mary whispered to prevent Benny from hearing. "Until he develops a complication that we cannot or might not want to treat. An infection. Usually a pneumonia from the ventilator or some other organ failure. He is being kept alive by purely artificial means. But ultimately the outcome will be the same."

He looked directly at Junior. "I've been involved in many cases like this in the past. I know you want to roll back the clock so you can say something to him and perhaps unsay others, but it will not change things." He paused. "I've spoken with Dr. Cummings and Dr. Reynolds. They understand the situation. Both recommended removing life support."

Why the hell didn't they come down here and tell us this themselves? Chet thought stiffly.

The neurologist bowed slightly, gave a wan smile and said, "If you'll excuse me. Have the nurses reach out to me if you have any further questions."

Chet hugged his mother as she began a muffled sob into his sweatshirt, a 'thank you.' "We need to talk to Rhee. She'll know what to do," Chet said as he held his mother. "I'll call her." He looked over his mother's shoulder at Benny who sat motionless, staring at his father. Only his father's head and face were visible outside the layer of blankets and Bear-Hugger heating blanket.

"We can't just let him die by pulling a plug out of the wall." "We need to talk to Rhee, Mother. Maybe she can offer us some enlightenment."

Chapter Eight
Words from Old Friends

Amy came into the cubicle and said, "Good afternoon. Shift change. How's Mr. Pettigrew this afternoon?"

"Apparently, dying," Junior said.

She stopped in her tracks and turned to him. "Yes, I heard in report. I'm so sorry. I know how close you all are. If you have any questions, I'd be glad to answer them as best I can or at least track down the answer." Her eyes were on Junior's as the words left her mouth.

"Thank you. This is a bit overwhelming to say the least. I'm sure you've seen this situation many times before."

"Sadly," she said. "I have. We could talk about it later if you'd like."

"That would be nice." Chet decided no decisions would be made until he had a chance to talk to the cute nurse in the pink scrubs.

"I'll swing by at the end of the shift."

"Thanks."

Rounds completed, she walked out of the cubicle. She suddenly turned. "Oh wait, here is some mail addressed to Mrs. Pettigrew." She pulled out the envelope. Likely a 'get well' card.

"Thank you." Their fingers touched briefly as Chet took the letter.

"It arrived at the Nurse's Station a little while ago." He handed the card to his mother.

Earlier Chet had received an email. It was from his boss.

> "Hi, Chet. I received your email two days ago and thought I'd get a quick note to you. From what you said, I know things are not going well with your dad. I extend the best wishes of all the Air

Wing. We hope he gets better soon and returns to his evil ways. He's a tough old coot and I know he will get through this. Take as much time as you need. The guys in the Squadron all send their best wishes.

Speaking of Squadrons, they all qualified without incident. Even that twit Zipper. Griswold"—he was referring to Clark the Squadron's exec— "has held the Squadron together well in your absence. You should include that in his next fitness. We are back at Norfolk, post-refit shakedown completed. We received orders to head to the Med at the end of the month. Hurry back but take your time. Get the Old Man well again. CAG."

"Oh, Chet. Look." Junior was not sure which Chet she was addressing. He saw she was talking to his father. "You got a card from Rosemary." She held it up as if her comatose husband could glance over and appreciate it. Junior was convinced she had no clear understanding of the predicament they were facing. As if the sound of her voice might magically reverse the whole dreadful situation. Sad. Pathetic. Rhee would set her straight.

...

There was a little breakroom off the floor in the main part of the mill. It had the usual snack, soda, coffee and sandwich dispensers against the back wall and a large table in the center, a large fluorescent light hung from the ceiling, making the room look harsh instead of an inviting place to rest for a few minutes during the overnight shift. Rosemary was a permanent fixture there. Her sole job was to keep all the breakrooms and restrooms in the plant clean. She did so with meticulous attention. If she walked through the mill and saw a stray piece of paper, she would go out of her way to address it. When she was first new to the job people were pleasant enough but after a while, she was unseen to them. What kind of meaningful conversation can you have with someone afflicted with Down's Syndrome?

Chet went into the breakroom at about three-thirty in the morning. It was snowing outside and some of the workers, especially those who lived out in the boonies had trouble making it in. Chet never missed a shift. Even when he had a kidney stone many years ago. If snow was in the forecast, he would go to the plant at the impact of the first flake of snow on the ground with the intention of staying there until the crisis passed. He would sleep in the locker room, anticipating overtime because of the no-shows.

Rosemary was sitting in the same chair she sat in every day. It was at the end of the table closest to the machines. She was preoccupied with her lunch and didn't notice Chet enter the breakroom, as isolated as if she were drifting alone in deep space.

She sucked on a straw drawing in her white milk. It was always white milk from the same machine at the same seat in the same breakroom at the same time every night. They could have set the atomic clock to her precision.

"How come you never drink soda?"

She looked up at Chet through coke-bottle glasses smiling broadly through her gapped teeth as if embarrassed.

"Soda makes me burp. It's not nice to burp in public. So, I wait 'til I get home. It makes me fart, too." She glanced down at her half-eaten sandwich still smiling.

"Soda makes me fart, too. I can't drink milk. It makes me fart," Chet replied.

"I only fart when I poop."

"Good to know." He smiled at her, her chubby cheeks red with embarrassment. He bowed his head, lifted his Coke can respectfully and, telling her to have a nice evening, left the breakroom, having bonded over lactose.

How optimistic and joyful her parents must have been when Rosemary was born. Only to have their hearts broken by a genetic accident. It was a heartbreak Chet understood.

Over time, during the weeks Chet was working the night shift, he would take his Coke in the breakroom with Rosemary knowing she would be there even if he was working a half mile away on the other side of the plant.

Rumors were that she had a bad heart defect and spent many months of her early life recovering from a complex heart reconstruction. The defect might have been God's way of recalling a bad model. But God also gave man the skills to address God's plan. At least most of the time.

Gradually their encounters became a regular thing. She would leave her seat, run over and give Chet a brisk, unsolicited hug. Initially, Chet found these spontaneous displays of affection annoying, as if she were flirting with him. He reassured himself that she didn't understand the boundary between friendship and acquaintance.

Then one day a man was sitting with her across the table. It was Roger, the deformed plant broom-pusher. Another one of God's misfires. Roger had some spinal deformity that caused his lower legs to be splayed out as he walked, his knees bowed inward. He essentially walked on his instep. It almost seemed a cruel managerial joke to give Roger the job of pushing a broom almost as wide as his splayed feet around the plant gathering the tons of stray paper, paper dust and loose butts, the discarded ends of the long logs of toilet paper that were sliced up and wrapped in tissue by a machine. The broom, nearly as wide as his gait, made his task almost painful to watch. But he was, like Rosemary, diligent, dedicated to his occupation and a relentlessly cheerful, if largely unnoticed, fixture around the plant.

"Your father gave Rosemary away at her wedding. Did I ever tell you that story? I found the wedding invitation in his pants one day."

Chet looked over at his mother as if she had just spoken Aramaic.

"He told me it was some couple at the mill who decided to get married. He said he had no intention of going. They were retarded and just people he knew around the plant. I, of course became livid and told him I didn't like that word and that he should keep a still tongue in his head." # "Hiya Roger," Chet said as he entered the breakroom.

Roger, carefully studying both ends both ends of his newly peeled banana, looked over saying, "Good evening, Mr. Chet. Boy am I glad to see you."

As the soda can dropped noisily through the machine, Chet asked, "Why? What's up?"

"Rosemary and I are getting married next month, and I want you to be my Best Man." "You're getting married to Rosemary?" At first, he thought it was a joke. "Yep."

"Why me? Surely you have other, closer friends you could ask."

"Everybody is either busy or can't." *Or won't.* Chet thought.

"Please? Here's the wedding invitation." Roger came to his feet and limped his way across the breakroom, handing the envelope to Chet.

"Okay, let me sleep on it and I'll tell you my decision tomorrow."

"I'd also like for you to give the bride away."

"Roger, you can't be Best Man *and* give the bride away."

Roger looked perplexed. "You can't? There's some sort of rule about that?" "It's in the Torah, I think."

"Huh."

"Lemme sleep on it." "Okay. Thanks."

When he got to the car, Chet pulled the wedding invitation from his pocket. He opened the envelope expecting to find an invitation written in crayon. Instead, the invitation was professionally printed on formal stationary. He folded it and stuffed it back in his pocket, thinking of how he was going to make some excuse to get out of this predicament.

...

"What the hell do you mean 'We're not going'?"

"Mary, I hardly know either of these people except for around the mill. You've never even met 'em."

"Not good enough, you asshole. We're going whether you have any role in it or not. That's final."

The nuptials were planned for a month hence.

"I'll do it, Roger. On one condition. I get to kiss the bride first." Roger was again perplexed.

"After you do, of course," Chet added. Roger hugged Chet.

...

The wedding was held outdoors in a small, flat area of the park. There was a chance of rain and the dark clouds that drifted overhead seemed to cast an omen in Chet's brain.

Roger was in a tuxedo and Rosemary was plumply splendid in her white gown. *A wedding for the ages*, Chet thought.

As Chet walked her down the aisle, he noticed their slow and deformed friends, dressed in their finest, were clustered together. Neither parents of the bridal couple were present and the back rows of chairs were unoccupied. Chet also noticed a particularly strident display of animation when Benny turned to look at his father as he escorted the bride down the aisle.

After the vows were exchanged and Roger kissed the bride, Chet couldn't help but wonder if he was an unwitting accomplice in a genetic apocalypse.

Later, the reception, which Chet nicknamed the Island of Dr. Moreau, proved far more entertaining than he expected, he kissed the bride, made a long, cheerful and hopeful toast and got thoroughly drunk as he worked the room. Rosemary gave Benny a hug. He stood motionless.

Mary smiled as she related the story, unaware that Rhiannon had joined them in the cubicle.

"Oh, Rhee. How are you darling?"

"Rhee, we need to talk," Chet said.

CHAPTER NINE
Vigil

"The neurologist confirmed that Dad is braindead," Chet said. Rhiannon did not look surprised.

"Oh, Chet. He didn't say that," Mary said.

"Mother, he didn't use those exact words, but it is surely what he meant." "He said there was still a little brain activity," she insisted.

"Mom," Rhee continued. "I interpret what he says as there is no hope for a recovery in any meaningful way. It is just not possible. We have to make a decision."

"*We* don't have to make a decision. *I* have to make a decision and *I* am not ready to make it. This is not like putting Rusty down because he had arthritis and couldn't walk. We don't put people down. *Especially* your father." Mary started crying. She took Benny by the hand and led him out of the Intensive Care Unit.

Chet looked at his sister. "He's being kept alive by Boston Power and Light. He was a dead man when they put him in the ambulance."

"Chet, please."

"No, Rhee. You're a trained professional. What do your years of experience tell you, huh?"

"Okay, Chet. Let's let this settle and we'll talk to her."

"Alright, but a decision is looming. You need to talk to her."

"I will," she said softly. "How are we going to explain this to Benny?"

"I think he already knows. Let's get her out of here for dinner. She hasn't left his side practically since he got here."

"I agree. But let's not bear down too hard on her. She needs to come to grips with this herself at her own speed."

"Do you see any value in a second opinion?" he asked.

"No."

Rhiannon sat down. Chet looked at her. "I have to go drain the lemon."

She stared at her father. He was still alive if only by artificial means. She hoped he remembered.

When Rhee was young Mary made sure she was brought up a devoted catholic. The same with her older brother. Chet, the Elder, had no use for organized religion. He confessed one day to uncertainty if he'd ever been baptized. How he coexisted with a wife so spiritually involved was a mystery that was never explained and remained so to this minute.

Her mother told Rhee that getting your father to church was nearly impossible and on those rare occasions when he did it posed significant risk to the parishioners for fear the man's presence would result in a lightning bolt smashing into the church. It became a running joke between Rhee and her mother. On the few occasions he entered the church she would lean over to her daughter and whisper, "Don't touch anything metal."

Rhee remembered the occasion as if it just happened only yesterday. She felt so special in her new, immaculate dress and gold cross around her neck. She walked down the aisle with her hands held against her chest in prayer about to receive her Confirmation into the Catholic Church. Rhiannon studied hard to become Catholic not just to please her mother but to please her dad and maybe convince him of the value of a pure and spiritual life.

She loved him so much. Why wouldn't he embrace God? Why, then, was he beaming so much as she walked past them when he couldn't even stand being in the place? As she passed him, she made a sideways glance and saw the rim of moisture in his eyes as he smiled broadly.

"Don't cry, Dad," she thought. "We'll be out of here soon."

She reached down and stroked his silver hair then bent over and kissed his forehead. She wished she could tell him how much she loved him and be sure he could her it.

...

Mary agreed to dinner and they went to Alonzo's for pizza and beer. It was awkward. Chet Senior's dead brain was the elephant in the room. Very little was said. There was very little to say. Finally, as the bill was being paid, Mary said, "Your father squeezed my hand yesterday." Rhee reached across the table and caressed her mother's hand. "Mom, it was probably a reflex." She wanted to add 'of a dying brain: a muscle spasm but chose not to.

"I'm certain he was telling me to hang on; don't give up. It's too soon. Don't let me go just yet."

"Okay, Mom. We'll give it twenty-four more hours then we'll decide." Mary nodded agreement.

After they left, Mary snuggled up against Benny. He was asleep but knew she was there as he pushed himself into her. After the beach-ball lesson and the death of the doe, there was a palpable change in her husband.

...

Mary was in the kitchen clearing the dishes when she heard Chet in the next room reading Benny a story from a book of parables for children. Might have been the one about the turtle and the rabbit but she could not be sure. She put down the dirty frying pan and peeked into the room quiet not to disturb them. Benny was sitting close to his father staring at the page. Chet took his time emphasizing certain words or images changing the tone of his voice to match the different characters.

She felt her heart fill with a peace and joy at the sight. She returned to the kitchen.

Half an hour later she noticed Chet had stopped reading. She returned to check on them and saw her husband's head arched over the back of the couch as if he was staring at the ceiling, a drop of spittle glistened on his chin. He snored softly. Benny's eyes were still fixed on the page waiting for the story to resume.

...

Chapter Ten
Day Seven: Life Support

Rhiannon had rounds at the hospital and was not there in the morning when Chet arrived. He was hoping a decision could be made. He thought about it all night. Today might be the day they unplug the machines and end their father's life. It was a grim thought and a particle of him wanted his mother to make the decision alone not by some vote or default.

He had concerns, and he assumed Rhee felt the same, that their mom would defer any decision indefinitely. Amy told Chet over coffee that they would be moving Senior to a private room on the floor. Close to the Nurse's Station, of course. He didn't need specialized care any longer and the Intensive Care Unit was expensive and needed for other post-operative heart patients. The only thing he needed besides tube feeding was a wall socket for the ventilator and the air mattress used to prevent bedsores.

"Do you think we can keep him where he is for another twenty-four hours?"

"For the moment, we are not pressed for beds and it is the weekend coming up, so I think he can stay put. But I am not in a position to make promises. If they really need the bed, he'll be moved regardless of your wishes."

"I understand. You've been very helpful. Sympathetic, too. Attentive not just to my father but my family. Thank you. We appreciate your help. Not that we don't appreciate everyone's care, but you seem particularly—well—dedicated to my father."

She smiled broadly, reaching over to touch Chet's hand. He was surprised but did not withdraw.

"When do you have to go back to the Navy?"

"Grim as it is to say it, I'm good until my father's buried."

"What do you have to do when you go back?"

"We are doing run-ups to a six-month deployment in the Mediterranean. We still have a month or so to get ready before we set sail."

"Gee. Will you be back this way when you return?"

"Sure. Why?"

"Well, I might be interested in seeing you again. Maybe we could meet up when you get back. I'd even make you a dinner. I'm a pretty good cook if I do say so myself."

"I think you'd be good at anything you do." He removed her hand from over his and grasped hers. Tightly. It was not what he expected while he waited for her in the coffee shop. There imposed a pregnant pause. "Have you ever been to Italy?"

"No. The furthest east I've ever been is Bangor. Why?"

"We will probably make a port call. I'd pay to fly you over. Show you the sights. No strings attached, of course."

"I would love that. And who knows? I might like strings."

"Make sure I get your cell and email. You on Facebook?"

"You know, I've never seen Norfolk either."

Mary was in the seat beside her husband's bed as she was most of the time. Benny snored softly coiled under a blanket on the small couch. Rhee sat near the light from the hall as she worked over her iPad. She gave Chet a slight wave when he returned to the cubicle.

In a low voice, he spoke, "Rhee, did you get a chance to speak to Mom?" "No, was I supposed to?"

"Well, yeah. I expected, you being a doctor and all, that you might help her make a decision."

"Chet, you poor thing. She has to make the decision on her own.

Were I in her shoes, I wouldn't want anybody forcing that decision on me. It would be my call and my call alone. He's her husband."

"Rhee, I— "

"Oh, Chet, darling. You're back. How was coffee with Amy?" Mary said.

"Fine, Mother." He hesitated in telling her about the bed situation in the ICU. The man was essentially dead. What else could Amy have said?

"She seems like such a nice girl."

Yeah, Chet thought, *and I'm old enough to be her much older brother.*

There was a long pause. Finally, Rhee broke the silence

"Mom, if you and Benny want to come home with me, I'm sure Chet will call you if anything changes."

"Oh, darling. I certainly don't want to impose. I could use a bath. Same for Benjamin. I can fix breakfast. I'm sure nothing will change. When your father wakes up, Chet could call us right away, I'm sure." Rhee looked at Chet, who was dumbfounded that she had volunteered him for the overnight shift by a lightning strike of subterfuge from his sister.

Yeah, he thought, *while you're gone, I will accidentally unplug him from the wall. End his silent torture and his family's prolonged grief. I could do it when nobody's watching and when his heart stops just plug it in again when his alarms go off.* It was a sinister and indulgent thought and he smiled at himself for being so clever. But he quickly admonished himself for his callous and selfish scheme. "Good night, Chet," Rhee said.

"Yes, good night, darling." His mother kissed his cheek. He gave Benny his hug. "You'll call right away with any change." "I will."

When they were gone, he walked over to the bedside and took his father's hand and squeezed. He waited for his father's grip to suddenly appear, alas it did not. He brushed some of the gray hair off Senior's forehead. He leaned over and said, "Hey Dad, want a beer?" If he didn't respond to that offer, the man was truly dead.

It was then Junior arrived at the awareness that this was one of maybe a half dozen times he was alone with his father since he graduated from the Naval Academy. He stroked the man's forehead again.

"I guess our shoes are on different feet this time. I want to speak softly and slowly while I tell you a few things. I want you to remember them and keep them in mind when you cross over to the other side.

"You are so, so very lucky. Maybe it was lost on you along the way or when you were sleeping off a beer buzz in front of the TV or listening entranced to Johnnie Mathis.

"You had the best wife a man could have, far better, I thought, than you were entitled to. You were harsh, inconsiderate at times, even to people you didn't even know. Selfish to a fault. But Mom, your dear, beautiful wife was always at your side, ready to pick up after you, literally as well as figuratively. She loves you with every cell in her body. Of this no one could ever doubt.

I worry about her when you are gone. You probably are already. You will be pleased to know she's hanging in there. She was always tougher than she appeared.

"Rhee is a beautiful woman and a dedicated pediatrician. 'Brilliant' is the word I've heard used to describe her. Dedicated to all those poor, helpless little kids with cancer. It breaks her heart when she loses and the cancer wins. But she is strong. No need to worry there.

"As for Benjamin, words escape me. I think Benny is a message. A message from God that we should be humble for the gifts He has bestowed on us for there but for His Grace we go.

"Now me. All those lectures as I sat on the floor for while you drank your beer, smoked your Marlboros and made me listen to that stultifying music worked. I am the commander of men. And I stand in the shadows of men far greater than me. You are one of them. You bow before no man. Except Uncle Simpson, maybe. He's a lot bigger than you. But I digress.

"We didn't always see eye to eye. I know I broke your heart by not becoming a Marine. I chose a different path. But I could tell you were still very proud. The expression on your face at graduation was worth every lecture and haranguing I ever got. Thanks.

"Sometimes, I think you were lonely. Longing for the mother you never had and resentful of the father who was no father at all. You missed that growing up. In return, you made up for it with us, all four of us. But especially Mom. But don't worry. She'll be fine. We'll see to it.

"That's about all I have to say. I love you. Safe travels on your next journey. I hope it won't be too hot. I'll probably catch up with you at some point. Wait for me." He leaned over the bed railing and kissed his father's cheek.

When he let go of his father's hand and stepped back from the bedside, he saw Amy in the dark entrance to the cubicle. She wiped a tear from her cheek.

"Oh, hi," Chet said.

Chapter Eleven
Day Eight: Saturday

When Rhee arrived at the cubicle, Chet pulled her to one side and asked his sister if she had spoken to their mother about turning off the machines.

"No."

"We need to. We both know he will not get better and this could drag out for weeks. At some point, I have to get back to the ship and you need to get back to work. You need to be rid of this distraction and concentrate on your kids."

"So, you think our dying father is a distraction?"

"Oh, Christ, Rhee. You know what I mean."

"No, I don't, Chet."

"Yes, you do."

"Chet, I'm not getting into an argument with you." "Nor I with you. Just think about it, will you."

"Okay. I'll be by after work and we'll talk to Mom."

"Fair enough."

...

Chet sat on the chair beside his father's bed. His brother and mother had not yet arrived. He reached over and touched his father's hand. It had an intravenous in it and was mostly covered by tape, but he felt enough of his father's skin to know his father felt him at whatever level of awareness remained.

"It's been a while since we talked. I don't count last night. I apologize for being out of the loop. You know I finally got my squadron. One day I will make Captain. I would like to be a carrier captain. It would be the high point of my career. I want you to know that you figured into every success I've had. I take sole possession of my failures.

"So often when I faced with a difficult decision, I would ask myself 'what would Dad do?' It often gave me a perspective that wasn't apparent. It's called wisdom."

"Hi, Son."

"Good morning, Mom. Hi, Benny."

"Talking to your dad?"

"Yeah. Think he can hear me?"

"I do."

Chapter Twelve
Forty-eight Hours

The eighth day after Chet's aorta tore was a Saturday. The cardiac operating room was handling only the few cases that could not wait until Monday or the occasional genuine emergency. It meant there was no pressure to move Chet out or yank the plug.

His condition had not changed. He did not squeeze his wife's hand again even as she held it for hour upon hour. Rhee showed up after morning rounds. Junior returned after a shower and change of clothes at Rhee's place. He stopped only for a quick bite at a coffee shop.

When he returned to the bedside, he hoped his mother had arrived at a decision. But she had not. Instead she was noticeably expressive, interacting with Amy as she tried to get her bedside chores done. She had picked up an extra shift, she explained. Chantelle, the day nurse assigned to the Chet Watch, called in sick and ended up getting her appendix out. Amy was quite animated as well. Maybe it was the fact she might one day get to see Norfolk.

Doctor Reynolds stepped into the cubicle.

"Good morning, all. Hi, Amy. I wanted to stop by to see how everyone was doing. Hope everyone is hanging in there. I know this has been a bad week for y'all. I wanted you to know I had an extended conversation with Dr. Cummings and Dr. Perov. We are in agreement about Mr. Pettigrew's current condition. As the surgeon on the case I want you to know we all feel any meaningful recovery here is not possible."

"Hopeless?" Rhee asked more for the benefit of her mother than her own.

"I never use that word. But it is likely this situation is irretrievable. In other words, he will not recover. He will never be the same man you last saw before his calamity. With good, and I mean perfect, medical management he can be kept alive until a situation arises, we cannot reverse. We can have him transferred to the floor where they know how to handle these kinds of cases until arrangements can be made to transfer him to an extended care facility that can manage patients on long-term ventilators. That might take a while. But we are willing to explore that possibility. It will be expensive. His Medicare benefits will run out quickly. Then the decision will be made on the basis of economics not compassion. But sometimes our desires exceed our judgement and our arrogance that we can fix the unfixable. That somehow we can change biology." Chet said softly, "The operation was a success, but the patient died." Reynolds snapped his head around but after a moment nodded.

"I meant no disrespect, Doctor," Chet said.

Still in the Doctor's crosshairs, speaking directly to Junior, Reynolds added. "Precisely." All eyes turned toward Mary who stood resolutely with her arm around Benny.

"Give us another twenty-four hours to decide about our course of action," she said.

"Yes, Ma'am. Why don't we give it until Monday morning? We will reconvene then. In the meantime, it will be status quo ante." He reached into his lab coat, took out a business card and wrote on it. "Here is my personal cellphone. I'll be around. If at any time you need me just call this number. I will stop by Monday morning."

Chet half expected the doctor to slap his hands together, as if the end of a locker room pep talk and yell, "Okay, people let's get with it and make a decision. The clock is ticking." Instead, he shook Chet's and Rhiannon's hands, touched Benny on his shoulder and gave Mary a gentle hug.

He nodded at Amy and left the cubicle toward the rest of the Unit no doubt, Chet thought, to see how the rest of his garden was growing. Amy followed him out.

As he was leaving, he nodded his head to Junior and his sister. He clearly wanted to talk to them outside the range of Mary's hearing.

"There is something I need to tell you. The aortic dissection caused the loss of the large artery to his spinal cord. Deprived of its blood supply the spinal cord died along the lines of a stroke. Even if Mr. Pettigrew survives and wakes up, he will be a paraplegic from mid-chest down."

Returning to the cubicle, Rhee spoke up. "Well, Mother. I guess we have forty-eight hours to arrive at a decision."

Had she not said it with such compassion in her voice, Chet might have wrung her neck.

"Yes. Perhaps," was all Mary said. She pulled her chair to the usual position beside the bed and placed Benny on the couch to her other side. Chet and Rhee went for coffee. "You think Reynolds got through to Mom?" Chet asked.

"Maybe. But you know Mom—the eternal optimist. Her glass will always be half full."

"But she listened to every word he said. I watched her. You think she will turn things off and let him go dust to dust?"

"I do."

"Wager?"

"Chet, you're a fucking asshole."

"True, but I come by it honestly."

"Okay, a fiver."

She reached across the table and shook her brother's hand.

When they returned to the cubicle, their mother was stroking Chet Senior's hand, talking to him as if at the dinner table. At first, Chet Junior could not make out what she was saying as her voice was barely above a whisper. Perhaps, he thought, she was trying to elicit another squeeze.

Amy came in with a fresh bag of intravenous fluid but stopped when she saw Mary talking to her husband. She turned and left.

Chet drew closer to his mother. Mary was talking about how she would take care of things after he was gone. She reviewed the status of all three of their children and what their futures held. Perhaps she had made her decision, finally yielding to the inevitable. "We're all going to go sometime," he had heard his father say. "Nobody gets off the planet alive. Unless of course you're an astronaut." Chet smiled as he recalled the conversation.

Chet had just completed flight training at Pensacola and had been awarded his wings as a bona fide Naval Aviator and had come home on a two-week furlough before starting FA-18 training. So, Senior took Junior to the lake to go fishing. It was one of the few things his father did voluntarily that he did not enjoy.

It was a clear, crisp Saturday morning in early spring. Junior did not particularly care for fishing either but when his father insisted they go, he felt compelled to join him. He feared another lecture. This time without the beer.

Instead, they spent most of the first hour in silence, casting and recasting their lines.

"What's on your mind, Pop?"

"Just keep fishing."

"No, really. What's up? We haven't fished together since I was in high school."

"I just wanted to spend some quiet time with you before you start flying those damned fighters."

"Pop, it's risky business. I know that. But it's what I've always wanted to do. I'm living my dream. Isn't that what you always told me? 'Find something you want to do and become the best at it.' Christ, if you said it once you said it a thousand times."

"Look at you. A Naval Aviator. Guess the lectures paid off."

Junior chuckled. "I guess so." After a protracted silence he said, "You're still pissed off I didn't become a Marine."

"Yep. I'll take that disappointment to my grave."

After a moment, Senior put his arms around his son and hugged him.

...

Chet walked around the bed, took his father's other hand and squeezed it tightly hoping his father would squeeze back.

They caught no fish that day. Even if they had, Senior would have insisted they toss the fish back into the water. Chet knew his father didn't like random, indiscriminate death. Even if it was just a fish.

Chapter Thirteen
Day Nine: Borrowed Time

This was one of the few Sundays in his mother's life that she didn't go to church. Raised Catholic, she went to Mass virtually every Sunday unless she was either too sick or in labor. She tried hard to get Senior to go with her to church, especially early on, but he resisted her efforts. He called the belief in religion a waste of a Sunday morning, especially during the fall when the Patriots were playing. He said people who went to church were hedging their bets. Religion was 'just in case' he liked to say.

During the vigil, Mary would leave the bedside to go down to the hospital's chapel. She would take Benny with her even though the experience was completely lost on him.

Senior would let her take the kids to Mass as they grew up, but the experience was lost on them too. Out of respect for his mother, but largely the result of habit, Chet continued to go to

Mass at the Naval Academy. Also, it was the one place, as a plebe, he didn't get harassed.

One day, Chet engaged his father in a philosophical discussion about the meaning of life and the origin of the Universe. They were on the back-deck drinking beer on a Saturday afternoon during summer break.

"You've heard of the Big Bang, haven't you Dad?"

"Sure. I may be crazy but I'm not stupid."

"How do you suppose it started? Who made it happen?"

"Got me, but I'll play along. Nobody. It just happened. You, Son, are falling into the teleological trap of thinking there has to be an active cause to something or even everything. A physical hand that moves a lever or pushes a button. If you want to call that active force God, be my guest. If there is a God, he's probably sitting up there on a chaise lounge working on His can of Pabst Blue Ribbon, laughing His ass off. Or else wondering where He went wrong."

"Now where the fuck did you learn teleology?"

"I read it in a book."

Chet stared at his father for a moment then put his thumb over the lip of the bottle, shook it fiercely and sprayed his father with beer. Senior erupted and grabbed his son pinning him to the deck. Mary saw the scuffle and went out to stop it before somebody got hurt. Soon she was laughing and soaked with beer too. When it was over, she made them strip to their skivvies and spray off with the garden hose before she would let anyone back in the house. It was the last time Chet remembered his father hugging him. It was also the happiest he ever recalled seeing him.

Please Dad, squeeze my hand.

...

They sat, as they had for over a week, around the bedside in the glass-enclosed cubicle in the corner of the ICU. Chet looked at the pinpoint trace on the EKG monitor as if it might reveal something other than the electrical activity of his father's heart. He did the mental calculation in his head: average 72 heartbeats a minute times 60 minutes in an hour times 24 hours in a day times 365 days a year (not counting leap years) times 70 years yielded 110 million beats. Give or take. Maybe more. He had spent two tours in Vietnam. It was hard to imagine, he thought, that any organ could do the same thing over a hundred million times and not break. But it could. It happened all the time.

Chet Junior was a pragmatist. As a Naval officer and pilot, one had to be. He recalled a biology lecture at the Academy.

"Darwin tells us everything," the professor said. "Everything in biology comes down to natural selection as enshrined forever in our genetic code." He was emphatic when he said it.

"Survival of the fittest. The most prepared. The strongest. The cleverest.

"Gentlemen, evolution allowed man, Neanderthal, Upright Man, Homo Habilis to live only into his late thirties or early forties. Just long enough for their progeny to reproduce and learn survival strategies. To be fed, reproduce and rear their young. Once the next generation has acquired those skills, all the mommies and daddies become superfluous. For them, everything else is borrowed time."

Borrowed time.

"Mom," he said finally, "we need to make a decision. What are we going to do?" "We have until tomorrow, dear."

"No, we don't," Rhee said. "The time is now. Dad can't go on like this. We can't. You can't."

Mary started sobbing softly. "Okay, we'll turn him off tomorrow. So, let's just spend the rest of this Sunday with him."

A short time later, Amy, dressed in street clothes, poked her head into the cubicle. "Hi," she said softly. "I hope I'm not intruding. I just stopped by to see how you all were doing."

"Oh, no dear," Mary said, wiping the tears from her cheek. "Please come in. We've decided to stop everything tomorrow and let him go."

"I see." She looked at Junior. "If there's anything you need or I can do, let me know."

Chet nodded to her saying, "Thanks, Amy."

"I guess I need to call a funeral home," Mary said, her composure restored.

"Mom," Rhee said. "It can wait."

Mary sat down beside Benny and pulled him to her.

"Soon, Benny, Daddy will be going away, and you won't be able to see him anymore except in Heaven. It will be a while before you can see him again. But I'm sure you will, and it will be a grand day that will last an eternity."

Two presumptions, Junior thought: A, there is a Heaven and B, he's on the list to get into heaven. He wanted to cry. He looked at the clock then the monitor. Even the sound of the respirator mocked him.

"Mom, I'll be back."

Chet turned and put his arm around Amy. Her eyes were wet. She seemed smaller, vulnerable. When they stepped onto the elevator, they were alone. Amy turned, reached her arms around Chet's neck and kissed him. He could feel her wet cheeks on his. He kissed her back. Her embrace tightened. As did his.

They walked out of the hospital. It was raining. *Even God is weeping,* he thought.

They sought shelter on a park bench under a large oak in the park across the street from the hospital. She pulled out a cigarette and lit it.

"I still find it disappointing that you smoke."

"Me too. Stress reliever."

"Gimme one." Chet took the cigarette from her, lit it and took a long drag. First cigarette since graduation day from the Academy.

"Chet, I hope you didn't mind me stopping by." "No."

"Over the past week, I have come to know you and your family. The sadness. Your dad must have been very proud of you. And your sister. Even Benny. Poor Benny."

"He still is."

"Yes, of course. It's not what I meant."

Chet wrapped his arm around her shoulder and hugged her.

"I know."

"How soon will you be going back to the ship?"

"In a day or so after he's buried. I am sure I am sorely missed."

"When will I see you again?"

"Up to you. We don't head out for deployment for another month or so."

"I will miss you."

"And I you."

They fell silent for several minutes and two more cigarettes. "We should get back in," Chet finally said.

"No, Chet. You go in. I don't belong there. I'll see you tomorrow when my shift starts.

You'll be around then?"

"Yes. We will be there."

She stood up, kissed the crown of his head and left. She stopped, turned around, pulled out

a cigarette and gave him her lighter saying, "Here. One for the road."

He watched her go down the block, cross the street and disappear into the parking garage.

"Thanks, Dad," he whispered. "Were it not for you, I'd'a never met her."

...

When Chet returned to the cubicle, Mary and Rhiannon were laughing. It provided Chet with a vicarious pleasure. They must have been reminiscing. Another Chet Story.

Around seven o'clock they had two large pepperoni pizzas delivered to the cubicle. Chet snuck in two six-packs of Miller Lite so they could have a last drink with their father and husband. Benny seemed particularly enamored with the pizza. They gave him a beer. Benny liked beer. Mary said it was the one thing he shared with his father. They drank together from time to time and when they did, often while listening to music. Benny burped for an hour. Drinking beer was one of the few things that ever made Benny smile and, in so doing, formed a bond between father and son that would last forever.

Chet wondered if he could drip some Miller Lite down his father's feeding tube. *I mean,* he thought, *what could it hurt?*

Chapter Fourteen
Day Ten: 'til Death do Us Part

"Good morning all," Dr. Reynolds said at the entrance to the cubicle. "Thoughts?"

Everyone was standing by the bed. Mary said, "We want my husband removed from the machines. We agree it is time."

"Okay. I'll let the nurses know. I want you to know, we are sorry he did not survive the dissection of his aorta. The care he received here is the finest anywhere in the world. His condition simply did too much damage and could not be reversed. He probably lost blood flow to his brain very quickly. Probably not long after he collapsed at his home. We, all of us, extend our deepest sympathies."

Mary walked over to Reynolds and hugged him, whispering, "Thank you for all you did for Chet."

He hugged her back. "Yes, ma'am."

She pulled away and Junior and Rhiannon shook Reynold's hand. The doctor then went over to Benny, standing at the head of the bed, reached down, took his hand and shook it.

Reynolds turned and walked out of the cubicle. He had done everything he could.

A short time later, a nurse came into the room and, assisted by a respiratory therapist, turned off the ventilator, gently removed the tubes from his throat and nose and put them in a disposal bag. The nurse then took Chet's arms from under the covers and placed them at his side and removed the two intravenous lines from his arms and another from under his collar bone. She fluffed his pillow and tucked the blankets up to the base of his neck as if she was settling him in for a nap. She took a small brush and combed his hair.

When the nurse was done, she turned to the family as the respiratory therapist removed the machine from the cubicle and expressed her sympathies. Before leaving she asked if there was anything she could do.

"No dear, you've done enough," Mary said, smiling wanly. Chet thought she might have chosen different words, but the sentiment was sincere.

Mary sat by her pale, still husband. He made no movement. Chet would have gone running for the nurse if his father had but he was dead still. Mary took his left hand in hers and rubbed it gently. She rotated his wedding band.

Rhiannon stood at the foot of the bed alongside her brother. Benny stood by the head of the bed and stared down at his father.

Mary thought of Rusty. She was with him when Chet carried him into the vet's. They were going to put him down. Chet was worried they had kept him alive too long. Chet placed him gently onto the exam table and said his goodbyes. Mary hugged the dog and gave him a kiss on the top of his graying head. The vet came in and with reverence, gave Rusty the medicine. Chet picked up the dog easily despite the dog's size and sat in the chair, Rusty in his lap. Rusty knew. In the last few moments of his life, the dog looked around desperately for Chet. Their eyes met and the dog breathed his last, laying his head on Chet's lap.

When Rusty was put down, they decided not to tell Chet. He was away at the Academy and they didn't want to upset him. Chet loved that dog and they would tell him the next time he was home.

Chet's focus was drawn to the monitor as his father's heart rhythm slowed. The bumps on the trace became less frequent. He could not take his eyes off the bouncing dot of light. He placed his hand on his father's foot beneath the blanket. The bouncing light became smaller and its trace widely spaced until, after several minutes the line went flat going from one side of the auburn glass to the other, its work done.

Chet stepped out of the cubicle to fetch the nurse who stood by with a clipboard in her hand.

"I think it's over," was all he said.

She nodded, saying, "Let me know when you are finished. Take as long as you need to."

"Give us five minutes."

"Of course."

Ten minutes later, the nurse returned to the cubicle and jotted down the time of her patient's demise and gently asked the identity of the funeral home.

Chet thought it might have been a detail that had not quite occurred to his mother, but she said, "Whittington's in Cherry Hill. They always do such a nice job." Whittington's in Cherry Hill.

"They are expecting a call." Dear sweet Mother. "Would you like me to call them?"

"No, Mrs. Pettigrew. I will call them for you. I have their number."

During the distraction no one noticed that Benny had silently slipped onto the bed, cuddling his father.

Chet went to Benny to remove the embrace of his father.

"Come on, Buddy. He's gone. He's dead now, Benny. We need to go now."

Mary and Rhiannon noticed Chet removing his brother's embrace of their father and husband.

They gathered outside the cubicle and the nurse pulled the curtain shut.

After a moment, Chet guided what remained of his family out of the hospital.

After driving for half an hour in silence, Mary said to no one in particular, "You know you reach a point in your life where the sad parts start to outnumber the happy ones. It should be the other way around."

"I did not know that the last time I saw him truly alive was when they put him in the ambulance. Let's just have a small, quiet service for your father. He was not big on funerals." Sitting in the back beside

Benny, Rhee started to cry.

Chet wondered if he should tell his ex-wife of his father's demise then realized he didn't want to tell her. She wouldn't give a shit. She never liked the man.

...

Arriving home, Mary fixed them an early supper. Tomorrow, she wanted to visit Whittington's and make appropriate arrangements.

CHAPTER FIFTEEN
Day Eleven: Arrangements

The sky was threatening when they arrived at Whittington's Funeral Home and Crematorium. Mr. Whittington was a short, smarmy little man wearing a gray suit, paisley tie and black, horn-rimmed glasses. He was annoyingly over-solicitous. He greeted Chet, his brother and his mother.

After appropriate sympathies expressed at their loss, Whittington told them he had sent the hearse to pick up Mr. Pettigrew. He directed them to his office so they could discuss the details of the service, pick a casket and where she would like him interred.

Why can't you just say 'buried?' Chet thought as if the man's choice of synonyms would somehow ease the blow.

"I want a small service," Mary said. "A small obituary in the paper. Chet didn't have a lot of friends. He was a Marine too. He won the Navy Cross in Vietnam, you know." Chet thought, *They gave out a lot of medals back then.*

"Oh," Mary added, "please put in the obituary that in lieu of flowers, please make a donation to the National Autism Network."

"Yes, of course

Whittington made quick notes. The discussion about the vault, the size and price of the

coffin was all lost on Chet. He couldn't focus on the details and heard very little of the exchanges between Whittington and his mother. He heard nothing of the time or date of the service. What minister or priest was officiating? Since he was a veteran, did she want a flag on the coffin? None of it. All he wanted to do was talk to Amy, give his dad a decent send-off and get back to flying. He had called Amy not long after they got home from the hospital.

"Hi, Chet. So sorry about your father passing away."

"I know you are. It was inevitable. Foretold as they were putting him in the ambulance."

"I just couldn't bring myself to be there when he died. I could not bring myself to pronounce him, so Laverne stepped in to help. Besides it was a private thing and I hardly know

you or your family. I would have felt like an intruder or interloper. Sorry."

"What's there to be sorry about? Don't be silly. Your job is hard enough." "Yes, but—"

"No 'buts.' We have some matters to attend to. I'll call you later."

"Okay. My best to everyone."

"Sure."

Chapter Sixteen
Day Twelve: Cancer

"I found a lump in your breast." The doctor said it as casually as if he was telling her she needed a little more air in her back tires. At first, she thought he had the wrong patient. She didn't feel anything every time she remembered to check. Mary remembered where she was and even what she was wearing when the doctor found the lump. The specific aroma of the doctor's cologne still burns in her memory. Her first thought was how she was going to tell Chet, not how much longer she had to live. He flipped out at even the slightest hint of a medical problem with his wife. Each pregnancy proved an ordeal. For him, not for her. But because of him, for her. She had a little spotting late in Rhiannon's pregnancy and she had to stop him as he sprinted to the phone to alert the authorities.

She now sat in the very same kitchen chair she was sitting in when she told him about the lump. She stirred her tea as memories of her dead husband streamed to the surface like the milk in the cup. She wanted just another few minutes to talk to him; ask him a couple of remaining questions she never got around to before he keeled over and was gone forever.

She left the doctor convinced her life had come to a premature end. How would she explain this to her husband? Who would look after her children? Chet would be okay. He was a survivor. Anybody who could come out alive at the other end of the black tunnel that was Vietnam had all the survival skills anybody could ever need.

No, she thought, *I'm wrong. Chet would be devastated. If I turn out to have cancer, he might sink into a funk from which he might never recover.*

Even as she thought of that moment in the kitchen, her heart started to ache. Her memory of those moments remained pristine.

"Chet, I have to tell you something."

"What is it, Benny finally recited the Gettysburg Address?"

"I have a lump in my breast. The doctor wants it removed."

He put down the paper he was talking into. "What did you say? You have a lump in your boob?"

"Yes. It might be cancer."

"I'm sorry. Start over again." He put the newspaper down and stared into his wife's eyes. It was as if somehow, she might be kidding.

"You have cancer?"

"I don't know, Chet. That's why they want to remove it. Do a biopsy." He could read the anguish on her face.

"Jesus."

Chet rocked back in his seat as if he was just one number short of winning the Powerball.

"So you lose a tit. It doesn't mean I'll love you any less."

"Jesus Christ, Chet! If I have cancer, I could die."

"You don't have cancer."

"I believe I do." She started sobbing, thinking about a sinister lump she could not feel.

Chet got on his knees and put his head on her lap. He started crying too.

She stroked his head as she regained her composure. She felt a hand on her shoulder. Benny. She reached back and grasped the hand, squeezing it gently.

"They are going to remove it at the surgical center Monday."

Over the weekend, Chet became overly solicitous toward Mary to the point of great annoyance. She knew he meant well but he was still a pain in the ass. She would have preferred to suffer in silence as the certainty of her malignancy would not leave her.

When Monday arrived, it was a relief. Chet took the day off and, with Benny in tow, drove his wife to the surgical center in Westborough.

He kissed her goodbye as she was wheeled away on the gurney. He then went to the waiting room and sat down with his son. He expected an answer right away, but they were told it would take three days to get the report back. Chet knew it would be the longest three days of his life. He was prepared to take off work until she heard so he could comfort her during the oppressive time of uncertainty, but she insisted she would be fine and preferred he go to the mill and, as she put it, stay out of her hair.

The nurse came out and told Chet and Benny that she was out of surgery, awake and doing fine. He could take her home in about two hours.

Ninety minutes later, the nurse led her to the waiting room. Benny saw her first and stood. Chet looked at Benny then saw his wife. He walked over to her and asked how she was. She deflected an exuberant embrace from her husband. She did not want her breast to suffer the compression of a hug.

"I'm fine," she said. "Just a little sore is all."

The nurse went over the post-operative instructions, but Chet heard not a word of it. His eyes remained fixed on his wife. She looked a little pale.

She napped off and on the rest of the day. Chet cooked dinner—macaroni and cheese out of a box. Mary ate little. The doctor had instructed her to wear a bra when she went to bed. Chet watched her closely. The bandage on her left breast was large. His first thought was that his wife might somehow never be the same as if some life force might have been left behind on the operating table or removed with a lump of breast. She had been exposed to vulnerability.

The next day she sent Chet to work. Benny, she said, would keep an eye on her. The thought of her husband hovering over her all day wringing his hands while he drank his beer was more than she could take. After she cleaned the breakfast dishes, Mary curled up with Benny and took a nap. Chet called her several times. In their entire life together, he had called her from work on maybe a half-dozen occasions.

When the phone rang the next day, her heart went to her throat when she heard it was the doctor's office. The biopsy results were in. *More like a verdict*, she thought. She had not expected them until tomorrow.

"Mary," the doctor said, "your biopsy came back benign. No cancer."

"Thank you, Jesus."

"Any problems with the incision?"

"What?"

"Is your incision okay?"

"Um… yes."

Benny was in the doorway to the kitchen. He cracked a small smile as his mother wiped away her tears.

Later, when Chet came home, she told him the good news. He smiled broadly. "See," he said, "told ya."

He turned and went to the bathroom. Through the door she could hear him crying.

CHAPTER SEVENTEEN
Day Thirteen: The Funeral

It was a dark, cloudy day when they buried Chester Pettigrew. *Fitting,* Junior thought.

An American flag was partially draped over the coffin. There was also the red Marine

Corps flag posted to one side. Chet was taken aback when he noticed the color guard of two young Marines standing at parade rest at either end of the catafalque. A captain stood unobtrusively nearby.

"Is all this pomp necessary, Captain? I'm not sure this is what my Dad would have wanted."

The Marine captain stiffened slightly. "It is what *we* wanted, Commander. Did you ever read your father's citation for the Navy Cross, Sir?"

"No, Captain. I must say I never did."

"You should, Sir. It makes for interesting reading. He should have been awarded the Medal of Honor. We're from the Marine Corps Recruiting District, Boston, Sir. It is our honor to be here." Chet noticed a wreath of red, white and blue flowers near the head of the casket. It was one of the few floral arrangements. There was a card on it saying, "To our fallen Comrade-in-Arms.

Have a safe journey." It was from the Legion Post. I guess, Chet thought, they didn't get the memo.

Chet stared at his father's corpse. His mother walked up behind him and gripped his arm. "Looks peaceful. Almost contented," Chet said. *Probably could use a beer,* he thought.

"Life well-lived?"

“I guess. I never got the chance to tell him how much I loved him.”

“Sure, you did,” she retorted sharply. “Never say that. You had plenty of opportunities. You should never say to yourself that ‘I wish I done one more thing or said one more thing’ or anything you could have done yesterday or the day before. The day will come, like they did for your Father, when you won’t have any more days.” She let go of his arm.

The priest from Saint Ignatius of Loyola parish was asked by his mother to say a few words. He walked up to the casket, crossed himself, bowed and stepped up to the podium. He wondered how his mother had gotten away with getting a priest to give the homily. Chet was not Catholic.

He took the podium to address the few people present, most of whom Chet did not know or had ever seen. “In the name of the Father, the Son and the Holy Spirit, Amen.

“Welcome to the service honoring Mister Chester”—Chet cringed, his father despised the name Chester—“Chet Pettigrew.” He half expected his father to sit up, red-faced and correct the priest. “Though Chet was not Catholic, his lovely and loving wife, Mary is. She is a faithful member of our Parish at Saint Aloysius. She attends Mass regularly. When she asked me to say a few words, I could hardly refuse. We are joined here today by his son Chet Junior, his daughter Rhiannon and his son Benjamin.

“I only had a few opportunities to meet and talk with Chet. He would occasionally drop by the parish to help Mary deliver baked goods to the bake sale or help with Christmas decorations.

He was a soft spoken and generous man.”

Chet wondered if he was talking about the same man. His father cursed indiscriminately and was a skinflint.

“He worked hard to support and educate his family.” That was true.

“He was a devoted father to his mentally and emotionally challenged son, Benjamin.”

Also true.

"He had a certain, *joie de vivre*: a zest for living." Perhaps. Most of the time he was cranky.

"But most of all, I remember Chet as a loving husband and dedicated and loving father." *Yeah, unless we pissed him off.*

"Our faults make us more human, not less. Who among us is perfect?" *Who is this asshole? Did he ever meet my Dad?*

"Chet was above all a devoted husband, a loving father and a patriot." All true. Even when he had a difficult time showing it.

"First Thessalonians chapter four, verse thirteen and fourteen: 'Brothers and sisters, we do not want you to be uninformed about those who sleep in death, so that you do not grieve like the rest of mankind, who have no hope. For we believe Jesus died and rose again, and so we believe that God will bring with Jesus those who have fallen asleep in him.'

"John chapter eleven, verses twenty-five and twenty-six. 'Jesus said to her, "I am the resurrection and the life. The one who believes in me will live though they die; and whoever lives by believing in me will never die."'

"Let us pray. Dear heavenly Father, we commit Your son, Chester to Your heavenly host. Watch over him as You watched over Your own Son."

God left His Son to die a horrible, gruesome death on the cross, if I'm not mistaken.

Chet could hear the rest of the service but did not listen. His father made cynicism look so easy. When he priest made The Sign of the Cross, Chet could not help but smile. Years ago, on one of the occasions when his father attended a service with his family, he leaned over to his son and whispered, "Watch. He's giving God the signal to lay down a bunt." He smiled again when he thought it was a stretch of credulity to use his father's name and the hope of resurrection in the same sentence.

When the time came for Chet and Rhee to speak of their father, they both declined, having told their mother and through her

Whittington and the priest that they did not want to say anything because it might hurt their brother who did not and could not speak.

Chet came by his cynicism honestly. His father could be one of the biggest cynics he ever knew. But, at the end, he thought it was a nice service. Understated without many tears. It had taken over a week to arrive at this moment, they all thought it through. They were all prepared.

Everyone, including the Marines exited the room, leaving Mary and her children alone with Chet. Mary asked them to wait outside after each said their goodbyes. Benny stood by the coffin until he was led away. Chet did not know if, even now, Benny truly understood what was going on or if he had any understanding of death let alone salvation.

Mary, alone a last time with her husband, leaned into the casket and kissed his cold, waxy lips and caressed his stiff face and stroked his gray hair. She wondered if he knew when they placed him into the back of the ambulance that that would be the last time they would glimpse each other.

"Wait for me," she whispered.

She turned and walked out to the lobby where Whittington talked with Chet and Rhee about the ride to the cemetery. Mary listened intently. She looked around. *All funeral home lobbies looked the same,* she thought. She wondered why the man spoke in such hushed tones. *Probably didn't want to wake the dead,* she thought and smiled. "Where's Benny?" Mary asked.

Rhee turned toward her mother. "We thought he was with you."

"No, sweetheart, the last time I saw him he was with you."

"I'll check outside," Rhee said. She turned and walked outside in case he had wandered off, something he never did.

Chet went into the parlor and walked up to the casket. Benny was lying in the casket beside his father. Benny's head rested next to his father's, eyes closed, his right arm across his chest.

"Oh, Jesus, look at this," Chet whispered. It was only the second time he ever witnessed any genuine emotional display by his brother.

"Come on, Champ. You've got to get out of there."

Chet slowly guided his brother out of the coffin and made him stand still while he adjusted the blanket over his dead father. He wanted to tell his brother that his father had gone to heaven, but Benny wouldn't understand the concept and he wasn't really sure if that was his father's final destination in any event.

"Come on, Benny. We have to go." Chet took his brother by the hand and led him out of the funeral parlor taking one parting look at his father before they closed the casket.

They watched the Marines lift the casket into the hearse. When they closed the door, Mary and her children climbed into the black limousine.

After the half-hour drive to the cemetery, they were ushered to their seats.

The Marines unloaded the coffin with as much care as if a president were inside. They took it to the gravesite and placed it carefully over the grave.

The Marine pallbearers lifted the flag from the coffin and with a grace and precision due a head-of-state, folded the flag in a brisk, well-rehearsed manner and presented it to the Marine captain. Receiving it, he slowly turned and walked with measured steps up to Mary and knelt. He spoke softly.

"On behalf of a grateful nation, I present you with this flag."

Mary nodded, thanked him with words only he could hear and placed it on her lap. He came slowly to attention and saluted. Before he dropped his hand, his eyes caught Chet's. Chet returned the salute and offered an appreciative smile.

Seven Marines marched in lock step beyond the gravesite and fired three volleys in rapid succession. Everyone saw it coming and did not flinch except Benny. Rhee grabbed his hand and squeezed tightly.

At the end, they placed the flowers, one by one, on the casket. The priest gave a final blessing, laid down another bunt sign and they were escorted away from the gravesite as if witnessing the lowering of the casket into the ground might elicit an emotional catharsis and public demonstration of uncontrolled grief.

As they walked away from the grave, Chet slipped his sister a five-dollar bill.

Chapter Eighteen
The Wake: What Would Chet Do?

It started to drizzle off and on as they reconvened at home. A few people, Charlie Simpson and his wife Tonya, Matt Dorsey, an acquaintance from the Legion Post that Chet Senior rarely visited (Matt's wife had passed away some years back from cancer) and Tom Skorskie and his wife came back to the house. They did not expect many others.

Chet Junior had set up a small bar in the kitchen, filled a tub with ice and Miller Lite and set out some hors d'oeuvres made by Rhiannon earlier that morning.

Mary walked into the kitchen and asked Chet to make her a stiff highball. As he handed her the drink, she said, "This is the way your dad would have wanted it: nice, quiet moments to reflect with a couple of stiff drinks." She raised the glass to her son and took a sip.

"Don't you mean the other way around?" Chet said. "A couple stiff drinks and then a pause to reflect?"

There was a soft knock at the door. It was Amy. She looked sad and almost embarrassed to be there as if she alone might have saved Chet from his inevitable demise. She brought cupcakes instead of the standard tuna casserole or pan of lasagna. She was the last arrival.

Amy greeted everybody, giving all a hug and Benny a soft kiss on the cheek. She could not dispel the feeling of being an intruder at a very personal event. This was softened by Chet's introduction to those present and the warmth she was shown. Rhee pulled her aside and they chatted not as doctor to nurse, but caregiver to daughter. Chet was blown away when they stepped out onto the deck and smoked cigarettes. It was all to surreal. Perhaps any second the world might crack open and they would all disappear.

Mary kept going into the dining room to make sure the snacks were arranged just so and there was plenty to drink. From other parts of the house there came a laugh, or a raised voice followed by a laugh. It was still a grim occasion because her heart was so empty, so broken.

The doorbell chimed and she went to open it. A couple Mary barely knew stepped into the house after exchanging a warm greeting and sympathetic hugs. They handed her a tray of cookies.

Chocolate chip. They were still warm under the foil.

Mary took the tray and thanked them profusely. She placed the tray beside the cupcakes. Amy had baked and offered them a drink.

"It's still early in the day but," the man said. "What the hell, what would Chet do?" He took a beer, cracked open the can and saluted Mary. His wife took a Coke.

Mary drifted back to the kitchen then to the living room. The doorbell rang again. It was answered by Chet. He exchanged words and then there was another chuckle. Chet brought a casserole into the kitchen and placed it on the counter.

"Who's there?" she asked.

"No clue. But they knew Pop."

Mary stood in the kitchen after Chet returned to the dining room. She heard Rhee laugh. The doorbell rang again, and Amy placed a bottle of Malbec and a six-pack of beer on the counter, turned, smiled at Mary and returned to the living room.

Tears welled in her eyes as she realized they were probably approaching the limits of Chet Senior's circle of friends and acquaintances. Perhaps ten, maybe a dozen people. They were congregating in the living and dining rooms. She made herself another highball. How could she commiserate with so many people she barely knew and some she didn't know at all? Most of all, she didn't want to get drunk. If it were the other way around her husband would be half lit by now.

Chet stood in the living room. The house was increasingly crowded with people, nearly all of them strangers. It was so warm with the concentration of bodies, he had to open the living room windows and the one over the sink in the kitchen. He did not know his father had so many friends. Perhaps they had journeyed to the wrong wake. He held a coffee cup as if it were a prop to avoid talking to people. But in his uniform, he was hard to miss. He looked at the framed *Life* magazine cover for the thousandth time.

"That's me."

Chet turned to the sound of the voice. "I beg your pardon."

"That's me in the picture. I'm the one he's carrying." It was only then Chet noticed the voice had an Asian face.

"My name is Sammy Nguyen."

Sammy extended his hand which Chet warmly shook.

"That's *you*?" Chet said not hiding his incredulity.

"It is. Your dad and I go way back."

"Explain, please."

"My mother was killed by a North Vietnamese rocket to our shop in Hue. It was the start of Tet. He heard me crying and pulled me out of the wreckage and took me to an aid station. A *Life* magazine photographer snapped the picture. I was evacuated with other orphans much later when Saigon fell. I was brought to San Francisco and adopted. My adoptive parents told me the story of the picture. How they came to know this remains a mystery. After I graduated from Stanford, I went to the magazine archives to find out who that Marine was, to see if he was alive, so I could thank him."

"You tracked down my father to thank him all these years later for saving your life?"

"Yes. He was quite surprised. From that point on, we became good friends, although, until today, I never met him. We exchanged birthday cards every year. I told him about my life, and he told me stories about his. He was regular as clockwork. Then I didn't get one. He was very proud of you."

"He never told us this. Any of it."

"I'm not sure he even told your mother. I think the war disturbed him too much. When I did not get a birthday card from him last week, I wondered if something had happened. That's when I found out he was dying. I flew right out so I could thank him one more time in person. But he passed away before I got to talk to him. I am sorry for your loss."

"That's the damnedest thing I've ever heard."

"I will miss our annual letters."

Uncertain as to what to say next, Chet asked, "What do you do?"

"I own a software company in Silicon Valley. I have a wife and three grown children. I owe it all to your father. Everything. I even named my first son after him."

"Does my mother know this?"

"I don't know."

"My sister?"

"I don't know. They looked at me oddly when I came in." "Don't feel bad, Sammy. I don't know most of these people either. I'll have to tell them. They won't believe it. I wonder why he would keep such an important story to himself. I've looked at that picture a thousand times."

Nguyen extended his hand again. It was a firm handshake. "It was like our little secret. I loved him so much. Sorry he passed away. He was a good man."

"You flew in for this?"

"Of course. Wouldn't you?"

Chet looked up at the picture for a moment. When he turned back to Nguyen he had melted back into the crowd. "I'll be damned," he whispered to himself.

Amy walked over, took the cup from Chet's hand and replaced it with a highball.

"Here."

"Thanks. You read my mind."

"I have found that easy to do. You wear your heart on your sleeve. Or at least on your face."

Chet spoke softly, "I was worried I might not get the chance to say goodbye."

"You did, Chet. He heard you."

There was a commotion at the foyer. He heard his mother get excited at the front door and handed the highball back to Amy for safe keeping. "Now what?" he whispered.

He saw a woman with obvious Down's Syndrome wearing thick glasses accompanied by a smiling man with a goatee and splayed legs step into the foyer. She gave Mary a huge hug. The woman had a baby in her arms. Mary made quite a fuss over them. Their embrace was tight, and Chet hoped they had not injured the infant in their exuberance. When she turned to introduce them, Mary had tears in her eyes. They were the joyful kind.

"This is our son, Chet." Rose, grinning from ear to ear, got up on her tippy toes and gave Chet a firm hug and a peck on the cheek. He was again worried some harm might come to the baby. Crush injury, perhaps.

"This is Chet," she said introducing the baby to Chet and Mary.

Wow was all Chet could think. He inspected the baby. He had no choice, Rose thrust the baby up into his arms. He pulled the blankets back a little to see its face. The new Chet wore a blue knit cap and matching onesie. The baby looked perfectly normal. Two hands, two feet. Ten fingers and ten toes. The little guy had dodged a genetic catastrophe.

People walked over to Rose and Roger to take part in greeting the baby and making small talk with the proud parents. Most already knew them from the mill.

The house had become so packed with laughing and drinking, Mary grew concerned there might be a violation of some Fire Department code or municipal ordinance about how many occupants were allowed in a domicile at one time. She went to the front door and saw more couples, often laughing or in otherwise good humor headed into their driveway.

There were enough casseroles, cakes and cookies arrayed on the flat surfaces of the house to feed a regiment. Most of the people she barely knew or looked familiar but couldn't precisely place. They greeted her as tough they had cocktails over lunch just yesterday. There was laughter, loud conversation and drinking; they were celebrating more than just a life. They were celebrating a legend, a legend of which she had no knowledge. She was pleased for her family and her friends.

It warmed her heart and, apparently, the hearts of her children. She went to the kitchen.

Chapter Nineteen
Closure

Junior walked to the back door. He sipped the drink he held in his hand and watched the men gathered on the back deck to drink and smoke. A short time later he felt Benny's arm around his shoulder. A few moments later Rhee stepped beside Benny and held his hand. They stood silently watching the men on the deck. They saw Charlie, of gray crown and paunch, his back against the deck railing, a concerned look on his face. There were raised voices. A big man Chet did not recognize was gesticulating wilding and poking Charlie in the chest with his finger. Charlie appeared to be having none of it. Violence was in the offing. Chet gave thought to intervening.

There was the sudden burst of laughter. Charlie threw his arm around the big man as they guffawed. Skorskie spilled his beer. Even Nguyen laughed with these perfect strangers.

Mary said softly, "Must have just told a Chet story. Sometimes your father was a difficult man to like. But he was an easy man to love."

The End

The First White Woman

Excerpt From the forthcoming novel
Ivory
A novel of Love and Murder

I pulled on my shoulder rig and made sure there was one in the chamber. I stepped out of the tent and zipped it shut. I loaded about twenty-five pounds of rocks wrapped in a towel into the ruck sack, closed it. I wished good morning to the resident baboon chieftain as he started each day perched on a tree stump a half dozen yards away. He turned and pointed his bulbous red ass toward me and squirted his morning greeting of liquid feces in my direction. Over the past week it had become a routine. I should have shot the revolting bastard the first time he did it. Maybe one day I will. If for nothing other than the unsanitary insult.

I trotted over to the dirt road and adjusted my earbuds, despite the resulting reduction in my situational awareness; but this was the Democratic Republic of Congo not the Hindu Kush. I turned on Rascal Flatts. My feet started pounding the road as "Life is a Highway" pounded against my eardrums.

Keno's was about five miles away and this was my first trip back to the small village since Dembe Keno dropped me off at the campsite a week ago. I longed for the first swig of cold beer.

The run was uneventful. No tigers jumped out to make me their lunch. No viper fell from a tree to poison me. No poacher mistook me for an elephant. It was a good run and I was covered with pleasing sweat.

The village, Nguadula, was spread out on both sides of the road, its main street—only street—was about a football field in length. There were only two brick buildings. The local constabulary and the UN clinic. There was a line waiting to get in. The door was open, and I could hear a baby crying.

Keno owned a general store attached to his bar on the near end of the town. He had a few rooms for rent above the bar, one in which I had spent my first full night in the DRC. Passible but not the Waldorf. The ceiling fan in the center of the room was in desperate need of oiling. The general store was actually well provisioned with everything from flashlights and car batteries to weapons and ammunition.

The road was lined on one side by women sitting on the dirt or stools in brightly colored dashikis selling fruit or potatoes, small clay pots and trinkets. Dead chickens hung by their feet from a clothesline; some were plucked naked. Others were not. Little kids ran around playing with one another. Some were wearing nothing but a tee-shirt.

The other side of the street was lined with trees, dirt plots and shanties of various construction.

Nguadula could easily pass for a town in the Wild West. The only thing missing were the horses tied up to hitching posts, piles of oxen droppings and a pair of gunfighters poised in the middle of the street awaiting their fate.

Keno's was the last building at the far end of the street. Parked on the side was his pristine 1955 Ford F100 pickup, the envy of any collector. I rode in it when he brought me and my gear down from Kivu. It ran like a swiss watch. Magnificent. Car show quality. Probably the only one on the continent.

I stepped into the bar for the second time. It was dark with a long counter, open, unscreened windows and three ceiling fans, one of which wobbled slightly and made a clinking noise with each rotation. The plank floor was covered with dirt and cigarette butts. It had a large crowd some of which were seated at the ten wooden tables; the others lined the bar. An unwitting, picture-perfect replica of a cowboy saloon.

The bar was filled, mostly with native Congolese. But, I noted as I stepped up to the bar and purchased a Tusker, two Eastern European fellows and a Middle Eastern gentleman with a janbiya dagger on his belt complete with a yellowed ornate ivory saifani handle reflecting the status of the man wearing it. I hadn't seen one of these since left Afghanistan. He stood alone, separate from the Europeans. His ilk and I had a shared history. Nobody seemed to notice me except the Arab. Figured.

As I worked my way past the crowded bar, I searched for an empty table or someplace I could enjoy my drink. I wondered how many of the patrons had their wives squatting out on the dirt hawking dead chickens and clay pots.

When I saw her, she was sitting alone at the table in the corner peeling the label off her beer with her fingernail. She was as incandescent at a naked light bulb in a coalmine.

I walked over and stared down at her. She looked up.

"Yes?"

"You are the first white person I've seen since I left Kinshasa."

She jerked her thumb at the Europeans. "What about them?"

"I saw you first. They don't count. Let me rephrase: the first white woman I've seen since I left Kinshasa." She stared up at me as if I were a leper. "May I join you?"

She pushed the chair away from the table with her boot.

"Sure. You're the first white man I've seen in a month. Sit. No monkey business or that man over there"—she nodded toward the bar— "will kill you."

The Arab had fixed his cold stare on me as he fingered the saifani of his janbiya. The saifani tells the status of the man who carries it. This was an important dude. I nodded, tipped my ballcap and smiled. He returned his cold stare to his drink.

"Duly noted."

I sat down on the chair placing my beer on the table as unthreateningly as possible.

"Let me ask you a question. Who are you and why are you here?" she asked.

"That's actually two questions. But I'll answer them in the order posed and then I get to ask you two."

"Fair enough."

I extended my hand saying, "My name is Aubrey Wickersham." I was reminded again by my mother's admonition never to shake a woman's hand unless she offered hers first. It was simple, if antiquated, etiquette. I extended my hand. She had a firm grip. She wore black, expensive looking aviator's watch on her left wrist. She combined Hope Hicks' beauty with a barnyard aroma.

"Ellie. Nice to meet you Aubrey."

"But people call me Jack."

"Why?"

He sipped his beer. "It's my middle name and I don't like Aubrey and 'Wick' is part of a candle."

"Aubrey Jack Wickersham. Sounds like Fifth Avenue."

"Just Jack. But I see your point."

"So, answer my question, what are you doing here?"

"I am here on assignment with National Geographic. I am a photographer. One of those Russians over there just commented on your tits. Admiringly so."

"You speak Russian?"

"Da."

She returned her attention to the task of mutilating the label. I studied her while she picked. She had a narrow-sculpted face and bright blue eyes that made her seem vulnerable. Her hair was blond with a few streaks of darker shade. It was pulled back in a ponytail and had a sheen to it that indicated she had not washed it in a week, probably longer. I wondered if the carpet matched the drapes. If there even was a carpet. She looked hot beneath a thin blouse that was unbuttoned down to the start of an appealing, rounded décolletage. She wore a dirty pair of khaki shorts and trail boots that were caked with dry clumps of red mud. Her lithe, tanned legs bore scratches at various angles.

She was beautiful as a debutante and probably equally fecund. Why she wasn't standing on the lawn of a split-level with a two-year-old tugging at her house dress, a one year old on her hip and pregnant was a question for the ages. Instead she looked like she belonged on the cover of either Cosmopolitan or Field and Stream.

"So how come you know Russian?" she asked.

"That's a *third* question. I studied it in college. Thought it might come in handy someday. So, my first question is what in the hell is a nice girl like you doing in a place like this?"

"Studying the genome of *Loxodonta cyclopigus.*" She made a disgusted face and shook her head almost imperceptibly.

"Absolutely fascinating. Making any progress?"

"Yes."

"What the hell is a *lexicon psychoclitoris*?"

"*Loxodonta cyclotis.* The African forest elephant."

"Ah, pachyderm genes. Sounds interesting." I said rocking back in my seat. I hoped he did not sound too incredulous. "Actually, sounds more like a clothing line at Babies-r-us."

"With all the poaching, it appears elephants are evolving into a tusk-less subspecies. That way they will stop being killed for their ivory. And I am trying to prove it."

"I thought poaching was for all intents and purposes stopped in this region."

"It has been. That's why those two Russians make me nervous."

"Maybe they're methane men. Or prospectors."

"Maybe. We shall see."

"Who's the Arab over there. Seems like he knows you."

"Khalid. My father hired him to look after me. I told the old fart I could take care of myself, but he insisted, or he would withhold his money. It was either Khalid or no funding."

"You're not from some hoity-toity university?"

"Well, Actually I am. Berkeley. But they cut the funding. So, my dad chipped in. What's your claim to fame before you became a photographer?"

"Who said I had one? I was a Ranger."

"Park Ranger?"

"No. the other kind."

Her interest piqued, she leaned forward becoming more animated, "Oh, you might know my Dad. What position did you play?"

"Position?"

"He's a minority owner of the Texas Rangers. Owns Trask Corporation."

"Trask of *The* Trask Corporation?"

"Yep, that's him."

"What do they do?"

"Build stuff like highways, buildings, you know, stuff."

"Say, didn't they build that bridge that fell down killing all those people?"

"No, I don't think so. What bridge? So, you didn't answer my question."

"I was an Army Ranger. The 75th Ranger Regiment. First Battalion."

"Oh," she said with the same inflection as if I had told her I had a sixth toe on my right foot.

I turned to look at Khalid. We exchanged cautious stares. "I don't think your boy there, Khalid, likes me very much."

"He's okay once you get to know him. He's no 'boy' as you say. Did you ever kill anybody?"

"That's a question you should never ask a man. But, since you asked, hundreds, maybe thousands."

She stared into my eyes with piercing contempt.

"When you call in an airstrike heads will roll. Lots of heads."

Her revulsion must have been picked up by Khalid because he walked over and bent down to speaking softly, "Are you ready to go, Miss Trask?"

Miss Trask. Jack wondered if Khalid had ever seen her moist little nest. Going native like this, it was anybody's guess.

"No, I'll have another." She looked at Jack. "He's buying."

"Damn nice of me." I took out some bills and handed them to Khalid. I noticed the tips of his ring and pinkie fingers were missing as he took the bills. "Get yourself another, Friend."

"I'm also tracking poached ivory by DNA analysis to see where it was taken and where it is seized. Fortunately, that business has slowed."

"So, the absence of tusks is a new thing? Makes them second-class elephants. Kinda like de Lamarck."

"Who?"

"You know, the guy who figured it out before Darwin. A bird gets a hankerin' for seafood and a couple generations later it's a duck. Elephant gets killed for its tusks so all of a sudden, he doesn't grow a pair. Cool."

"No, you twit. The mutant elephant without a tusk is left alone to reproduce. He or she has no value to the poachers. The new mutant gene is passed on saving the species from a negative survival pressure."

"I'm siding with the duck."

"What community college did you go to?"

"Princeton. Lacrosse scholarship. Full ride."

"Incredible. That explains everything."

Khalid placed two beers on the table and said, "I'll go check on the horses."

"Where'd you find that dude?"

"Dude? My Dad knew people who knew people with certain skill sets, and he was hired to look after me. I don't think they made him take some sort of blood oath or anything but he's attentive and careful. Watch your step around me, Ranger. I give him the word and they won't find your headless body."

"Lovely. You must feel pretty safe then."

"Especially from any horny strangers."

"Married?"

"Nope."

"Fiancé?"

"Used too."

"Boyfriend?"

"Gee, I'm beginning to think you've used up all your twenty questions."

"You counting questions? I take that as a no. It always concerns me that you San Francisco prima donnas think we're all lug-heads who can't spell, think for ourselves, drag our knuckles when we walk and don't give a fuck about the environment. Save the planet. Use just the minimum amount of toilet paper so as not to draw flies to the seat of our pants."

"Oh no. Not usually anyway. And I'm from Atlanta."

"You don't sound like it."

"I grew up in New Jersey."

"Hey, what do you know? Me too."

"Yeah? What exit?"

"Is there any poaching around here?"

"Poaching? There's been no poaching for almost a year that I am aware of and I've been keeping a lookout for it. The authorities ran them out. Bloody affair. At least I can say I haven't heard of any for a while. Not sure about other places in the Kahuzi-Biega Park. It's a big park. There may still be a few out there but not like it was. To their credit, the park scouts and the burgeoning tourist trade has kept them out. Same with bush meat."

"Aren't you worried about being out here all alone?"

"No, not really. Khalid looks after me. Besides, I was a Brownie."

"What does worry you?"

"That you're going to continue to sit there." She leaned back and started working on her next beer label. "One of these days the universe is going to run out of protons. Then where would we be? The Universe is negative enough already."

"What? You know the handle of Khalid's rat-stabber over there is made of ivory."

"He said it was from a walrus."

I rocked back on the chair's two back legs and said, "And you believed him?"

She turned around to snatch a glimpse out the window. There were dark clouds looming on the horizon. Looks like I am going to have a wet run home. Maybe it will cool off a little. As her face was turned, I noted a small smudge of dirt on her cheek. I wanted to lick my thumb, reach over and wipe it off like my mom did as I found its presence distracting. She probably would have reacted to the gentle gesture with a karate chop to my Adam's Apple. Or else have Khalid stroll over and gut me right there in the bar.

"You know, you're really annoying."

"It's a gift. So why do you Georgia debutantes think we're all lug heads who can't spell and drag our knuckles when we walk?"

"Boy, you're a real dick."

"Well, I used to be a staff sergeant at basic training so the moniker fits."

"Got any good pictures lately?"

"Yeah, I was trying to catch some elephant piss in a special container from a small elephant. The mother took exception to me collecting her calf's tinkle, so she charged me. Got some great pictures of a very pissed off elephant baby-momma."

"Oh pishaw.? You must be the dumbest male I've ever seen. Somebody is making an ass out of you. Who told you that, seriously?"

"The guy in charge of the elephants at the Bronx Zoo."

"Tried it yet?"

"Yeah."

"How'd it go?"

"Like I said, I was almost stomped flat."

Khalid dropped off two more bottles of beer on the table and said, "I'm going to go check on the horses." She pulled some loose hair back behind her ears. She did it frequently almost like a nervous tic.

"And you sit around sprinkling foreign elephant piss trying to get a rise out of the king. Don't make him mad."

"Got it."

"If he's in musth he's already working on a hair trigger."

"Okay."

"Piss is piss. Musth is another matter entirely. Be careful who you piss off." She suddenly pushed back, slapping the table with her hands. "Shit! I just made a funny!"

I could not suppress a smile. "Thanks for the heads-up. I kinda figured that."

"Elephant piss marks territory and will draw out aggression."

"Where'd you hear that again?"

"Read it in a book and the aforementioned zookeeper."

"I don't even want to talk to you. You're a moron."

"Who's convinced I'm not?"

"You don't know the least bit about elephants, do you?"

"You could teach me."

"It would be like transferring knowledge to an aardvark. You're such a twit. You should have stayed in New Jersey. If for no other reason than the sake of the dignity of these animals."

Without warning, she pushed back from the table. "I gotta pee and go home. See you around, Ranger."

She nodded to Khalid, stood and without a second glance or another word, walked out of the bar, Khalid in trail.

I was in love.

Siren

There is nothing so compelling as a siren in the middle of the night.

The Beast of Train 317

I remember praying that I didn't want to die: a frozen, anonymous and forgotten corpse buried under the snow. Looking back, I wish I had if I'd known what was in store. Some selfless act of heroism and sacrifice for which I might have won a Medal of Honor or a least a posthumous Bronze Star. This might give succor to my grieving parents that I died a hero.

We held our position as long as we could in a foxhole sitting in front of a small stand of fir trees. But they kept coming. Yelling and screaming and laughing as if it were all fun. Sometimes they tripped and fell in the snow as if they were drunk. Their laughing was inappropriate to the circumstance. Bordering on hysterical. I was trying to kill them, and they were trying to kill me. They were either drunk or drugged. Maybe both. But they prevailed by numbers and ruthlessness. We were on the losing side of this martial equation.

Miller, on my left, stood up stupidly to fire his Tommy gun and took a round in the forehead instantly filling his helmet with bone, hair and wet brains. I turned to see Jones on my right. In the brief moment

I looked away he was hit in the throat spouting blood like a fountain. He gurgled a bloody sigh and fell back, eyes wide open so he could get a good look at eternity.

A German charged at me ready to pull the trigger. I threw down my rifle and stood up both hands extended as far above my head as I could reach ignominiously shouting, "*Nicht schiesen*! *Ich ergebe mich*! *Nicht schiesen*!" over and over loud as I could. Often mortality trumps a futile, insane act of sacrifice. The instantaneous visceral act of self-preservation sometimes wins. No medal today.

A second Nazis grabbed me and pulled me out of the blood-spattered, snow-filled foxhole and threw me to the ground. He kicked me savagely twice in the gut. I grabbed my stomach and yelled hoping his jackboot had not broken some important organ inside. I shielded myself awaiting the next blow, but it did not come. A comrade came running past only pausing long enough to kick me in the back. The second captor banged something against my helmet. It was either his boot or the stock of his rifle. Roles reversed I'd have killed me without a second thought.

No sooner had I struggled to my feet than they pushed me down onto the bloody snow landing onto poor Miller. One of the two Germans went to his knees and pulled off my rubber overshoes and started congratulating himself over his find. The other Kraut started rifling through the pockets of my two dead comrades finding two D-ration chocolate bars, three packs of cigarettes and the picture of a sweetheart. He kissed the picture, said something certainly lewd and put it in his pocket. They turned their attention to poor Jones. They yanked off my companions' overshoes. They pulled off our watches and rings and stuffed the booty into their pockets. They even took Miller's glasses from his face.

"*Raus! Raus! Herraus mit uns*!"

I pulled myself to my feet and they pushed me in the direction from whence they had come down a long, sloping, open field. I fell in the snow and they took turns kicking me and swearing until I was able to get up.

I was joined by other GIs, some in terrible shape. The number of

Germans escorting us increased too. By guarding us, I figured, they were no doubt eager to get as far away from the bloody maw of battle as they could.

We walked past tanks and halftracks covered with jeering krauts. They threw snowballs at us and spit on us.

There were probably thirty captives by the time we came to a halt five miles behind their lines. An angry looking officer separated the officers from the enlisted and took them away.

We walked another few miles before we reached a large muddy field. We had heard of the massacre in Malmedy and, as they pushed us into a compact cluster, some started crying and whimpering figuring this was it. It all ended here. I was resigned to being murdered feeling lucky to have survived this long. A truck came up and pushed a dozen shovels out the back. They were making us dig our own graves. We remained passive as sheep.

"Where are the Jews?" said the *feldwebel* in densely German-accented English. No one moved.

"Jews step forward! Now!"

Same result.

"I will ask only one more time." He raised his burp gun toward us. "Where are the Jews!"

Finally, two brave souls stepped forward and the *feldwebel* pushed and kicked them into a patch of woods at the end of the field. A moment after they disappeared two shots rang out.

Several minutes later, the *feldwebel* returned. This bastard was so depraved even the SS wouldn't have him.

"Now dig!"

There weren't enough shovels to go around, so he told us to dig with our bare hands or our helmets. One poor lad had a bad shoulder wound and could not use the shovel, so he stood. One of the guards walked over and pulled him out of the crowd and pushed him to the ground. I suspect most of us expected him to be shot but, he wasn't. He just fell to the snow in his own private agony.

We were digging a mass grave. When we were done, they were going to kill us and bury the evidence.

As I chipped at the frozen ground with a dull, wooden spade, I noticed a dark, amorphous mound near the edge of the clearing. Bodies had been stacked like cord wood. I could not discern at this distance whose army the corpses belonged to.

"Bigger! Deeper! Faster! You swinehunds! Don't make me kill you too soon."

After two hours of digging, we finally reached unfrozen earth and the task became a little easier. Finally, the hole reached acceptability.

"Stop! Get out!" He kicked a few who were too exhausted to move quickly enough. By now we were so thirsty we started eating the snow still clean enough to suck on.

"Come vis me. All of you! *Schnell! Macht Schnell!*" Some walked, some staggered or limped in the direction of the amorphous pile. Growing closer, we saw the pile of a dozen frozen Germans corpses.

"Pick zem up respectfully and carry zem to their grave. If you drop zem, you will soon join zem."

We collectively grabbed zem by their tunics and pant legs and carried zem to the pit. One by one we laid them to rest side by side in the shallow pit under the watchful eyes of a corporal with a rifle.

I heard one of us say just above a whisper, "Here lies Hans and Franz, brave *soldatin* of zee Turd Reichhhh."

A few of us snickered. One surreptitiously dropped a long string of saliva onto a body and whispered, "Sleep well, *mien* kinder. Listen for the Valkyries."

"You! Vat were you sayink?"

"A prayer for the dead, *Feldwebel*."

"No talking or the shooting vill begin. Now get out! Fill it. Kvickly. My name is *Feldwebel* Klaus Richter. You vill do as I say, do it kvickly or you will die."

I knew some of us enjoyed burying these dead krauts. Could we have anointed the bodies with piss and gotten away with it, we would have.

Task completed, we were sent back to the road and marched east. As we passed the small section of trees, I looked for the dead Jews but could not see them. Missing in Action for all eternity. A short time later, sleet started pecking at our faces. It became dark quickly. Every few minutes, we had to clear the road to allow movement of tanks, halftracks and troops to pass. Bringing up the rear were dozens of horse-drawn wagons filled with jeering, spitting Krauts. I hoped they would all be dead by sunrise either slaughtered by a resurgent defense or ripped apart by aerial or artillery bombardment.

A few men collapsed with exhaustion. Hungry, thirsty, tired and scared, we helped them along as best we could. A few just fell dead by the road.

Finally, as the snow took the place of the biting sleet, we stopped, moving a short distance off the road. After a while, a horse-drawn wagon arrived and pulled off the road. A steamy broth of water with a few floating pieces of what looked like grass was ladled out in metal cups to each of us. The swill warmed us even if there was nothing of substance in it.

After this brief respite, Richter strode up, "*Steh auf*! On your foots! Move!"

All but two were able to stand. One was dead, the other not strong enough to rise. We helped him up, but he could not walk. More shouting, we placed him back to the ground being as caring and gentle as we could. We walked on. I looked back at him as we rounded the bend and he passed out of sight.

I figured we had gone at least ten miles as a freezing drizzle pelted us, stiffening our uniforms. I had no idea how many had fallen by the wayside. Our collection looked smaller perhaps down to a count of thirty.

A few hours later, we could hear the low monotonous rumble of planes. Probably hundreds of them. Likely RAF bombers high above the clouds headed into Germany. It was my fervent wish they would pulverize and set fire to the city Richter's mother lived in and incinerate her.

It was the middle of the night I guessed when we finally stopped alongside a railroad siding after walking or staggering, off and on for ten hours. We joined a larger group of about two hundred GIs. We collectively collapsed onto the side of the roadbed. Another buckboard drawn by two sickly, emaciated horses pulled up with two steaming kettles in the back. One contained a thin soup with potato peels floating in it. The peels were soft and easy to chew. The second kettle contained ersatz coffee nearly as thin as the soup. They handed out loaves of hard, black bread. We each tore off a piece and passed it on.

An hour or so later, a line of weathered, reddish-brown, four-wheeled goods wagons was backed into the siding by the puffing 'little engine that could.' Each wagon was stenciled: 'Hommes 40: Chevaux 8.' Forty men or eight horses.

Richter and his sidekicks opened the doors and made us climb into the cars. We could hear subdued voices coming from some of the wagons. We climbed aboard helping those who could not manage the task themselves. Others from the roadside collection of prisoners were also told to climb into our wagon. By the time we were all on, Richter slammed the door shut, engaged the latch. We did our best to sit. There were so many GIs jammed into the wagon most of us had to stand.

One guy slumped in the corner sobbing. I never saw him move again.

In another corner of the boxcar, there was a round opening clearly meant to be a place for us to shit and piss through. It would take many minutes to push through the throng to get to it. By then the urgency of the moment would take hold and they would piss or shit our pants. By the time the train started moving the place started to smell like a sewer.

There were two small rectangular openings near the roof where we could see sky and trees pass by. After a time, the heat generated by all the jostling bodies caused the steam from our breath to cease.

A small commotion developed in one of the corners. Tempers flared as a guy collapsed to the floor. Their comrades separated them, but the swearing continued. I did not know what the raucous was all about. I didn't care to know.

Things quieted except for some moaning, frequent coughing fits and an episode of swearing that accompanied someone's fingers or crotch getting stepped on.

The raw smell of piss and shit saturated the wagon. I finally worked enough room to sit. If there was a Hell, this was it. There was low conversation and the occasional sobbing episode.

At one point, I suspect around midday, we slowed and pulled onto a siding. A heavy train raced past us causing our forty and eights to vibrate, creak and rock gently. More fodder for the front. Good.

We started up again. After an hour, we heard the distant approach of aircraft. It drew rapidly closer as the pitch of its engine changed. Suddenly, we heard the firing of machine guns and saw instantaneous shafts of angled light through holes in the ceiling There was screaming as some of the guys were hit crumbling to the floor as the train speeded up. Some lost our footing and fell into writhing, disoriented human jumbles on the floor causing more yelling and cursing. I could hear the moans of those who had been hit by Allied bullets.

We listened to changes in the pitch of the engine to hear if the plane was going to bank around for a second run. But it quickly receded and did not return.

Hours passed in this private corner of perdition as it grew dark outside. The wounded and dying moaned and wept. The train slowed, pulled into a siding and abruptly jerked to a stop causing some to fall like bowling pins and robust swearing. The door was opened, and a kettle of luke-warm soup with three small floating potatoes and a radish was lifted up to us followed by two loaves of black bread. We were all starving but we shared as equitably as we could. The potatoes were cut apart with a small jackknife that had escaped confiscation and the small pieces were passed to the ones who seemed most critically sick.

After half an hour, the door opened, and the empty kettle was removed. The door was slammed shut, latched and shortly the train lurched forward again. The train continued into the night.

By morning, two more men had died. They were removed when we next stopped to let an express through. Their bodies were laid on the road ballast and left there as we pulled away. I didn't know their names hoping that one day the kid's family would know their loved one's fate.

It was a bright sunny morning. A good day for the Air Corps guys to pound the living shit out of this God-forsaken, hell-bent country. Pummel and smash everything into the ground and if anything tried to rise like an evil Phoenix, grind the place into sawdust again.

Men in the boxcar started getting dysentery with foul-smelling shit running down their pantlegs like an evil, wretched hot lava. I was lucky but I knew eventually it would afflict me.

After several hours, we pulled over again. This time we were allowed out of the car and made to stand on the ground beyond the train. It was then apparent we were part of a larger train with perhaps a dozen cars all disgorging GIs. It was difficult for the men to move as muscles were weak and our bones and joints ached. We hobbled weakly like invalids forced to their feet. We helped each other. Looking up and down the train, with the cars finally empty, I estimated there were two hundred of us standing in a long line. I took little comfort that they looked even worse than we did. The two or three guards covering us with their rifles slung from their soldiers looked bored. They lit cigarettes hoping some of the smoke would get exhaled in our direction.

Finally, Richter, clearly in charge of the whole train, came strutting to the center of the captives looking one way then the other.

"Jews. I'm looking for Jews. Which vons of you are Juden? Step forward. Now!"

No one moved. The only sound was the coughing.

"I'm not going to ask again. Who are the Jews?"

Frustrated by the silence, Richter strode over to our boxcar pointing to one of the men a few down in line from me.

"You! Vot is your religion? You look like a dirty little Jew."

"I'm not Jewish."

"Well you look like a Jew."

"Too much sun. I have a tan. My long nose I get from my auntie. She lives in Hoboken." Suddenly, Richter pulled him out of line and shot him at point blank range in the chest.

He crumpled to the ground, twitched twice and was dead.

Richter was a mere two feet from me. I could smell him. I wanted to reach out and kill him with his own bayonet. It would take me but a second becoming a worthy gesture of sacrifice on my part as the two guards filled me with lead. But alas I controlled my rage.

Richter moved up the line to the GIs in the car beside us.

"What's your religion? You look like a Jew."

"I am catholic." He reached into the front of his shirt and pulled out a crucifix, dangling it in front of Richter's nose.

Visibly disappointed, he yelled for everyone to get back into the 40 and 8s.

Private Hennessy, an ammo carrier in our weapons platoon whom I met at the Repple Depple, apparently didn't move fast enough to suit Richter so he pushed him to the ground. Hennessy was so weak there was no protest left in him. As he made a feeble attempt to get up, Richter bent down and yelled in his ear, "*Aufstehen*! *Raus*! *Swinehund*!" Hennessey pulled himself onto all fours, but he fell back over onto the ballast. He lifted his head up and moved his right arm, Richter kicked him square in the head with the power of an opening kickoff. The impact of the boot knocked him out cold and tore his scalp which started to bleed profusely. No one wanted to assist him lest they feel the jackboot or a bullet. Unconscious and incapable of further movement, I feared the boy would be shot and left on the roadbed as the train pulled away. Instead, we gathered him up and lifted him gently back into the boxcar yielding enough space for him to lay down. His breathing soon became a wet gurgle, slowed and stopped with an agonal snort.

I had help as I moved the dead boy to the door. I held him in my arms as he passed. At least he wasn't alone when he died.

The train rattled on. Above the clatter of the train, I could hear bombs exploding in the faraway night. Eventually, I fell asleep, my arms still cradling the boy.

It was well into the night when we stopped again. I curled the boy deeper into my arms. His body had begun to stiffen. Outside I could hear yelling. Then some laughter. I heard the unmistakable sound of Richter's voice. He seemed to be standing right outside our door. I banged on the door with my fist as hard as I could. Those around me stepped away. After a moment, I heard the latch release. I braced myself as the door slid back. When I saw Richter, I shoved the body of Private Hennessy onto the fucking bastard. Richter fell back onto the ground losing his grip on the rifle. I followed Hennessy out landing full square onto Richter. Using all my strength, I grabbed the rifle, lifted it above my head and crashed the butt into his face as he tried to push me off. I could feel the satisfying crunch of bone transmitted through the rifle. The pleasing power of each blow surprised me considering my how weak I was. With his face turned to bloody pulp, he still stared back at me through one eye. I stood over him as he struggled to move. I pulled his bayonet from its scabbard and plunged it deeply into his chest. I twisted it from side to side to make sure his black soul felt it. He twitched once or twice and died. I tried to pull his body over to the woods that lined the tracks, but all of my strength had been exhausted. Suddenly, the load became lighter as several of the men jumped down to help me ditch the body.

Returning to the boxcar, I hurled the bloody rifle and bayonet into the woods. We climbed back into it and I collapsed on the floor. Though no word was spoken, several of the men came over to pat me on my head. One reached down and shook my hand. I was also lucky Richter was the only German who stepped off the train when it stopped.

I was sorry we had to leave Hennessy by the tracks. It was his last good act as a soldier.

The Chihuahua

It was 2AM and things were quiet. Pleasingly so for a change. I was catching up on computer medical records of the patients I had seen earlier. Two cases of the flu. One fractured ankle. One acute MI. One scalded baby. All since I took over at eleven. Praise Jesus for copy and paste. What a great invention.

The third-year medical student was anxious to see the next patient who rolled into the ER. Clearly, he wanted something to do. He begged me to allow him to see the next patient that came in. Regardless of what it was. He danced around like he had ants in his pants.

"Have at it, Dude," was all I needed to say.

Twenty minutes later he ran over to me and said, "I just saw a patient." He was so excited there was perspiration on his upper lip.

"Okay, give the details." I put my feet onto the desk.

"Twenty-nine-year-old female presents with the chief complaint of a dead chihuahua in her vagina."

"You don't say?"

"She said it was a little puppy. She couldn't find him when she went to look."

"How does she know the puppy's dead?" I asked as I dropped my feel to the floor.

"She didn't say."

"Is it her puppy?"

"She didn't say that either."

"Has this ever happened before?"

"Not sure."

"Any allergies?"

"I didn't ask."

"Any pre-existing illnesses?"

"I don't know that either."

"Well, so far this has been a very incomplete history of the present illness."

"Shall I call the psyche resident on call?"

"No. How do you know we don't need an obstetrician? Did you do a preliminary examination?"

"No."

"So, you don't really know if there is a chihuahua puppy in her vagina?"

"No, sir."

"You cannot make a preliminary diagnosis of anything without at least a quick examination, now, can you?"

"No."

"Get a nurse, put her up in stirrups and take a look."

"She said not to pet him, he might bite."

"Go! Be glad it's not a pit bull she lost. Git!"

Paris or the Lost Generation, part duex

My summer vacation was brief. Mid-August I packed two suitcases, kissed my parents and sisters goodbye and took the train to New York. I spent the night in a hotel and next morning embarked on the *SS Champlain* of the French Line, *Compagnie Generale Transatlantique*, setting sail for Le Havre. I was nicely accommodated in tourist class. The cruise lasted seven days. On the way, I met a dark-haired French delight named Monique De Velban.

I was fascinated by the big ship. After dinner, the second evening at sea, I stood by the railing gently buffeted by the sea breeze mesmerized by smell of the ocean, the lapping waves against the hull and the soft roar of the bow pushing through the water. I was smoking a cigarette and daydreaming of Barbary pirates and Jutland when Monique sidled up to me and asked in heavily French-accented English if I had a light. She was surprised when I spoke French back to her obviously, and correctly, taking me for an American. It immediately disarmed the moment and we freely conversed in both French and English. She was a student at the *Institut d'études politiques de Paris*. Science Po. She wanted to be a diplomat. Her father was an assistant attaché at the consulate in New York. She was returning after spending the summer with her parents. I told her my story. The sun dipped below the western horizon and, even though it was August, it was still the North Atlantic and we both got chilled. I took a blanket from a deck chair and placed it around her shoulders and exposed arms. We hit it off right away, so after about an hour of bilingual chit-chat we retired to the lounge.

The smell of cigars hung heavy in the lounge. It was a beautifully appointed room with dark wood and a fireplace. Warm and inviting. We sidled up to the fire alongside people in evening dress and ordered a bottle of champagne. She wore the blanket like a shawl. We smoked, drank and chatted until one AM. She smiled warmly and started to slur her French. I imagine my English was not so pristine either. I could not tell if the not-so-subtle *bon ami* we were experiencing translated into seduction or intoxication. She kept crossing and uncrossing her legs with sufficient lack of concern to allow me to catch a glimpse of her magnificent white thighs. Not once but, repeatedly.

At last she stood up, extended her hand and wished me a good evening. I shook it warmly and brought it to my lips and kissed it. It was probably the silliest thing I had ever done. I had never kissed a woman's hand before. Or ever had the need to. She smiled, gently withdrew her hand and left. She continued to wear the blanket as if it were a priceless ermine.

I slept soundly, the gentle roll of the ship like a rocking cradle.

The next morning, I went to breakfast as we sailed into a rainstorm. The seas were a little angry but, it did not bother me. I was hoping I might run into Mademoiselle De Velban. But I did not see her. I had eggs benedict, baked salmon and toast, finished with fresh melon. I leisurely smoked some cigarettes, read the papers and drank coffee. Two Bloody Marys blunted my disappointment at not meeting Monique again.

Breakfast completed, I returned to the room, picked up a book, a history of the French Revolution as I recall, and a pad of paper and pencils to be prepared for note taking, poem writing or whatever random burst of creativity might fill my brain. As I left the stateroom, I grabbed a fresh pack of cigarettes and headed for the library as the conditions on deck were windy and wet.

It was a small, quiet room with elegant mahogany paneling and bookshelves from floor to ceiling. As is always my habit when spying a collection of books, I started to peruse the volumes. To my surprise I found quite an eclectic assortment. Everything from Tolstoy to Twain. They had *The Adventures of Huckleberry Finn* in both English and French. Hemingway's *To Have and To Have Not.* And a new novel entitled *Gone with the Wind.* Also in English and French. Margaret Mitchell would be pleased. She was in good company. Proust. Montesquieu, Rostand and a bounty of novels the authors of which were obscure to me.

I settled into a deep, comfortable, leather chair and started reading; the only sound was the constant humming of the engines deep in the bowels of the liner. The only movement the gentle roll and pitch of the ship over the ocean and the passing of an occasional steward. I began to wonder where Monique was or what she might be doing.

Sadly, I did not see her at all that day. I looked for her at dinner. Maybe she was seasick in her cabin. I had drinks in the salon hoping she might stroll in. Or perhaps she knew I would be there waiting and didn't have the heart to tell me she had met someone more interesting who was fluent in Russian.

That night the storm grew more intense and pushed the ship around. I grew queasy but did not vomit. The morning, however, was gorgeous. Not a cloud in the sky. A cool breeze across the deck, the sea as smooth as glass. I scanned the horizon for icebergs but didn't see any. I napped on a deck lounger and when I woke up Monique was stylishly reclining on the one beside me, a broad hat shading her face as she read a magazine. She must have sensed me stirring because when I turned to look at her, she was smiling.

"Beautiful afternoon, no?"

"*Oui*," I said.

She put down her magazine.

"Last night was—how you say—more bouncier." She made an up and down pitching motion with her hand.

"I missed you yesterday," I said.

"I am sorry. Did I disappoint you?"

"Yes."

"Pity," she purred. "Shall we meet for dinner?"

"As you wish."

"Meet me in the salon for a drink around seven-thirty."

"*Absolument*."

She rose to her feet, smiled down at me and walked off, her broad hat bending to the wind. She left her magazine.

After a delightful dinner and a few drinks in the salon, she invited me back to her room. Jackpot. It was much more elegant than mine which in comparison was a large broom closet. I had no prior frame of reference. At twenty years of age, my frames of reference were still limited.

I finally got to kiss more than her hand. I woke up in her bed. Two things stand out in my memory. The enormous tuft of course black hair, thick as the Amazon jungle, that nearly reached halfway to her belly button and how well she could lick an ice cream cone. Things would never be the same. She revealed she was a communist. And I don't think she bathed with any frequency.

I saw her twice more during the remainder of the voyage. Her virginal, mysterious charm now lacking, I found her slightly less captivating. I also noticed that when she contorted her face in pleasure, she was even less appealing. When she spoke during coitus it was as if she were speaking in tongues. Incoherent grunts and moans. And something that passed for a laugh. It was so guttural I could not differentiate between release or pain.

To be chivalrous, I escorted her off the ship. As she stepped off the gangway, she turned to me, gave me a peck on the cheek and said we should meet again in Paris as we would be in such close proximity. I believe she meant it.

I never saw her again.

. . .

The train from Le Havre was delayed taking the better part of two hours to get going. We had disembarked in the late morning and I had hoped to get to Paris by the early afternoon. The process proved much more tedious than I had anticipated. Customs was perfunctory.

As might be expected, the ship disgorged a large number of people from the New World all urgently wanting to get to Paris. The great rush of humanity toward the nearby train station made the transition from ship to train problematic and caused the initial delay as the first train became full and the subsequent one was late. The various classes of accommodation made finding one's ticketed compartment challenging and only added to my frustration. I was glad to get out of the grimy, smelly station and be on my way. I looked for De Velban in the shifting crowds but never caught glimpse of her. Being the daughter of near-royalty, she was probably whisked away by fawning chauffer.

The train took us to Rouen where we stopped for nearly an hour. Then down to Giverny again letting off some passengers. I ticked off each town on a tourist map I had purchased at the station marking my progress. The countryside was green and somewhat hilly. I guess I expected it to be flat as a prairie, but it was not. Vineyards scaled each hill in orderly rows of vines heavy with grapes. There were small, ancient villages constructed around narrow roads and intersections populated by stone houses with tiled roofs and small, squat homes with thatched roofs. Huge trees dotted the fields like magnificent sentries, silent witnesses probably dating back to the Romans. Hundreds of fat cows whipped their tails and munched on the sweet, green grass. I saw small cathedrals in each town their sharp, narrow spires poking the bottom of the sky. By the time we reached Paris it was raining.

Paris was incredible. My first impression was of its vastness and filth. Upon arrival in the 5th arrondissement I went to the rental office near the university that managed the flats leased for exchange students. I was lucky to get there before they closed. I was assigned a fifth floor flat not much bigger than the kitchen in the cottage back in Virginia. It had a Murphy bed, a small table by the window flanked by two wooden chairs in desperate need of fresh paint. A tiny sink and cupboard containing a few cups, saucers and dishes, two battered pots and a cast iron skillet flanked a gas stove with two burners. I later found this was a luxury for student apartments as many only had electrical hotplates. There was a cold radiator by the window. The heat, despite the summer rain, was oppressive and I broke into a sweat. There was a small electric fan on top of a chest of drawers, but it did not work. The floor creaked loudly when weight was applied.

Trying ever to be the optimist, I unpacked and placed my books in a neat row beside the fan. I sat on the bed and watched the rain streak the window. Paris beyond the glass was gray, crowded and mysterious. I was famished.

I stepped out into the early evening and quickly purchased an umbrella from a local apothecary. I walked north toward the river, passing several small shops and dirty, gray apartments. I expected the place to be chic and pristine; instead it was grimy, filthy and littered with trash. A few people were sitting under awnings drinking and munching on small sandwiches. They looked my age or slightly older. I suspected they were students as well.

I finally settled on a café that looked appealing. It had booths against one wall and a big wooden bar lining the other. I took a seat and was quickly approached by a waiter in a stained white shirt, sleeves rolled up, open at the neck, with a long apron that folded redundantly over his worn black loafers. Despite his promptness he looked annoyed that he actually had to wait on somebody. He pulled out a pad and lifted the pencil from behind his ear.

"What do you want?"

My jaw dropped. He spoke in perfect English. Well, not quite perfect. He had an accent which I suspected was from New York or New Jersey.

"You're American," I said.

"You act like you just got off the boat."

"Actually. I did."

He seemed put out.

"You work here?" As if the rolled-up sleeves and long apron were some prop.

"No, this is my hobby. Look chum, I can translate the menu for you, or you can let me pick out something you might like."

"No, I can read French."

"How about I get you a glass of wine while you mull over your destiny."

I was flummoxed. "That would be fine."

As he walked away, I could hear laughter in French further back in the bar. There was a large cluster of people sitting and standing around a group of tables. My waiter pushed past them and disappeared. Outside there was a clap of thunder and the rain intensified. I took it as an omen. Good or bad, I could not tell.

A short time later, the waiter from New York or New Jersey returned with some bread and a glass of red wine. He placed it in front of me with such disdain that a few drops spilled over the rim and landed on my fingers. I asked for a napkin but by then he was gone. I licked the wine from my fingers and listened to the reverie at the back of the bar. I could make out most of what was being said but they would lapse into whispers and I lost the train of the intermingling conversations all of which would resume simultaneously. Whatever it was, they laughed a lot.

I had a bowl of soup: noodles, with a few shards of onion and scattered particles of meat. I honestly could not tell if it was chicken or fish. Another glass of wine. I asked the waiter's opinion with regards to the main course and he recommended the ham, potatoes and cabbage.

I asked if it was any good and the corner of his lip lifted slightly. I suspect I had either said something really stupid or I was directly challenging the wisdom of his recommendation.

"Of course, it is good. The name of this place is 'Spirit of the Pig.'"

"I had not noticed. "

"Coming right up." He walked away but stopped and turned, "Alabama?"

"Virginia."

I expected a conversation, but he delivered supper without further ado. I ate, paid for the meal and left.

The rain stopped and I walked down the street stopping at a couple of bistros and had a glass of wine at each. I guess my reconnoitering was motivated by my desire to find another American as I was feeling lonely despite all the novelty. But mostly, I was just getting tipsy.

I found my way back to the flat and climbed into bed. A cool breeze came in through the window furling the curtains.

I thought of Monique and her dark, wiry escutcheon and, with my old friend, my right hand, addressed the issue.

...

Initially, with Sunday off and the academic offices not open till the next morning, I took in the sites. With most of the universities, the Sorbonne, *Collège international de philosophie*, the École des Mines de Paris and *Grandes écoles* contained therein, it was a delight to be this close to so much ancient history. The Quartier Latin was lively with restaurants and cafés lining the narrow streets packed with students. It was so named because of the Latin spoken there as it was the language of education in the Middle Ages. I did not know that until I actually stepped foot on the place. I felt silly in the revelation as previously I had thought it related to ethnicity. Upon further inquiry, I found out

Sciences-Po was located in Paris' 7th arrondissement. My search for naught. The Eiffel Tower is also located in the 7th arrondissement. I did not see it except at a distance. The Pantheon was one of the most magnificent structures I had ever seen. I strolled along the Left Bank until it was nearly dark. Again, I was tipsy. Again, I visited the slightly malodorous Monique in my dreams. With similar result.

...

Classes commenced mid-August and were to continue until mid-December. Following which there were to be several days of final exams, pack my bags and head home in time for Christmas.

We dove into the works of Honoré de Balzac, dissecting his *La Comédie humaine* and his influence on Zola, Dostoyevsky and Poe. It was all rather exciting. I found myself up to the challenge when it came to my French.

I finally befriended the haughty waiter at the Spirit of the Pig. He was a medical student from Brooklyn. He came to France to study because he could not get into an American medical school. I did not find him particularly bright, his odyssey explained. He was part of an informal group of expatriate American students in the 5th arrondissement into which I was quickly accepted. They would gather as if by unheard signal in various places, seemingly quite at random, often at the Pig. They were a free-spirited bunch and thought of themselves as the continuation of The Lost Generation. Or more accurately, The Lost Generation, *part duex*. They fashioned themselves as artisans, but I found their artwork pedestrian. Or budding Fitzgeralds or Gertrude Steins without the style or polish. Perhaps in a different age and time they would become so, but not yet, not here. Their Bohemian life was raucous and occasionally erotic but also frequently boring and self-indulgent. But they took me in and helped ease my homesickness until, by the end of September, I felt like I was one of them. The hard core of our collection of émigrés was a half dozen eastern intelligentsia who attended the university without any obvious field of study or interest for that matter. The women in our little group outnumbered the men almost two to one. This made for curious, oft-times revealing conversations. They were uninhibited in their discussions of the ins and outs of sex and fornication. So much so, in fact, that I was frequently embarrassed by their detailed revelations and alleged erotic dexterity. They had lost any sense of decorum long before I got there.

Their talents were often misdirected or dormant and undeveloped; diamonds in the rough, as the saying goes. There was one chap from Tennessee who was there to study physical chemistry who, in the evening, would play the piano with such virtuosity that he could be the star attraction with any philharmonic. He made a little money doing it, too, working in bistros or coffee shops. One night he played the piano while a young, ordinary-looking girl from Oswego, New York sang some show tunes with riveting expertise. Their rendition of "Someone to Watch over Me," would have brought tears to the eyes of George and Ira Gershwin causing them to leap to their feet, look at each other, point at the duo and declare that was how they intended their song to be heard.

Often, however, the bacchanalia and debauchery would fatigue, and our conversations turned inevitably to geopolitics. When our chats rolled deep into the night, we would adjourn to one or another local apartment so some could sleep, and others continue our discussions until dawn. The free flow of wine and a warm, odd-tasting beer cultivated our candor and camaraderie. Some of the insights were so compelling I began to think the little cadre without declared field of study were spies as they would listen intently and give each other slight, almost imperceptible nods.

By this time, the fall of 1938, the world had started to take a dark turn. The ugly, brutal Spanish Civil War had been raging for two years and the appalling history of reprisals, terror bombings and atrocities festered on liberal, western civilization like open sores. Hitler annexed Austria. Then, when he demanded the annexation of parts of Czechoslovakia to unite the Germanic tribes and make a Greater Reich, we all knew that there would be another war.

The French Third Republic was nearly schizophrenic. Some in the government, desirous of avoiding trouble with Germany, told the Czechs to cede territory to Germany in accordance with the ratio of German to non-German population; Britain their unwitting accomplices. Others wanted immediate war with Germany to solve the Hitler problem once and for all. Had they done so it would have saved a lot of people a lot of trouble. The Munich Agreement was just the first step in an inevitable, terrible inertia towards the collapse of humanity.

Chamberlain gave his 'peace in our time' speech on September 30. It was the beginning of the end. War had been averted but only for the time being. Poland, with its strong ties to Germany would be next. Alsace-Lorrain soon thereafter.

There were rumors of mobilization of French reservists. I just hoped I would be back home before the explosion. I had no confidence the coming cataclysm could be avoided.

. . .

One warm, sunny, September afternoon, I walked around Science Po to see if, by chance, I might encounter the delightful, mysterious, malodorous Mademoiselle De Velban but the effort did not yield a positive result. In fact, I could find no one who knew her, of her or where I might go to locate her. Crazy American.

I stopped by a small café for coffee and a pastry after picking up a copy of *Liberte*. A young lady with a fresh, pretty smile nodded to me. I smiled and nodded back. Most of the women around here were aloof and conceited so I took her friendliness as a moment for approach. I moved the chair opposite me slightly as an opening. She smiled again and, picking up her coffee, walked over and sat down. She looked well-heeled and about eighteen or twenty.

"Bonjour," I said.

"Are you a communist?"

Am I a what? A communist? Do I look like a communist?

"No, an American." I spoke in English.

She looked a little flustered. It was not the answer she was looking for nor was it in a language she spoke. She clearly understood the American part, however.

I reverted to French. "I am not a communist." In saying it, I smiled again and caught her glancing at the paper. *Liberte* was a communist organ. Here I was, a kindred spirit. A lot of young people in France, especially those connected to the universities, were enticed by the worker's struggle. It was at once hard-nosed, naïve and romantic. It was like they all caught the same cold. If I played along, I might get laid.

"I am an exchange student from America. I was reading this"—I was about to say to broaden my intellectual and political horizons but truthfully it was the only paper I could find— "because I am trying to understand the condition of the proletariat." It was the silliest thing that had ever rolled off my tongue. I tried to be sincere but inside I was laughing my ass off.

She bought it.

We ordered more coffee and began a deep, animated conversation about socialism and shared repression of the masses. I could barely contain myself. She took my humor to represent earnestness. I was sure she could be seduced. She was from Lyon and a freshman at the Sorbonne. She studied art. How useful a degree in art would be to the revolution was not made clear. Maybe design heroic posters of Lenin or Trotsky. Finally, the sun started to settle behind the buildings and the café darkened. A car pulled up outside and caught her attention. A chauffeur stepped out and opened the door.

"Ah, I must go." She stood, leaned over to kiss my cheek and left. The chauffeur closed the door behind her, and she was off.

I raised my fist and said, "All power to the soviet!"

I watched the limousine pull away.

"Workers, you are the cogs that turn the wheel!"

I ordered wine and a sandwich.

Dunderheads.

...

One weekend in October, several of us went off to Normandy. We took a train to Bayeux and Caen. I got my first taste of calvados. The countryside was magnificent. We found a small youth hostel to bed down for the night. It was rather cool after the sun went down and we snuggled in a small group to keep warm, drinking wine and conversing. I cuddled close to Susan Sharpe from Pittsburgh. She was sweet and let me get to second base. No ecstasy was to be found on this brief sojourn into rural France. It didn't matter. We became close friends until I left. Later, I continued corresponding with her until she got married after the war started.

I spent most of November writing my thesis on the influence of Guy de Maupassant on the works of O. Henry and the art of the short story. It was brilliant. I got a 'C'.

Alas, in early December, I packed my bags and bid my friends, especially Susan Sharpe, a fond adieu and took the train back to Le Havre. I embarked on *Ile de France*, a truly magnificent vessel.

The return trip to New York was torture. The North Atlantic in the winter was snowy, unforgiving and, under any other climatic circumstance, the voyage would have been a memorable indulgence. I was seasick practically from the time we entered the Channel until we reached the entrance to New York harbor. I even had to see the ship's doctor who felt I was getting dehydrated from the vomiting. He prescribed some potion to settle my stomach, but it came up too without alleviating anything. Even so, I was glad to be leaving France. I left a place that was doomed by a tragic inertia it was powerless to control. In less than a year, events would prove me correct.

Susan later wrote that, by the end of the spring semester, she and all our friends had left France. It resembled more of an evacuation, she said.

When to Quit

There is not more compelling or focusing sound than a 'stat' page from the operating room. As a surgeon, there are few other sequences of words that captivates the attention quite like it. This happened several times to me in my career as a thoracic, vascular and general surgeon. You never knew what you might find or what kind of mess you had just inherited because once you scrubbed in it was now elevated to *my* mess. Once it was for a gynecologist friend of mine. He got into some bleeding in the pelvis he could not control. You don't want to drop sutures into the pelvis willy-nilly. There's are a lot of important stuff down there. But once I got scrubbed in and took over, I found the problem and fixed it. When everything seemed in order, he graciously thanked me, and I left.

He was getting up in years and had already stopped doing deliveries. He had pissed away a lot of his money over the years but still managed to live well and, most importantly, he loved what he did. He was a bit of a character and a popular doctor about the town. (He broke his pelvis falling off a horse at a Civil War re-enactment many years before I met him. He was dressed as Jeb Stuart. It was said that this may have triggered the long decline.) So, he continued to practice gynecology.

I was Chief of Surgery at the time (a blessing and a curse) and mentioned to him in a fairly firm but gentle way to have an extra pair of hands at the table when he operated. After that he had a colleague assist him and things worked out fine. For a time.

Then, even with the help, he got into trouble again. But this time it was for catastrophic hemorrhage. And I don't mind saying it took everything I had to get control of the bright red flood. So much so I figured something had to be done and I quietly took him aside several days later and respectfully and with all the dignity I could muster, told him it was time to hang it up.

I think he knew it, too. It is human nature to be in denial. He kept his practice open for a while longer, but he never operated again. This was one of the most unpleasant things I ever had to do. The conversation still haunts me.

So how did we get here?

Before I delve into this difficult subject, let me say the practice of medicine is not what it was when I decided to become a doctor back in the late 1950s. Technology has exploded. Accountability has become a yoke around are necks. (Not that there is anything inherently wrong with that. Accountability was by self-policing, honoring our own profession and maintaining the dignity of what we all perceived as a higher, almost sacred calling. I mean think about it. I used to cut somebody's body open with a knife, stop their heart, fix it, then sew 'em shut. Gee.) Then things changed. We as a profession bled to death by a thousand tiny cuts.

What went wrong? I was once posed a question on rounds one day. The Chief, a world-renowned, pioneering heart surgeon, waxed philosophical asking me what I thought had ruined medicine. The first thing that popped into my head a nanosecond later was malpractice. He smiled that whimsical smile of his and said, "No. It was Medicare. Because Medicare suddenly put a price on everything. Along with control of the money came accountability. "We control the money; you do what we tell you. This is what you will get paid for each and everything that you do for anyone over the age of sixty-five." A light went off in my head. It was not long before everyone, private insurers, Medicaid, everybody fixed the value of everything we did. It became them versus us. Our noble, self-sacrificing efforts suddenly reduced us to mere prostitutes who know the price of everything but the value of nothing. But I digress.

Oh, and then, along came the computer and eventually the electronic medical record. Installing and utilizing EMR was not a suggestion, it was mandated. Instead of streamlining things it became a voracious waste of time like trying to slay the ancient Hydra. It has been estimated that for the average ER doctor's ten-hour shift, he will be required to make four thousand keystrokes. So instead of poking your sore tummy to see where it hurts or checking out your kid's earache, he either delegates it to somebody else or you wait until he gets around to it.

The EMR has been directly linked to the rising suicide rate of doctors. But I digress.

Where was I? Oh, yeah, the impaired physician.

What caused me to ruminate over this was an article in Medscape, April 11, 2018 by Shelly Reese asking "Would You Report an Impaired Physician? Many Doctors Won't." The upshot: 78% said they would but 22% said they either weren't sure or would not. Interesting. That statistic reveals the brotherhood we all, as physicians feel. As well as the stresses: rapidly advancing technology, medical school debt, increasing competition for shrinking reimbursement and of course, the burdensome, burnout, mandated EMR. (It has been suggested recently that the rising incidence of suicide among doctors is related directly to the draconian electronic medical record.)

In her context, Ms. Reese refers to impairment as addiction to alcohol, drugs or illness. Conspicuously absent was a full examination of the impact of declining skill or competence in an aging cohort especially in these hyperacute days of concern for patient safety. Ten percent of physicians will experience an addictive disorder at some point in their career. Drugs, alcohol. In a survey, one third of doctors said they personally knew of someone by direct knowledge who was afflicted. Yet they are reluctant to report it for many reasons. How impaired is impaired, fear of retribution, or the depth of professionalism? It has gotten to the point where there is a push to require mandated random drug testing for all physicians. Okay, what about police officers or airline pilots?

These are complex issues that need to be addressed.

I had a long, highly successful career as a surgeon. I enjoyed every minute of it. I felt I was bestowed a sacred honor and trust. I have a loving, supportive wife and children, and like Jackie Stewart, famed F1 driver who quit while he was top, I decided to quit before a decline was apparent to me, my wife or my colleagues. Let alone my public.

www.ingramcontent.com/pod-product-compliance
Lightning Source LLC
Chambersburg PA
CBHW051433050726
47593CB00005B/1764